Gothic Shakespea

CU00803012

Readings of Shakespeare were both influenced by and influential in the rise of Gothic forms in literature and culture from the late eighteenth century onwards. Shakespeare's plays are full of ghosts, suspense, fear-inducing moments and cultural anxieties which many writers in the Gothic mode have since emulated, adapted and appropriated.

The contributors to this volume consider:

- Shakespeare's relationship with popular Gothic fiction of the eighteenth century
- how, without Shakespeare as a point of reference, the Gothic mode in fiction and drama may not have developed and evolved in quite the way it did
- the ways in which the Gothic engages in a complex dialogue with Shakespeare, often through the use of quotation, citation and analogy
- the extent to which the relationship between Shakespeare and the Gothic requires a radical reappraisal in the light of contemporary literary theory, as well as the popular extensions of the Gothic into many modern modes of representation.

In *Gothic Shakespeares*, Shakespeare is considered alongside major Gothic texts and writers – from Horace Walpole, Ann Radcliffe, Matthew Lewis and Mary Shelley, up to and including contemporary Gothic fiction and horror film. This volume offers a highly original and truly provocative account of Gothic reformulations of Shakespeare, and Shakespeare's significance to the Gothic.

Contributors include: Elisabeth Bronfen, Steven Craig, Dale Townshend, Susan Chaplin, Angela Wright, Robert Miles, Michael Gamer, Peter Hutchings, Scott Wilson, Fred Botting and Jerrold E. Hogle.

John Drakakis is Professor in the Department of English Studies, University of Stirling. He has published articles, chapters and books on a wide variety of literature, drama, critical theory and cultural studies. He is also the series editor for Routledge's 'New Critical Idiom' series.

Dale Townshend is Lecturer in Gothic and Romantic Literature in the Department of English Studies, University of Stirling. He has published many articles and co-edited several books on the Gothic.

Accents on Shakespeare Series

General Editor: Terence Hawkes

It is more than twenty years since the New Accents series helped to establish 'theory' as a fundamental and continuing feature of the study of literature at the undergraduate level. Since then, the need for short, powerful 'cutting-edge' accounts of and comments on new developments has increased sharply. In the case of Shakespeare, books with this sort of focus have not been readily available, **Accents on Shakespeare** aims to supply them.

Accents on Shakespeare volumes will either 'apply' theory, or broaden and adapt it in order to connect with concrete teaching concerns. In the process, they will also reflect and engage with the major developments in Shakespeare studies of the last ten years.

The series will lead as well as follow. In pursuit of this goal it will be a two-tiered series. In addition to affordable, 'adoptable' titles aimed at modular undergraduate courses, it will include a number of research-based books. Spirited and committed, these second-tier volumes advocate radical change rather than stolidly reinforcing the status quo.

In the same series

Shakespeare and Appropriation
Edited by Christy Desmet and Robert Sawyer

Shakespeare Without Women
Dympna Callaghan

Philosophical Shakespeares
Edited by John J. Joughin

Shakespeare and Modernity: Early Modern to Millennium
Edited by Hugh Grady

Marxist Shakespeares
Edited by Jean E. Howard and Scott Cutler Shershow

Shakespeare in Psychoanalysis
Philip Armstrong

Shakespeare and Modern Theatre: The Performance of Modernity
Edited by Michael Bristol and Kathleen McLuskie

Shakespeare and Feminist Performance: Ideology on Stage
Sarah Werner

Shame in Shakespeare
Ewan Fernie

The Sound of Shakespeare
Wes Folkerth

Shakespeare in the Present
Terence Hawkes

Making Shakespeare
Tiffany Stern

Spiritual Shakespeares
Edited by Ewan Fernie

Green Shakespeare
Gabriel Egan

Shakespeare, Authority, Sexuality
Alan Sinfield

Presentist Shakespeare
Edited by Hugh Grady and Terence Hawkes

Gothic Shakespeares

Edited by
John Drakakis and
Dale Townshend

First edition published 2008
by Routledge
2 Park Square, Milton Park, Abingdon, OX14 4RN

Simultaneously published in the USA and Canada
by Routledge
270 Madison Ave, New York, NY 10016

Routledge is an imprint of the Taylor & Francis Group

Typeset in Baskerville by
Taylor & Francis Books
Printed and bound in Great Britain by
TJ International Ltd, Padstow, Cornwall

British Library Cataloguing in Publication Data
A catalogue record for this book is available from the British Library

Library of Congress Cataloging in Publication Data
A catalog record for this book has been requested

ISBN 13: 978-0-415-42066-2 (hbk)
ISBN 13: 978-0-415-42067-9 (pbk)
ISBN 13: 978-0-203-88574-1 (ebk)

In memory of Julia Briggs,
1943–2007

Contents

Contributors

Fred Botting works in the Institute for Cultural Research, Lancaster University. He has written extensively on things Gothic and has two books in preparation, *Limits of Horror* (Manchester University Press) and *Gothic Romanced* (Routledge).

Elisabeth Bronfen is Professor of English and American Studies at the University of Zurich, and since 2007, Global Distinguished Professor at New York University. Her book publications are *Over Her Dead Body: Death, Femininity and the Aesthetic*; *Death and Representation* (co-edited with Sarah W. Goodwin); a four-volume German edition of Anne Sexton's poetry and letters; *The Knotted Subject: Hysteria and its Discontents*; *Sylvia Plath*; *Dorothy Richardson's Art of Memory: Space, Identity, Text*; *Home in Hollywood: The Imaginary Geography of Cinema*; *Feminist Consequences: Theory for the New Century* (co-edited with Misha Kavka); *Die Diva: Geschichte einer Bewunderung*; *Liebestod und Femme Fatale: Der Austausch sozialer Energien zwischen Oper, Literatur und Film*. A cultural history of the night, *Tiefer als der Tag gedacht: Szenen der Nacht*, will appear in 2008. Current research projects include a book on Queen Elizabeth I as the first diva, an introduction to the writings of Stanley Cavell and a book on war cinema.

Glennis Byron is Professor of English Studies at the University of Stirling and director of Stirling's MLitt in The Gothic Imagination. She has published various books and articles on the Gothic, including 'Where Meaning Collapses: Tunku Halim and the Global Gothic', in *Asian Gothic*, ed. Andrew Ng Hock Soon (Macfarland, 2008); 'Bram Stoker and the Resources of Science', *Critical Survey*, 2007; (with David Punter) *Gothic* (Blackwell, 2004); (with David Punter) *Spectral Readings: Towards a Gothic Geography* (Macmillan, 1999); (ed.), *Dracula: New Casebook* (Macmillan, 1999). She is presently working on the concept of a 'Global gothic'.

Sue Chaplin is a Senior Lecturer at Leeds Metropolitan University where she specializes in eighteenth-century and Romantic literature, Gothic fiction and theories of the novel. She has published two monographs, *Speaking of Dread: Law, Sensibility and the Sublime in Eighteenth-Century Women's Fiction* and *The Gothic and the Rule of Law, 1764–1820*. She is also involved in the interdisciplinary 'Law and Literature' movement and has published several articles in this field.

Steven Craig is a PhD candidate in the Department of English Studies, University of Stirling. He is working on a dissertation provisionally entitled '"Our Gothic Bard": Shakespeare and Appropriation, from Enlightenment to Romantic'.

John Drakakis is Professor of English Studies at the University of Stirling. He was the editor of *Alternative Shakespeares*, and he is the current general editor for the Routledge *New Critical Idiom* series. He has edited the Arden 3 *The Merchant of Venice*, and has contributed many articles and book chapters on Shakespeare and on literary theory to journals and collections. He has edited *Shakespearean Tragedy* for the Longman Critical Reader series, and the New Casebooks *Antony and Cleopatra* and *Tragedy* (with Naomi Liebler) for the Longman Critical Reader series. He has been appointed to the general editorship of the *New Narrative and Dramatic Sources of Shakespeare* series, and he is currently working on a monograph entitled *Shakespearean Discourses*. He is also a Fellow of the English Association, director of the Scottish Institute for Northern Renaissance Studies, and a member of the editorial boards of a number of international journals including *Textual Practice*, *The Journal of Semiotics*, *Shakespeare*, *SEDERI* and *Critical Survey*.

Michael Gamer is Associate Professor of English at the University of Pennsylvania. He is author of *Romanticism and the Gothic: Genre, Reception, and Canon Formation* (Cambridge University Press, 2000) and editor of Penguin's edition of Horace Walpole's *Castle of Otranto* (2002) and Charlotte Smith's *Manon L'Escaut* and *The Romance of Real Life* (volume 1 of Pickering and Chatto's *Works of Charlotte Smith*). With Jeffrey Cox, he co-edited *The Broadview Anthology of Romantic Drama*. He also has published a number of additional essays in *PMLA, Novel, ELH, Nineteenth-Century Contexts, Studies in Romanticism*, and other journals on popular culture, national collections, the novel, pornography, authorship and dramas of spectacle.

Jerrold E. Hogle is Professor of English and University Distinguished Professor at the University of Arizona. He is long noted for his work on Romantic poetry and theory, especially for his *Shelley's Process* (Oxford University Press). The recipient of Guggenheim and Mellon

Fellowships, he has also written extensively on the Gothic and served as the elected President of the International Gothic Association. In 2002 he published both *The Cambridge Companion to Gothic Fiction* (which he edited and introduced) and *The Undergrounds of the Phantom of the Opera* (from Palgrave). As his recently published essays show, he is currently at work on the functions of the most Gothic features in Romantic writing.

Peter Hutchings is a Reader in Film Studies at Northumbria University, Newcastle upon Tyne. He is the author of *Hammer and Beyond: The British Horror Film* (1993), *Terence Fisher* (2002), *Dracula* (2003), *The Horror Film* (2004) and *The Historical Dictionary of Horror Cinema* (2008) as well as co-editor (with Joanne Hollows and Mark Jancovich) of *The Film Studies Reader* (2000).

Robert Miles is Professor and Chair of the Department of English at the University of Victoria, Canada. He is the author of numerous books and articles on Gothic and Romantic topics, including *Gothic Writing, 1750–1820: A Genealogy* (1993, 2002); *Ann Radcliffe: the Great Enchantress* (1995); *Jane Austen: Writers and their Work* (2003); and *Romantic Misfits* (2008). He has also edited Radcliffe's *The Italian* (2000).

Dale Townshend is a Lecturer in the Department of English Studies, University of Stirling, where he teaches on the MLitt in The Gothic Imagination. He is the author of *The Orders of Gothic: Foucault, Lacan, and the Subject of Gothic Writing, 1764–1820* (2007), as well as a number of essays and chapters on critical theory and late eighteenth-century Gothic writing. He has also co-edited, with Fred Botting, four volumes in the *Gothic: Critical Concepts in Literary and Cultural Studies* series (2004).

Scott Wilson is Reader in Cultural Theory at the Institute for Cultural Research, Lancaster University. His most recent publications include *Great Satan's Rage: American Negativity and Rap/Metal in the Age of Supercapitalism* (Manchester University Press, 2008) and *The Order of Joy: Beyond the Cultural Politics of Enjoyment* (SUNY Press, 2008). He is also the co-editor of *Journal for Cultural Research*.

Angela Wright lectures in Romantic Literature at the University of Sheffield, UK. She has published widely on Gothic literature and its reception in the periodical press between 1764 and 1820. Her particular research interests include Anglo-French Gothic exchanges and women's Gothic writing during this period. She is the author of *Gothic Fiction: A Reader's Guide to Essential Criticism* (2007), and has recently completed a second book, *The Import of Terror: Britain, France and the Gothic, 1780–1820*.

General editor's preface

In our time, the field of literary studies has rarely been a settled, tranquil place. Indeed, for over two decades, the clash of opposed theories, prejudices and points of view has made it more of a battlefield. Echoing across its most beleaguered terrain, the student's weary complaint 'Why can't I just pick up Shakespeare's plays and read them?' seems to demand a sympathetic response.

Nevertheless, we know that modern spectacles will always impose their own particular characteristics on the vision of those who unthinkingly don them. This must mean, at the very least, that an apparently simple confrontation with, or pious contemplation of, the text of a four-hundred-year-old play can scarcely supply the grounding for an adequate response to its complex demands. For this reason, a transfer of emphasis from 'text' toward 'context' has increasingly been the concern of critics and scholars since the Second World War: a tendency that has perhaps reached its climax in more recent movements such as 'New Historicism', 'Cultural Materialism' or 'Presentism'.

A consideration of the conditions – social, political, or economic – within which the play came to exist, from which it derives, and to which it speaks will certainly make legitimate demands on the attention of any well-prepared student nowadays. Of course, the serious pursuit of those interests will inevitably start to undermine ancient and inherited prejudices, such as the supposed distinction between 'foreground' and 'background' in literary studies. And even the slightest awareness of the pressures of gender or of race, or the most cursory glance at the role played by that strange creature 'Shakespeare' in our cultural politics, will reinforce a similar turn toward questions that sometimes appear scandalously 'non-literary'. It seems clear that very different and unsettling notions of the ways in which literature might be addressed can hardly be avoided. The worrying truth is that nobody can just pick up Shakespeare's plays and read them. Perhaps – even more worryingly – they never could.

The aim of *Accents on Shakespeare* is to encourage students and teachers to explore the implications of this situation by means of an engagement with the major developments in Shakespeare studies over recent years. It will offer a continuing and challenging reflection on those ideas through a series of multi- and single-author books which will also supply the basis for adapting or augmenting them in the light of changing concerns.

Accents on Shakespeare also intends to lead the way as well as follow. In pursuit of this goal, the series will operate on more than one level. In addition to titles aimed at modular undergraduate courses, it will include a number of books embodying polemical, strongly argued cases aimed at expanding the horizons of a specific aspect of the subject and at challenging the preconceptions on which it is based. These volumes will not be learned 'monographs' in any traditional sense. They will, it is hoped, offer a platform for the work of the liveliest younger scholars and teachers at their most outspoken and provocative. Committed and contentious, they will be reporting from the forefront of the current critical activity and will have something new to say. The fact that each book in the series promises a Shakespeare inflected in terms of a specific urgency should ensure that, in the present as in the recent past, the accent will be on change.

Terence Hawkes

Acknowledgements

This collection originated in a series of informal discussions between three of us engaged in teaching on the MLitt in The Gothic Imagination and supervising Doctoral students in the Department of English Studies at the University of Stirling. What began as a naïve observation of the high levels of Shakespearean quotation and allusion in Gothic writing gradually expanded into a more sustained investigation of the possibility of a collection of essays on that theme, essays that might address the historical range of the encounter between Shakespearean texts and motifs and the emergence of particular literary and dramatic forms that imitated them, engaged in dialogue with them and re-inscribed them in new cultural contexts, conferring upon them not only the status of a legitimising source, but also a plural identity: 'Shakespeares' rather than 'Shakespeare'.

The natural home for this collection was the Accents on Shakespeare Series, and it is to the infectious enthusiasm, the generosity and the intellectual adventurousness of the general editor, Professor Terence Hawkes, that we owe a considerable debt of gratitude. The commitment of our contributors, all of whom have done far more than we originally asked of them, is encouraging testimony to a truly international spirit of collegiality. Polly Dodson and Emma Nugent at Routledge, in their usual cordial and efficient manner, have done more than we could reasonably have expected of them to maintain the overall momentum of the project. We are also extremely grateful to Jerrold E. Hogle for having agreed to write an Afterword for the collection.

Finally, we wish to record with considerable sadness that the late Professor Julia Briggs, whose initial endorsement of the project we were privileged to receive, and who had herself originally agreed to contribute an essay, was forced by ill health to withdraw at a late stage. She was unable to complete her essay, and the world of literary scholarship is much the poorer for her untimely death. Her own range of intellectual interests far exceeded the scope of this project, but we feel that it would be appropriate in the circumstances to dedicate this collection of essays to her memory.

John Drakakis and Dale Townshend
Stirling

1 Introduction

John Drakakis

> We do not hesitate to pronounce this to be one of the most interesting, and most elegantly written, novels which have fallen under our inspection during the present year. Many of the passages would not disgrace Shakspeare; but the anxiety which the author still possesses to imitate the immortal bard, leads him into absurdities, which deteriorate the real merit of the work; these are the frequent introduction of *witches*, *demons*, and *ghosts*, which have so little relation to the chief incidents of the story, that we hope to see their officious interference dispensed with in a future edition, which we doubt not will be demanded.
>
> (Review of W. H. Ireland's *Gondez The Monk* (Blagdon 1805: 423)

Francis William Blagdon's review of W. H. Ireland's Gothic novel *Gondez the Monk* affirms explicitly a connection between 'Shakespeare' and Gothic writing of the early nineteenth century, one in which the authority of the national poet is invoked as a legitimizing strategy to recommend the fiction of a writer who, for some time, passed off forged documents as Shakespearean manuscripts. Within a larger context, Shakespeare's investment in the resources of the supernatural, his predilection for spectres, graveyards, the paraphernalia of death, moving statues, magical transformations and the emphasis upon the 'non-rational' as a category of human experience all render his plays open to the descriptive term 'Gothic'.

In addition to forming part of the pre-history of a movement that only comes into its own at the dawn of the Enlightenment, Shakespearean texts function as a resource for a particular style of writing that, by the beginning of the nineteenth century, had become sufficiently established as a literary genre to attract parody. For example, at the beginning of Jane Austen's *Northanger Abbey* (1817/18) the young Catherine Morland's life undergoes a momentous transformation. The narrator tells us that up to the age of fourteen she 'had by nature nothing heroic about her' and that she 'should prefer cricket, base ball, riding on horseback and running about the

country' (Austen 2003: 7). Catherine had no objection to books 'provided
that nothing like useful knowledge could be gained from them' and 'provided
they were all story and no reflection', but this was about to change:

> from fifteen to seventeen she was in training for a heroine; she read all
> such works as heroines must read to supply their memories with those
> quotations which are so serviceable and so soothing in the vicissitudes
> of their eventful lives.
>
> (Austen 2003: 7)

Poets such as Pope, Gray and Thomson provide her with a vocabulary of
censure, but it is from Shakespeare that 'she gained a great store of information', from *Othello* the power of jealousy, from *Measure for Measure* the
universality of suffering and from *Twelfth Night* the art of patiently concealing anxiety in the face of frustration.

By late 1817, drawing attention to Shakespearean quotations – an off-
shoot of the editions of Rowe (1709) and Pope (1725) – had grown into a
more extended practice of anthologization. Margreta de Grazia observes
that the first of these anthologies, William Dodd's *The Beauties of Shakespear*
(1752), contained quotations and 'evaluations based upon Johnson's
authority', but that by 1818 the contextual apparatus had been removed
(de Grazia 1991: 202–3). It is to this process of anthologizing that Austen's
narrator refers, although this is the last we hear in the novel of
Shakespearean quotation; rather, the narrative is confined to citations of
plot, Gothic architecture, spectres, the discovery of ancient manuscripts
and the behaviour of her 'literary' heroine, all of which were characteristic
of the novels of Ann Radcliffe. Indeed, the irony of *Northanger Abbey*
appears to extend to a self-denying ordinance that refuses to include epigraphs at the beginning of each chapter, a feature prevalent in much early
Gothic writing, and does not have Catherine cite one Shakespearean
quotation beyond the period of her 'training'. Rather, Austen focuses her
satire primarily upon Ann Radcliffe and the 'un-English' behaviour of her
fictional characters. For example, following one particular flight of fancy
involving the nature of the relationship between Henry Tilney's father and
his dead mother, a reverie that might easily have featured in Gothic fiction
per se, Catherine is taken to task:

> Charming as were all Mrs. Radcliffe's works, and charming even as
> were the works of all her imitators, it was not in them perhaps that
> human nature, at least in the midland counties of England, was to be
> looked for. Of the Alps and Pyrenees, with their pine forests and their
> vices, they might give a faithful delineation; and Italy, Switzerland,

and the South of France, might be as fruitful in horrors as they were then represented. Catherine dared not doubt beyond her own country, and even of that, if hard pressed, would have yielded the northern and western extremities. But in the central part of England there was surely some security of the existence even of a wife not beloved, in the laws of the land, and the manners of the age. Murder was not tolerated, servants were not slaves, and neither poison nor sleeping potions to be procured, like rhubarb, from every druggist. Among the Alps and Pyrenees, perhaps, there were no mixed characters. There, such as were not as spotless as an angel, might have the dispositions of a fiend.

(Austen 2003: 147)

The anxiety generated by a threat to 'national' identity goes well beyond the concern with Radcliffe's writing, and, as we shall see, extends to embrace the debate about the 'national' poet, Shakespeare. But we should pause here to consider for a moment the strands that comprise this type of novelistic discourse. As an *explicit* critique of Radcliffe's style, this is not the clearest example of Bakhtinian 'heteroglossia' (Bakhtin 1981: 301), although its parodic invocation of an 'other' discourse as well as the invocations throughout of particular 'Gothic' features of the narrative qualify it as 'a double-voiced discourse' that is 'always internally dialogized' (Bakhtin 1981: 324; Novy 1998: 2). There are, of course, throughout early Gothic fiction examples of precisely the kind of free indirect discourse in which one kind of language is 'internally dialogized' as part of a narrative. Indeed, Jane Austen was herself the butt of occasional irony as Gothic writing itself wrote back. In Charles Maturin's *Melmoth the Wanderer* (1820), Chapter 35 begins with an epigraph from Dryden's *King Arthur* (1691), followed by a coarse parody of the opening sentence of *Pride and Prejudice* (1813):

It is a singular, but well attested fact, that women who are compelled to undergo all the inconveniences and uneasiness of clandestine pregnancy, often fare better than those whose situation is watched over by tender and anxious relatives; and that concealed or illegitimate births are actually attended with less danger and suffering than those which have all the aid that skill and affection can give.

(Maturin 2000: 576)

Maturin's novel, coming at the end of the initial flourishing of Gothic writing, discloses, through its complex invaginated narratives, the fundamental literariness of the genre. But, like its predecessors, it contains both explicit quotation from Shakespeare, as well as 'internally dialogized' narrative that requires the reader to keep in mind the two elements of a complex dialectic that is anchored in the text, but that expands its horizons.

Horace Walpole's *The Castle of Otranto* (1764), a text generally thought to have initiated the genre, was published shortly before Samuel Johnson's edition of Shakespeare, and in his preface to the second edition of 1765, Walpole cites the authority of Shakespeare for the mixture of comedy and tragedy that his narrative contains:

> The very impatience which a reader feels, while delayed by the coarse pleasantries of vulgar actors from arriving at the knowledge of the important catastrophe he expects, perhaps heightens, certainly proves that he has been artfully interested in, the depending event. But I had higher authority than my own opinion for his conduct. That great master of nature, Shakespeare, was the model I copied.
>
> (Walpole 1968: 44)

This is another perspective upon the 'mixed' characters that Jane Austen defended as being peculiarly 'English'. *The Castle of Otranto* is a version of *Hamlet,* and the secret passageways, ghosts and general atmosphere of foreboding have informed performances of the play up to and including Laurence Olivier's 1947 film. But Walpole is concerned to defend the 'English' practice of mixing genres against the neo-classical strictures of French writers such as Voltaire whom he describes as 'a genius – but not of Shakespeare's magnitude' (Walpole 1968: 45). In his account of the process of eighteenth-century century adaptations of Shakespeare Michael Dobson observes that

> Shakespeare's enhanced status provided new incentives for modifying his texts, however discreetly such rewriting had to be performed: the more securely Shakespeare was enshrined as a figure of national authority, the greater were the potential legitimating rewards of appropriating that authority by adaptation.
>
> (Dobson 1994: 186)

He goes on to argue that in the case of two adaptations in particular, *Florizel and Perdita* (*The Winter's Tale*) and *Catherine and Petruchio* (*The Taming of The Shrew*), Shakespeare became 'an exemplar of middle-class domestic virtue' but also 'the foe of mid-century Britain's favourite personifications of aristocratic vice, the French – however vigorously nationalist writers were now prepared to execrate the practice of adaptation altogether' (Dobson 1994: 198). Dobson's general thesis draws the practice of performance into its aegis, and he notes throughout his argument the relationship between the adaptation of Shakespearean texts for actual performances, and the public perception of the literary and cultural value of particular texts (Dobson 1994: 201). Clearly, the Gothic annexation of what from a modern standpoint might be regarded as idiosyncratically selected examples of the Shakespeare *oeuvre* needs to be viewed in the larger political context of the challenge to national identity, as well as to the incidence of performance and the burgeoning domestic industry of editing the texts and the debate that this process stimulated. We are still a long distance from T.S. Eliot's reconstruction of an Elizabethan past whose organic culture could be set against the alienating and fragmenting processes of modernity. But there is more to the engagement of the 'Gothic' with Shakespeare – and with Milton, that other towering 'literary' influence on Gothic writing – than simply a question of legitimizing a particular form of what was, at the time, 'popular' literary production.

The Gothic and 'the Gothic'

The 'political' interest in Shakespeare during the eighteenth century is multifaceted and is an important part of an even larger interest in what we might call the historical Gothic at the end of the century. In the first of his 1818 lectures on European literature Coleridge encouraged 'contemplation of the works of antique art' because 'it excites a feeling of elevated beauty, and exalted notions of the human self', stimulated by the nature of Gothic architecture:

> the Gothic architecture impresses the beholder with a sense of self-annihilation; he becomes, as it were, a part of the work contemplated. An endless complexity and variety are united into one whole, the plan of which is not distinct from the execution. A Gothic cathedral is the petrifaction of our religion.[1]
>
> (Coleridge 1987: 60)

But he also went on to claim a direct historical connection between the pre-Christian beliefs of 'the northern nations' and Christianity itself. According to Coleridge these nations 'received it [Christianity] gladly, and it took root as in a native soil. The deference to woman, characteristic of the Gothic races, combined itself with devotion to the idea of the Virgin Mother, and gave rise to many beautiful associations' (Coleridge 1987: 79). This attempt to establish a continuity with the past, displaced into its material religious remains and aligned with a Romantic sense of the sublime, finds its way into the preoccupation with buildings and landscape in novels such as Ann Radcliffe's *The Romance of the Forest* (1791) and *The Mysteries of Udolpho* (1794). Coleridge seems to have had a tolerably 'objective' view of the Gothic past of the kind that might, in part, satisfy a modern historian,[2] although one of the number of differential equations to which it draws attention is that between the level-headedness of what Chris Baldrick has described as 'Northern Protestant nationalisms' and 'the southern Catholic cultures [that] could be represented as the barbarously superstitious antagonist' (Baldick 1993: xii). But this is not quite borne out in a poem such as 'The Pains of Sleep' (1803), where the urge to pray 'aloud' is prompted by the speaker's

> Upstarting from the fiendish crowd
> Of shapes and thoughts that tortured me:
> A lurid light, a trampling throng,
> Sense of intolerable wrong,
> And whom I scorned, those only strong!
> Thirst of revenge, the powerless will
> Still baffled, and yet burning still!
> Desire with loathing strangely mixed
> On wild or hateful objects fixed.
> (Coleridge 1951: ll.14–24)

Such images, whether produced under the effects of opium or not, recall the garish fantasies of Thomas Nashe's *The Terrors of the Night or a Discourse of Apparitions* (1594), and are much closer to the ethos of 'Gothic' fiction than to a more accurately historical sense of the Gothic. They are not too far removed from the violent ethos of the only Shakespeare play to deal explicitly with 'Goths', *Titus Andronicus* (c. 1594), a play for which Coleridge had little affection. Indeed, he castigated its 'rhymeless metre' (Coleridge 1962, I: 131) and thought 'it was obviously intended to excite vulgar audiences by its scenes of blood and horror – to our ears shocking and disgusting' (Coleridge 1962, II: 27).

Clearly, Coleridge's own sense of the Gothic as a historical moment and the precursor of a specifically Christian ethos conflicts with those disturbing anxieties that refuse to submit to rational explanation, but that are, at the same time, paradoxically, the justification for religion. Baldick attempts to unravel this complex psychological paradox by drawing attention to the double sense in which we interpret the epithet 'Gothic'. It is, as Coleridge adumbrates, a means of describing a particular style 'of European architecture and ornament that flourished from the late twelfth to the fifteenth century'; but it is also, in a literary and cinematic sense, a term that describes 'works that appeared in an entirely different medium several hundred years later' (Baldick 1995: xi). What Baldick calls the 'anti-Gothicism of Gothic' (Baldick 1995: xiii) is enlisted as part of a larger argument in support of its radical political potential, its invocation of 'the fables and nightmares of a past age in order to repudiate their authority', exorcizing on the one hand 'the ghosts of Catholic Europe' and more recently, in the fiction of writers such as Angela Carter, an exploitation of 'the power of a patriarchal folklore, all the better to expose and dispel its grip upon us' (Baldick 1993: xiii–iv). At its simplest, Baldick argues that 'Gothic fiction is characteristically obsessed with old buildings as sites of human decay', but this historical obsession with the material evanescence of human life is also connected with a series of timeless and universal anxieties (Baldick 1993: xx). It is this intersection between the historical and the a-historical that allows us to locate the emphasis placed upon Shakespeare in Gothic fiction: the resurrection of a past and the re-fashioning of its elements to represent a complex series of preoccupations and attitudes in the eighteenth-century present. What is true of the use of Shakespeare applies equally to the amalgamation of 'ancient' and 'modern' that Horace Walpole identified in the preface to the second edition of *Otranto* as the hallmark of *The Castle of Otranto*: 'the attempt to blend the two kinds of romance, the ancient and the modern' (Walpole 1968: 43). Here the 'modern' addition to 'ancient' romance consisted in the damning up of 'imagination and improbability' by the imitation of 'nature' that involves 'a strict adherence to common life' (Walpole 1968: 43). At the other end of this burgeoning of 'Gothic' fiction, Coleridge's scathing, and perhaps partisan, dismissal of Charles Maturin's play *Bertram* in 1816 concentrated on unmotivated 'effects' in his observation that the tempest in the play was 'a mere supernatural effect, without even a hint of any supernatural agency; a prodigy without any circumstance mentioned that is prodigious; and a miracle introduced without a ground, and ending without a result' (Coleridge 1951: 401). Coleridge is even more vitriolic in his judgement of the ending of the play in which the distraught figure of Imogine laments the loss of her child. Her lines 'The forest field hath snatched him – / He rides the night-mare thro' the wizard woods' are dismissed as 'a senseless plagiarism from the counterfeited madness of Edgar in *Lear* … and the no less senseless adoption of Dryden's forest-fiend and the wizard-stream by which Milton, in his *Lycidas* so finely characterises the spreading Deva, fabulous Amnis' (Coleridge 1951: 418).

Even though, as E. J. Clery has rightly pointed out, the term 'Gothic' used to describe a genre of fiction was not initially deployed by its early exponents (Clery 2002: 21), the term had already begun to creep into the vocabulary of those, like Coleridge, whose engagement with, and veneration of, the past was exploited, to very different effect, by writers such as

Walpole, Radcliffe, Lewis, Maturin and Mary Shelley. Shakespeare became a model for two reasons: first because he was an indigenous poet of 'Nature', a claim that had been substantially initiated by Dryden, and one that had persisted throughout the Augustan period, notwithstanding the textual improvements effected by editors; second, the 'common repertoire of shared anxieties' that Chris Baldick has catalogued were there in abundance in plays like *Hamlet*, *Julius Caesar*, *Othello*, *Measure for Measure*, *Macbeth* and *The Tempest*, although other plays such as the *Henry VI* plays, *King John*, *The Two Gentlemen of Verona*, *As You Like It* and *Twelfth Night* also provided sources of quotation. But Coleridge's allegation of 'plagiarism' levelled against Maturin raises a series of questions about the use of Shakespearean (and in this case, Milton and Dryden) 'quotation'.

Shakespearean intertexts

In a recent book, the late A.D. Nuttall cites the passage in *Hamlet* that describes the death of Ophelia. He suggests that this description may have had its origins in the real-life drowning of Katherine Hamlett in 1579 (Nuttall 2007: 5–6). He draws attention to the eighteenth-century practice of anthologizing 'beauties from Shakespeare' and suggests, provocatively, that Shakespeare himself 'sometimes seems to write "anthology pieces" as if he had such future treatment in mind' (Nuttall 2007: 7). This is, of course, another version of the claim made for the 'universality' of Shakespeare, and aligns Nuttall with his own Romantic forebears, but it is what Nuttall goes on to say that is of crucial interest. He refers in passing to John Everett Millais's nineteenth-century painting of the scene of Ophelia's drowning, and he concludes that 'It might seem then that the original, low-life incident has been wholly erased by this exercise in "heightening"' that began with Shakespeare's description. Transposed into a Coleridgean language, the passage describing Ophelia's death is the product of the poet's 'secondary imagination' that 'dissolves, diffuses, dissipates in order to re-create', in short to vitalize (Coleridge 1951: 263) what may have been an actual historical event. Subsequent quotation, however, provides a language for the filtering and the internalization of experience through a Shakespearean vocabulary that only attracts the allegation of plagiarism once texts become the intellectual property of authors. In this respect Shakespeare becomes one of the main mediating forces through which the 'Gothic' experience passes, and that process of mediation varies in its level of sophistication from writer to writer. In the case of Maturin's novel, or even Matthew Lewis's *The Monk*, relatively sparse quotation from Shakespeare is subsumed into an operatic finale that owes much to Marlowe's *Doctor Faustus*, while Mary Shelley's *Frankenstein* (1818) leans heavily on Milton. But in all these cases a series of literary intertexts are interwoven with the narrative and with each other to provide a dynamic vocabulary for the mediation of fictional experience. And it is a fictional experience that processes, even as it seeks to resurrect, a particular sense of the past.

We should, however, take care how we use the term 'intertextuality' as a means of describing this activity. In its domesticated form the term has simply come to mean the coexistence in one text of other texts, and it derives its explanatory force from a dilution of Roland Barthes's observation that any text is 'a multi-dimensional space in which a variety of writings, none of them original, blend and clash. The text is a tissue of quotations drawn from the innumerable centres of culture' (Barthes 1977: 146). In his book *Shakespeare and the English Romantic Imagination* (1989), Jonathan Bate, citing Horace Walpole and John Hollander, proposes a weak Freudian reading of the difference between quotation and allusion (Bate 1989a: 31–32). He genuflects towards literary theory with the claim that 'a quotation or an allusion may merely invoke a canonised text as authority' (Bate 1989a: 31). But he then goes on to argue that 'as more sophisticated forms of imitation transform their originals by establishing an interplay between the old and the new which will involve difference as well as sameness, more sophisticated forms of quotation and allusion establish creative tension between the original and the new contexts of an admired text' (Bate 1989a: 31). Of course, what Bate claims for 'admired texts' is the condition of all language and of textuality per se in Bakhtin, Barthes, and latterly, Julia Kristeva. Moreover – and Bate misses the full implication of this claim – Walpole did not dissociate himself from the view that imitation and quotation might *improve* the original.[3] Would it be too wild a speculation to entertain that Walpole may have thought that *The Castle of Otranto* was an *improvement* on *Hamlet* in exactly the same way that contemporary editors sought to 'improve' the detail of Shakespearean texts?

Bate's opportunistic negotiation of the imitation / quotation / allusion distinction is also an attempt to broker a concord between English criticism, North American formalist poetics and some scraps of French theory, a modern version of a part of the very debate that in the late eighteenth century enlisted Shakespearean texts as part of a larger literary currency. His sparse mention of 'Gothic' writing (only some three references to Walpole, Lewis and Radcliffe) reinforces the tacit assumption that their prolific deployment of Shakespearean texts in a variety of guises is not to be taken seriously, and that it is sufficient to treat only of the textual relations between 'canonical' writers. In this way Bate tacitly reinforces the very literary 'authority' and the hierarchical order from which it derives its legitimacy that the Barthesian theory of intertextuality was designed to dismantle.

Towards a minor literature

Writing of Franz Kafka, Gilles Deleuze and Felix Guattari note the extent to which the German language that his texts deploy is 'a deterritorialised language, appropriate for strange and minor uses', and that everything in the minor literatures that such language generates 'is political' (Deleuze and Guattari 1986: 17). At one level such minor literatures acknowledge the superior political authority of the languages they deploy, but in the cases of Ann Radcliffe and Mary Shelley (women), or Maturin (an Irishman), their deployment of Shakespeare, and of other literary vocabularies, is a form of utilization that results in a 're-territorialisation' of a 'major' literary language, reduced to a series of quotations. It is an acknowledgement of literary exemplarity but, at the same time, an absorption of its 'universal' themes into another linguistic register altogether. In some respects they function as what Deleuze and Guattari would call 'the skeleton(s) of sense' or 'paper cutout(s)' (Deleuze and Guattari 1986: 21) that Gothic fiction relocates. To take the example of the opening of Lewis's *The Monk* (1794), the epigraph from Shakespeare's *Measure for Measure* that opens the first chapter is prefaced by an 'Imitation of Horace', in which the writer acknowledges the 'novelty' of his enterprize, along with his 'passions strong', his 'hasty nature' and his 'graceless form and dwarfish stature' (Lewis 1973: 4). More importantly, he castigates his own inadequacies in matters of judgement:

> In forming judgements never long,
> And for the most part judging wrong;
> In friendship firm, but still believing
> Others are treacherous and deceiving,
> And thinking in the present aera
> That friendship is a pure chimaera [...]
>   (Lewis 1973: 4)

The epigraph in Chapter 1 is taken from the opening scene of Shakespeare's play, and is part of the Duke's scheme to test his puritanical deputy Angelo. The 'Monk' Ambrosio's treatment of the pregnant nun Agnes in Chapter 2 does little more than acknowledge the legal complexity of the Shakespearean reference, in part because Agnes is not an equivalent character to Shakespeare's Isabella. In the face of Ambrosio's unwillingness to be merciful, Agnes can only appeal to God's mercy in the face of human depravity:

> Insolent in your yet-unshaken virtue, you disdained the prayers of a Penitent; But God will show mercy, though you show none. And where is the merit of your boasted virtue? What temptations have you vanquished? Coward! you have fled from it, not opposed seduction. But the day of Trial will arrive! Oh! then when you yield to impetuous passions! when you feel that Man is weak, and born to err; When shuddering you look back upon your crimes, and solicit with terror the mercy of your God, Oh! in that fearful moment think upon me! Think upon your Cruelty! Think upon Agnes, and despair of pardon!
>
> (Lewis 1973: 49)

The structure that this utterance might have suggested is alluded to directly only once more in the novel, when a further one-line quotation from *Measure for Measure* is deployed. It is the final line from Act 2, Scene 2, after which Angelo muses on his own dilemma provoked specifically by the appeal of Isabella. In *The Monk*, Ambrosio's secret that he safeguards before the other monks who regard him as a 'Superior Being' is that 'the different sentiments, with which Education and Nature had inspired him, were combating in his bosom: It remained for his passions which as yet no opportunity had called into play, to decide the victory' (Lewis 1973: 238). The complex juridical ethos of *Measure for Measure* is discarded later in the novel for a tawdry sequence of seductions, incarcerations and attempted murders that lead Ambrosio to a Faustian despair. Indeed, the struggle in the novel is between a hypocritical Apollonian restraint that seeks to keep at bay the world's invitation to pursue libidinal desire unchecked, and the Dionysiac forces that promote and encourage it. The initial epigraph is one of only five quotations from Shakespeare, but the two from *Measure for Measure* indicate an undermining of Shakespearean authority at the same time as they appear to uphold it to the extent that they invoke and misread the text from which they are taken.

Deleuze and Guattari address the desire of genres and literary movements to 'assume a major function in language', and they propose a revolutionary alternative:

> How many styles or genres or literary movements, even very small ones, have only one single dream: to assume a major function in language, to offer themselves as a sort of state language, an official language (for example, psychoanalysis today, which would like to be a master of the

signifier, of metaphor, of wordplay). Create the opposite dream: know how to create a becoming-minor.

(Deleuze and Guattari 1986: 27)

The deployment of Shakespearean language and quotation in Gothic writing appears to share, whether consciously or not, the single dream to which Deleuze and Guattari here refer. But the manner of the quotation as it appears in a novel such as *The Monk* inadvertently perverts that dream, even as it enunciates it, and it might be of strategic advantage to think of Gothic writing as a 'minor literature' in this very specific sense of the term.

Quotation, allusion, appropriation

Clearly, at one level, the invocation of Shakespeare through the deployment of selected quotation (or, in Walpole's case, the wholesale dialogic encounter with one play as a model) reinforces the canonical status of a writer whose dual identity inheres in an uncomfortable amalgam of the literary and the theatrical. One means for a 'popular' literature to assert its own credentials is to align itself with other forms of writing whose cultural capital has already been established. Ann Radcliffe's *The Romance of the Forest* (1791) may have been nearer the forefront of Jane Austen's consciousness when she began writing *Northanger Abbey* in the late 1790s, since Radcliffe's novel possesses in abundance the very Shakespearean quotation that furnished the utterance of the Gothic heroine that Austen's genial parody presents. Radcliffe's novel has many of the ingredients that Claudia Johnson has recently identified as being standard fare of the Gothic novel:

> In gothic novels, excess and overstatement are indulged in their darkest and most egregious forms: lustful, tyrannical, and rapacious fathers, corrupt monks, and other diabolical villains work their evil upon forlorn heroines far away from the reach of reason, restraint, or effectual aid in secluded castles full of trap doors, hidden panels, dank dungeons, where storied spectres disclose in fragmentary pieces truths that can be neither fully spoken nor fully suppressed.
>
> (Johnson 2003: ix)

As the relationship between the heroine Adeline and Theodore begins to develop, so Radcliffe's narrator comments that 'Their discourse was enriched by elegant literature, and endeared by mutual regard'. Adeline's exposure to reading, we are told, was limited, but 'upon a taste peculiarly sensible of the beautiful and the elegant', the books to which she had access (including mainly Shakespeare) 'had impressed all their excellences upon her understanding. For his part, the 'Shakespearean' Theodore 'had received from nature many of the qualities of genius, and from education all that it could bestow; to these were added, a noble independency of spirit, a feeling heart, and manners, which partook of a happy mixture of dignity and sweetness' (Radcliffe 1986: 190). For Adeline, canonical literature provides a means of diversion from her present miseries, but one that is not without a distinctly nationalist bias:

> Adeline found that no species of writing had power so effectually to withdraw her mind from the contemplation of its own misery as the higher kinds of poetry, and in these her taste soon taught her to distinguish between the superiority of the English from that of the French.
>
> The genius of the language, more perhaps than the genius of the people, if, indeed, that distinction may be allowed, occasioned this.
>
> She frequently took a volume of Shakespeare or Milton, and, having gained some wild eminence, would seat herself beneath the pines, whose low murmurs soothed her heart, and conspired with the visions of the poet to lull her to forgetfulness of grief.
>
> (Radcliffe 1986: 273–74)

A little later the even-handed M. Verneuil provides an amusing counterbalance with his comment that 'When we observe the English, their laws, writings, and conversations, and at the same time mark their countenances, manners, and the frequency of suicide among them, we are apt to believe that wisdom and happiness are incompatible' (Radcliffe 1986: 268–69). National temperament, the literature that exemplifies and sustains it and the diversionary power with which the 'higher kind of poetry' is endowed mingle in the novel with a much deeper entanglement of 'awe' and 'terror'. When La Motte first sets eyes on the ruined abbey that features as a refuge, he feels 'a sensation of sublimity rising into terror – a suspension of mingled astonishment and awe!' (Radcliffe 1986: 15). In the novel, landscape, ruins and 'great' poetry are deployed, in part, for momentary effects in much the same way that a modern film might deploy music, although there are also, as in other examples of the genre, occasions when particular Shakespearean situations are imitated as models to be adapted. But there is also something else that is involved in the conjunction of the ruins of Gothic architecture, the Shakespearean literary and cultural heritage, and the sensation of the 'gothicized' present. To borrow a formulation from Gérard Genette's analysis of the metaphoric style of Marcel Proust, the Gothic is not merely ornamental, but is 'the necessary instrument for a recovery, through style, of the vision of essences, because it is the stylistic equivalent of the psychological experience of involuntary memory, which alone, by bringing together two sensations separated in time, is able to release their *common essence* through the *miracle of analogy*' (Genette 1982: 204). Shakespearean allusion and quotation in Gothic fiction function as invocations of sensation, as reminders of 'lost time', but they also indicate a tension between the receding past with its irrationalities and superstitions, and the rational, 'realistic' present whose political tensions, socio-cultural anxieties and uncertainties can be universalized, essentialized even, through the invocation of a mythology in which Manichean forms of good and evil are distributed. For example, the deployment of epigraphs from Chapters 4, 6 and 7 of *The Romance of the Forest* invokes metaphors of decay, the shadows of the supernaturally horrific and the horror of the perverse imagination all as essential states of being that inform the narrative rather than simply shadow Shakespearean plotting. The epigraph in Chapter 3 is taken from *As You Like It* and focuses upon the difference between harsh but honest Nature and the corruption of the court, while the epigraph in Chapter 8 from *Julius Caesar* pinpoints the irrational superstitions attendant upon the conjunction of 'prodigies'.

This is merely one example of a pillaging of the Shakespeare canon that venerates *and* dismantles its intertexts at the same time, setting up a tension between a literary opportunism on the one hand, and an assertion of artistic (and national) permanence and unity on the other. To this extent, we can say that the invocation of Shakespeare in this context traces 'the psychological experience of involuntary memory' where effect and practice culminate, not in unity but in tension. To this extent, Radcliffe's texts are palimpsests of narrative, the poetry of others, her own poetry and philosophical statements of Romanticism proper. Insofar as we can think of this as 'adaptation' then we may think of it as 'a transpositional practice', refashioning and relocating elements of one genre in another, or more widely, presenting a more extended narrative revision of a Shakespearean 'source-text' (Sanders 2006: 18–19), as in Walpole's *The Castle of Otranto*. Julie Sanders distinguishes 'adaptation' from 'appropriation' by ascribing to the latter the practice of taking 'a more decisive journey away from the informing source into a wholly new cultural product and domain' (Sanders 2006: 26). Of course, the judgements that contribute to that decisiveness can range from the neutrally formal to the intensely political, and throughout the range of early Gothic fiction these judgements combine, and in a more sophisticated manner than that attributed to Jane Austen's hapless heroine in *Northanger Abbey*. This is not the place to tease out the complex dialogue between literary avatars and narrative in Mary Shelley's *Frankenstein* (1818/1831) but we may look briefly at Chapters 11 and 12 that deal with the monster's attempts to learn language, and the history of the 'stranger' Safie who has come to the de Lacey family's cottage. The monster's learning of language aligns him in part with Shakespeare's Caliban in *The Tempest*, although the reading of monstrosity that Shelley produces presents a genuine alternative to Caliban's negative anti-colonial outburst: 'You taught me language, and my profit on't / Is I know how to curse. / The red plague rid you / For learning me your language' (1.2.366–68).[4] Following the treatment he has suffered at the hands of 'the barbarous villagers' (Shelley 1994: 106), the monster resolves to win the affection of the cottagers by learning their language, and the narrative of his progress is a reading against the grain of *The Tempest*'s manifest conception of monstrosity:

> These thoughts exhilarated me and led me to apply with fresh ardour to the acquiring the art of language. My organs were indeed harsh, but supple; and although my voice was very unlike the soft music of their tones, yet I pronounced such words as I understood with tolerable ease. It was as the ass and the lap-dog; yet surely the gentle ass whose intentions were affectionate, although his manners were rude, deserved better treatment than blows and execration.
>
> (Shelley 1994: 110–11)

In a sense we might claim that Shelley's reading at this point represents an early post-colonial critique of Shakespeare's play, a break with the 'Gothic' past, a critique of the 'involuntary memory' of Shakespeare, rather than an acceptance of the universal validity of its narrative of experience. The history of Safie in Chapter 14 is an even more complex interweaving of strands, this time of *Othello* and *The Merchant of Venice*. The narrative is sensitive to cultural and religious difference, and couches the Lorenzo–Jessica plot strand of *The Merchant of Venice* in a contemporary European context. Saphie's Christian mother had married a Turk, but the 'Turkish' Saphie had been taught 'to aspire to higher powers of intellect and an independence of spirit forbidden to the female followers of Muhammad' (Shelley 1994: 119). Consequently, for Saphie 'The prospect of marrying a Christian and remaining in a country where women were allowed to take a rank in society was enchanting to her' (Shelley 1994: 120). In pursuit of her lover, and taking with her 'some jewels that belonged to her and a sum of money, she quitted Italy with an attendant, a native of Leghorn, but who understood the common language of Turkey, and departed for Germany' (Shelley 1994: 122). This is a conflation of Jessica's elopement in *The Merchant of Venice* and Desdemona's in *Othello*, intercalated with the history of Shelley's own time. It is in many respects a 'creative' reworking of particular episodes in Shakespeare's texts that resonate with the larger narrative of *Frankenstein* in which the themes of the 'stranger', oppositions between 'Christian' and 'Turk', and questions of gender identity interact dynamically to enlarge meaning. As with other parts of Shelley's narrative, these elements have an independent existence, but the *knowledge* of other, canonical texts furnishes a dynamic humanistic alternative to the misguided and ultimately destructive knowledge of science.

This 'Gothic' Shakespeare, with its emphasis upon the darker aspects of the canon, is taken much further in Charlotte Brontë's *Jane Eyre* (1847), where Shakespearean quotation is used both to exemplify experience but also to point up ironies unavailable to readers ignorant of their location. Marianne Novy has argued that "[i]n the world of *Jane Eyre*, where passion is so important, Shakespearean allusions give tragic depth and other-worldly qualities to Jane and Rochester' (Novy 1998: 42). She notes the ways in which Brontë's text moves between references to the tragedies, mainly *Macbeth* and *King Lear*, adding authority to the psychological turmoil of the characters and implying 'the woman writer's relation to tradition' (Novy 1998: 38). She later observes, in regard to George Eliot in particular, that the stimulus derived from contemporary critical interest in Shakespeare's female characters, and from her immediate predecessors' deployment of quotation from Shakespeare, that 'women novelists could rewrite Shakespeare from their own points of view' (Novy 1998: 43). But in Brontë's novel there are subtle variations in the ways in which Shakespeare is deployed, as universal exemplar, as a means of establishing a cultural bond between writer and reader, and as a source of irony shared by the narrator and the 'knowing' reader. For example, the theatrical atmosphere of Thornfield Hall provides the backdrop in Chapters 18 and 19 for a series of disguises culminating in Rochester's appearance as the gypsy woman come to tell the fortunes of members of the household. In the ensuing interrogation of Jane by the 'old woman' on the subject of marriage, Jane maintains a rational composure in the face of 'Gothic' passions:

> 'I see no enemy to a fortunate issue but in the brow; and that brow professes to say "I can live alone, if self-respect and circumstances require me to do so. I need not sell my soul to buy bliss. I have an inward treasure born with me, which can keep me alive if all extraneous delights should be withheld, or offered only at a price I cannot afford to give." The forehead declares, "Reason sits firm and holds

the reins, and she will not let the feelings burst away and hurry her to wild chasms.

The passions may rage furiously, like true heathens, as they are; and the desires may imagine all sorts of vain things: but judgement shall still have the last word in every argument, and the casting vote in every decision. Strong wind, earthquake-shock, and fire may pass by: but I shall follow the guiding of that still small voice which interprets the dictates of conscience.'

(Brontë 1985: 230)

This statement of reason and the appeal to morality are uttered in the face of an assault from the world of pagan superstition towards which she is drawn. Even more disturbing in this episode is the gradual and uncanny transformation of the 'old woman' into Rochester, a change that leads Jane to wonder whether she is in the middle of a dream: 'Where was I? Did I wake or sleep? Had I been dreaming? Did I dream still? The old woman's voice had changed: her accent, her gesture, and all were familiar to me as my own face in a glass – as the speech of my own tongue' (Brontë 1985: 231). Of course, Rochester is the least reliable of mirrors, as the role he adopts once having removed his female disguise indicates: 'There, then – "Off, ye lendings!" And Mr Rochester stepped out of his disguise' (Brontë 1985: 231). The irony of this moment is intensified by the appropriation of a quotation from *King Lear*. In the case of Shakespeare's Lear, the stripping down of the king to the status of 'unaccommodated man' is genuine, but in the case of Rochester, it is merely the assumption of yet another role that points up his disingenuousness. The point is that Rochester is no Lear, although his later blinding in the fire caused by Bertha Mason returns his past errors to him in the same manner as Shakespeare's Gloucester is punished for his indiscretions. Here the Shakespeare allusion involves an active fashioning of *King Lear* in order to produce an ironic restatement of its ethical concerns as theatrical posturing. Rochester is not himself, nor is he Lear, and the knowing reader is invited to share a narrative scepticism of which Jane herself is not fully aware. The heteroglossic density of this moment points towards one of a number of Gothic Shakespeares available to subscribers to the genre of Gothic fiction.

A little later, in Chapter 24, Rochester affects to reveal 'himself' again to an inquisitive Jane who questions him about his past relationship with Miss Blanche Ingram. Jane thinks of him as 'King Ahasuerus' (Brontë 1985: 290), but when she reveals her anxiety to be other than he had feared, Rochester 'unknit his black brows' (Brontë 1985: 291), an echo from Kate's final speech from *The Taming of the Shrew* directed at recalcitrant brides. This curious feminizing of Rochester is carried a step further into duplicity through his response to Jane's observation that he has 'a curious designing mind' and that his 'principles on some points are eccentric' (Brontë 1985: 291). Just how devious and eccentric Rochester is emerges in the assurance he gives to Jane that no-one else will suffer as a consequence of his attraction to her: 'That you may, my good little girl; there is not another being in the world has the same pure love for me as yourself – *for I lay that pleasant unction to my soul,* Jane, a belief in your affection' (Brontë 1985: 291–92; emphasis added). This slightly emended quotation from *Hamlet* where the lines read 'Lay not a *flattering* unction to your soul / That not your trespass but my madness speaks' (3.4.136–37) casts Rochester this time as Gertrude who has now accepted the advice of Hamlet. And yet, this is another theatrical posture since the quotation does not intensify the emotional content of the moment so much as deepen the gulf between Shakespeare's text and Brontë's recasting of it. Jane's later appropriation of a line from *Macbeth* in Chapter 26, and from *The Winter's Tale* and *Much Ado About Nothing* in Chapter 31, draws from Rochester's posturing and is in danger of imitating its theatricality; the quotation from *The Winter's Tale* is particularly revealing in this respect: 'I must not forget that these coarsely-clad little peasants are of flesh and blood as good as the scions of gentlest genealogy; and that the germs of native excellence, refinement, intelligence, kind feeling, are as like to exist in their hearts as those of the best-born. My duty will be to develop these germs: surely I shall find some happiness in discharging that office' (Brontë 1985: 385).

The shift from quotation to appropriation increases in intensity and complexity from Ann Radcliffe to Charlotte Brontë. The movement is from enlistment of the *authority* of the national bard, and, in particular, from explicitly 'Gothic' resonances of Shakespearean texts to more subtle dialogues that incorporate radical re-writings. By the time we reach Charlotte Brontë, a genuine 'minor literature' emerges that is capable of subverting the exemplary status of Shakespeare in order to facilitate the emergence of new literary voices. The following collection of essays variously pursues the practical and theoretical consequences of recognizing this particular species of heteroglossia: Gothic Shakespeares. They range from historical beginnings in the early eighteenth century through to current manifestations.

We begin with Elisabeth Bronfen's exploration of the 'Gothic' sensibilities that reside at the heart of Shakespeare's nocturnal scenes in plays such as *The Merchant of Venice, Romeo and Juliet* and *A Midsummer Night's Dream*. Such nocturnal scenes and the work of fantasy combine to produce heterotopias in which desire generates 'Gothic shapes'. Steven Craig's essay pursues a parallel line in his exploration of the 'Gothic' ethos *within*

Shakespeare's *Titus Andronicus*, if only to conclude that Shakespeare's sense of the Gothic is in no way commensurate with the eighteenth-century construct that is a 'Gothic Shakespeare'. Craig extends the discussion to consider the moralistic reading imposed upon the text by one modern editor. In the process Craig touches on the debate concerning 'presentism' that leads directly into Dale Townshend's wide-ranging survey of early Gothic appropriations of Shakespearean texts. Townshend emphasizes mourning, the world of the spectre and the ways in which they figure as constitutive elements in particular appropriations of *Hamlet*. In a recontextualization of the 'fantasy' that Bronfen explores, Townshend deploys psychoanalytical theory as a means of unlocking the investments of Gothic writers in an exemplary Shakespearean text. Sue Chaplin's essay is more firmly directed towards an articulation of the perception of the Gothic within the framework of a Derridean account of genre and the juridical discourse of Law. She considers Walpole's *The Castle of Otranto* as an exemplary text that challenges the illusion of 'presence' implied in the discussion of literary origins, and she mounts a theoretically sophisticated assault on what she terms 'the operation of literary and juridical fictions of authority'. Angela Wright's essay on Ann Radcliffe proposes a fully nuanced and dynamic engagement between novelist and dramatist in which certain Shakespearean topoi recur in Radcliffe's fiction and in her personal writing. Wright contends that much of Radcliffe's interest in Shakespeare was stimulated by the appearance in the late eighteenth century of new editions of Shakespeare's plays, as well as by a series of memorable theatrical performances. Wright's concerns provide an entrée into Michael Gamer and Robert Miles's account of the Shakespeare forgeries of W. H. Ireland, and in particular the cultural and political context of his mock-Shakespearean Gothic play *Vortigern*. They tease out a complex politics in which the act of forgery becomes, paradoxically, a strategy designed to legitimate and authorize facets of a contemporary national cultural politics, and they demonstrate how a Gothic Shakespeare may be forged (in both senses), and subjected to allegorical reading.

With Peter Hutchings's essay on Shakespeare and modern horror films, we move into contemporary appropriations of Shakespeare and the Gothic. Hutchings explores the complex intertextual relations that permeate films that draw together examples of the canon of Gothic writing, Shakespeare, theatrical performance and film itself, and his essay deals with Shakespeare films that incorporate elements of the 'horror' genre, as well as horror films that cite and quote Shakespeare. Glennis Byron extends the parameters of this investigation into the area of the investments that an exemplary form of teenage vampiric romance, Stephenie Meyer's

Twilight series, make in a text such as Shakespeare's *Romeo and Juliet*. She demonstrates the dynamic interaction of play-text and fiction, and she explores some of the surprising implications of re-writing that result.

Byron's essay treads a careful line between analysis and *performance*, commenting on the fiction and locating the critic within it. Fred Botting and Scott Wilson's concluding essay to the collection pushes this boundary further in its amalgamation of analytical and creative styles. They take the debate beyond Hutchings and Byron into the wider sphere of cultural politics, in which they juxtapose the Shakespeare of Romantic mythology with the Shakespeare of pluri-religious origins whom they align with the Gothic as a revolutionary force. In Botting and Wilson's adventurous formulation the endless fictionalizing of 'Shakespeare' can be projected into a dystopic future whose narratives oscillate between orient and occident. As a guarantee of future 'Shakespeares' they locate in the Bard a volatile convergence of conservative and radical energies, the latter cluster of which they identify as 'Gothic', and they assert that whether as the 'Shakespeare' of the occidental imagination, or his oriental (and implicitly Gothic) avatar 'Sheik al Zoubir', the celebration of a sentimentalized transnational past will always be challenged by the forces of political alterity, of which the Gothic is an exemplary configuration.

Notes

1 Coleridge continues as follows in Lecture 2:

> But the Gothic art is sublime. On entering a cathedral, I am filled with devotion and with awe; I am lost to the actualities that surround me, and my whole being expands into the infinite; earth and air, nature and art, all swell up into eternity, and the only sensible impression left is 'I am nothing!' This religion, while it tended to soften the manners of the Northern tribes, was at the same time highly congenial to their nature. The Goths are free from the stain of hero worship. Gazing on their rugged mountains, surrounded by impassable forests, accustomed to gloomy seasons, they lived in the bosom of nature, and worshipped an invisible and unknown deity. Firm in his faith, domestic in his habits, the life of the Goth was simple and dignified, yet tender and affectionate.
>
> (Coleridge 1987: 79)

2 See *Gothic: Art For England 1400–1547* (Marks and Williamson 2003).
3 Bate cites the following Walpolean obervation: 'a quotation from a great author, with a novel application of the sense, has always been allowed to be an instance of parts and taste; *and may have more merit than the original*' (Bate 1989a: 32; emphasis added).
4 All Shakespearean references in this chapter are taken from *The Arden Shakespeare Complete Works* (Shakespeare 1998).

2 Shakespeare's nocturnal world

Elisabeth Bronfen

1

While the night, as privileged stage for transgressions, is most readily associated with the Gothic imaginary, Shakespeare's plays also deploy this chronotopos (Bakhtin 1984) as the domain for encounters and insights that fall outside the business of the everyday. Presaging a Gothic sensibility which will come into its own two centuries later, his comedies as well as his tragedies construct the night as site of refuge for lovers who seek to perform clandestine amorous rites. The nocturnal darkness supports the inflamed imagination and infection of these lovers' eyes, encouraging them in their revolt against the symbolic laws of the day. Yet the night is not simply a lawless chronotopos. Rather, in it a different law comes into its own, namely that of fate. Thus, even though Shakespeare's nocturnal world functions as one of our cultural imaginary's most resilient heterotopias (Foucault 1998), a space where lovers can successfully contest paternal authority and give free reign to their fantasies, it is informed by its own law of necessity. Once Shakespeare's lovers have left the realm of the ordinary and everyday, they must accept the course their transgressive desire takes, even as they insist that they could not have acted otherwise. Indeed, in Shakespeare's nocturnal world the consequences of desire can not be avoided, regardless of whether they veer towards self-destruction or marital happiness (Cavell 1969).

In the last act of *The Merchant of Venice*, Jessica and Lorenzo remind each other of famous night scenes in the tragic love stories of antiquity, in order to insert their own transgression into this set of mythic texts. Disguised as a page, the daughter of the Jew Shylock had stolen from her home, so as to flee from her father's protection as well as refute his religion. To mark the gravity of her betrayal, the night was so dark that although Jessica recognized the voice of her clandestine lover, she could not see him, and was thus compelled to ask for further proof of his identity. Yet at the time she was grateful for the complete obscurity of the scene, because the darkness protected her from Lorenzo's gaze. 'I am much ashamed of my exchange', she had explained to him, 'but love is blind, and lovers cannot see the pretty follies that themselves commit' (2.6.35). The absence of light, however, not only served to cover up her cross-dressing as a boy. The darkness also allowed her to hide her dual betrayal of her father – her willingness to convert to Christianity and the theft of his jewels and his gold. Precisely because she was well aware of her own guilt, she refused to serve as Lorenzo's torchbearer. 'What, must I hold a candle to my shames?' she had declared, 'They in themselves, good sooth, are too too light' (2.6.42). By keeping her external appearance unseen, she had hoped to keep the double disownment of her gender – as a woman and as a Jewess – obscured. To allow the light of the torch to illuminate her person would have been tantamount to an 'office of discovery' (2.6.43), disclosing her moral transgression as well.

A second act of concealment is at stake when, after her arrival in her new home in Belmont, Jessica, in a scene poignantly illuminated by moonlight, seeks to translate the transgression she has committed into pure poetic language. During their lovers' quarrel, Lorenzo and Jessica compare the scene in front of Shylock's house with other scenes in literature, in which the obscurity of the night sets the tone for the fatal outcome of a clandestine romance. 'In such a night as this', Lorenzo begins, 'Troilus, methinks, mounted the Trojan walls, / And sighed his soul toward the Grecian tents / Where Cressid lay that night' (5.1.1–8). Jessica, in turn, recalls the night in which Thisbe, terrified by the appearance of a lion, runs away from the place where she promised to meet her lover, while Lorenzo counters with an image of Dido, standing on the wild sea bank, gazing in despair out to sea, because her lover Aeneas has abandoned her. After Jessica reminds them both that on such a night as this, Medea went to gather the enchanted herbs which successfully rejuvenated the father of her lover Jason, Lorenzo finally invokes their own nocturnal misdemeanour. 'In such a night', he exclaims, 'did Jessica steal from the wealthy Jew / And with an unthrift love did run from Venice / As far as Belmont' (5.1.14–17).

By competing in their descriptions of the emotional injuries they have inflicted on each other, the two lovers transform themselves into literary characters. In retrospect Jessica recalls how Lorenzo stole her soul with false vows of faith, while he reminds her of how she slandered her love and he forgave her. In any rational light of day, these recollections would appear to be intolerable offences or fanciful delusions. Illuminated by moonlight, however, this verbal celebration of transgressive behaviour takes on the form of a jovial boast: 'I would outnight you' (5.1.23), Jessica declares, before she is interrupted by the arrival of a friend. While Gothic sensibility in general dictates a correspondence between nocturnal scenes in literature and the work of fantasy, precisely because darkness encourages and sustains any flight into imaginary domains, Jessica and Lorenzo's dialogue in the moonlit garden in Belmont performs a very specific passage. Because a night like the one they find themselves in is found to be the common denominator in a sequence of images commemorating fatal romantic transgressions, their entrance into the Parthenon of mythic texts is assured. Jessica and Lorenzo give birth to themselves as literary figures, yet do so by transcoding generically the texts they invoke. The outcome of their love nights is not tragic, even though – and therein lies the Gothic note of Shakespeare's comedy solution – they change their shape, passing from mimetic figures appearing on stage in a particular drama to figures of poetic speech.

Jessica and Lorenzo's quarrel, however, also points to a seminal aspect of Renaissance theatre practice, where the night was primarily performed linguistically. Plays were initially staged in daylight, in the middle of the afternoon. Any nocturnal mood, indeed any all-encompassing darkness, had to either be invoked through poetic language or dramatically indicated with the help of props like lanterns, candles or night clothes. As Marjorie Garber notes, in Shakespeare's *Romeo and Juliet* the night functions as an interior world, 'a middle world of transformation and dream sharply contrasted to the harsh daylight world of law, of civil war and banishment', which is to say, it is 'a state of theatre, and a state of mind' (Garber 2004: 195). So as further to qualify the specifically Gothic sensibility of Shakespeare's nocturnal world, it is useful to recall how in our cultural imaginary, the theatre of the Renaissance itself has come to stand for a particularly resilient heterotopia. On Shakespeare's stage – in the middle of the ordinary everyday, yet on the margin of London's jurisdiction – the law of the imagination overrules the symbolic order's law of rationality and obedience (Montrose 1998). The heterotopic quality of theatre, however, continues to resonate beyond its historic moment of emergence, particularly when the nocturnal scenes performed on stage present actions that explicitly break with the harsh laws of the day by privileging the work of fantasy.

Two plays by Shakespeare, both written around 1595, illustrate this juxtaposition of nocturnal scene and psychic scenario. Both *Romeo and Juliet* and *A Midsummer Night's Dream* enact the *rite-de-passage* of disobedient lovers, lovers who transgress the strict forbiddances of paternal authority by fleeing into the night and, concomitant with this, into a Gothic state of mind. In both plays the lovers privilege their fantasy of love over the symbolic conventions forbidding it. As stage and state of mind, the night in both cases represents a commentary on, and an alternative to, the day. The violence of the young Montagues and Capulets mirrors the ancient grudge of their parents and turns this hatred into the Gothic enactment of a death-marked love, the consequences of which none of the survivors can ignore. The violent peregrinations of the Athenian lovers in the nocturnal wood, in turn, contest the relentlessly severe paternal law of Athens which punishes disobedient daughters by sending them to a nunnery or to the scaffold. The confusion that ensues will ultimately end in an acknowledgement of Hermia's right to choose her own husband.

The two plays, furthermore, can be read as tragic and comic variations on the same story. Owing to chance, the lovers in both plays suddenly find themselves separated from each other, thus revealing the fickleness of any love based on a magic infection of the eye. Moreover, the coincidences that change the course of action in both plays render visible the speed with which romantic desire can turn into hatred and violence. Precisely because both plays mirror each other, however, one must interrogate the different resolutions Shakespeare finds for these nocturnal passages, dictated by the demands of genre. In *A Midsummer Night's Dream* Theseus and Hippolyta find the lovers, on the morning after their nocturnal adventures, sleeping peacefully next to each other. Why can all three couples celebrate their nuptials at the end of the next day, while Romeo and Juliet consistently veer towards an eternal night, so that their corpses are discovered by the Prince in the gloomy light of dawn, lying in a deadly embrace in the vault of Juliet's forefathers? What attitude towards the night must one assume in order to be able to leave this stage and state of mind? Which knowledge, won in the night, can be transported into the day? Which insight must once again be repressed?

2

While Jessica, standing in front of her father's house, embraces the darkness of the night because it helps her cover up the guilt she feels, Juliet, standing on her balcony, impatiently appeals to a 'love-performing night', asking her to spread her 'close curtain' (3.2.5) over the world. The man to whom she has secretly been betrothed can only come to her arms 'untalked of and unseen', that is, if the nocturnal darkness makes him invisible to the eyes of the other members of her household. Lovers, she declares, do not require daylight, for they 'can see to do their amorous rites / By their own beauties' (3.2.8–9). Love, furthermore, 'best agrees with night', because both are blinding forces. If Jessica wanted Lorenzo to see neither her masculine attire nor her shame, Juliet calls for the darkness of night to make sure that Romeo can notice neither her lack of sexual knowledge nor her unbridled desire. She bids the 'sober-suited matron all in black' to cover her 'unmanned blood, bating in my cheeks, / with thy black mantel till strange love grown bold / Think true love acted simple modesty' (3.2.11–16). Like Jessica, she is grateful for this darkness because she draws courage from it.

At the same time her apostrophizing of the night serves to install the wedding-bed as one of the pivotal heterotopic sites of this tragedy. Juliet claims that as a bride she is her own source of light, even while she places her husband on the same level of address as the love-performing night, calling to him 'Come night, come Romeo; come, thou day in night' (3.2.17). When Romeo saw her for the first time at her father's feast, he had maintained: 'O she doth teach the torches to burn bright! It seems she hangs upon the cheek of night as a rich jewel in an Ethiope's ear' (1.5.41–43). Now Juliet deploys a similar visual contrast to paint a picture of the arrival of her husband: 'thou wilt lie upon the wings of night whiter than new snow on a raven's back' (3.2.18–19). Her poetic language produces a nocturnal scene of love, a scene which contests the harsh diurnal world by transforming its civil war into a celebration of her sexual desire. In so doing she not only performs the night linguistically as stage and state of mind for her transgression. Rather, Juliet also gives birth to herself as the heroine of this heterotopic counter-site. In her apostrophe she produces herself as the queen of a nocturnal world which is not only independent of the garish sun, but which also surpasses it.

The wedding night, which Juliet and Romeo will consummate a few hours later, unfolds outside the diurnal strife of her parents. But although it serves as a stage for the transformation of hate into love, the two clandestine lovers cannot assert themselves against the 'continuance of their parents' rage' (Prologue 10). They can only consummate this violence as well, by insisting that from this moment on they can live only by night. After the wedding night, Juliet is able to pit her love against her parents' ancient grudge, yet she retains their unrelenting attitude. True to Gothic sensibility, the love she lives at night with Romeo is a death-marked love. Indeed, once she has consummated her marriage, her world is exclusively nocturnal. She senses in advance that death will be the price for her unyielding passion. To the 'loving, black-browed night' who will give Romeo to her, she promises her husband as a posthumous gift. As an homage to her nocturnal desire she images a sculpture with Romeo's body that will immortalize not only their love, but also the night as privileged site for its display: 'when I shall die / Take him and cut him out in little stars, / And he will make the face of heaven so fine / That all the world will be in love with night / And pay no worship to the garish sun' (3.2.21–25). The night Juliet invokes in her monologue thus epitomizes the emotional state of the star-crossed lovers. They can illuminate their amorous rites with the light of their own beauty, creating an intimate day in night, which they alone share with each other. What they cannot do, however, is introduce this intimacy – an intimacy which obliterates the distinction between light and dark, hate and love, forbiddance and enjoyment – back into their everyday. The inflexibility of their parents' grudge engenders their children's equally absolute flight from their diurnal world.

The world of day is introduced in the first act of *Romeo and Juliet* as the site of a relentless civil war. Tybalt declares that he hates the word peace as he hates hell, provoking the two fathers to once again raise their swords against each other. The Prince, in turn, seeks to contain the blind hatred of the two houses, in dignity so alike, by issuing the stern edict: 'If ever you disturb our streets again / Your lives shall pay the forfeit of the peace' (1.1.89–90). It is from this vicious day that Romeo flees, stealing away at the sight of dawn's light to hide in the privacy of his chamber. Here he 'shuts up his windows, locks fair daylight out and makes himself an artificial night' (1.1.134), so as to indulge in his love melancholia. As hopeless as it may be, his unrequited love for Rosaline offers him emotional protection. Though he is cognisant of the painful paradoxes of romantic desire, speaking of a 'brawling love' and a 'loving hate', he attributes to it the creativity that the civil war surrounding him lacks, calling it 'O anything of nothing first create' (1.1.170). While the hate-infected eyes of his relatives clearly divide the world into friends and foes, his love-infected eye allows him to partake of the spectacle of 'misshapen chaos of well-seeming forms' marked by the blurring of fixed categories: 'feather of lead, bright smoke, cold fire, sick health, still-waking sleep, that is not what it is' (1.1.172–73). Owing to his presence, the nocturnal feast at the Capulets, where Juliet is to meet her designated bridegroom Paris for the first time, is transformed into the stage for a different encounter. Romeo suddenly and unexpectedly exchanges the object of his love, because Juliet's appearance creates out of nothing a counter-site both to his melancholia and to the strife-ridden everyday love it is meant to assuage. While the old Capulet had promised Paris that in the person of his daughter he would 'behold this night / Earth-treading stars that make dark heaven light', the son of his enemy will be the one to claim this nocturnal light as his possession.

Initially Romeo agrees to go to the feast merely as 'candle-holder and look on' (1.4.38) so as to spy on Rosaline. Yet he prefaces his forbidden entrance into the home of the Capulets by recalling the portentous dream he had the night before. Taunting him, Mercutio claims that Queen Mab had been with him, 'the fairies' midwife' (1.4.55), who 'gallops night by night / through lovers' brains, and then they dream of love' (1.4.71–72). Romeo's objection to his friend's ridicule – 'thou talk'st of nothing' (1.4.6) – nevertheless implicitly gives voice to the co-dependency of love and dreams. After all, Mercutio's retort that dreams are 'children of an idle brain begot of nothing but vain fantasy which is as thin of substance as the air' (1.4.97– 98) adequately describes Romeo's attitude. Indeed, Romeo admits that his love is precisely that which creates anything out of nothing. The emphasis is on the act of creation, not on what is being created. And like Queen Mab's dreamscapes, the nocturnal festivities at the home of the Capulets are marked by the principle of shape-shifting, making unexpected encounters possible because, for a brief period of time, the law of enmity has been suspended. Juliet's father insists that Tybalt leave Romeo alone, explaining that he will have no fighting among his guests this night, and, as if to underscore his decision, he calls to his serving men for more light.

Yet even before he lays eyes on Juliet, Romeo senses that to visit the nocturnal festivities of his parents' enemy will have fatal consequences and 'expire the term of a despised life, closed in my breast, by some vile forfeit of untimely death' (1.4.109–11). The law of love, under the auspices of which the two star-crossed lovers meet, proves to be strict in its own way. Once Romeo's eye falls on Juliet, he immediately recognizes the delusion of his prior romantic fantasies: 'Did my heart love till now? Forswear it, sight, for I ne'er saw true beauty till this night' (1.5.49–50). Suddenly he is no longer the victim of fickle passions but rather overwhelmed by a true love at first site, the object of which is neither random nor exchangeable (Dolar 1996). Once the hands, and then the lips, of Romeo and Juliet touch, their mutual dream of love, which may initially have been of a substance thin as air, assumes an unequivocal reality, the consequences of which neither can nor wish to avoid. Both lovers willingly submit themselves to the fate Romeo already found 'hanging in the stars' (1.4.107) before his arrival, and insist on sustaining their nocturnal world of love. Significantly, it offers an alternative to the violence of the day not only because it transforms hate into love, but also because it declares the 'still-waking sleep' of their mutual rapture to be a state of emergency, occluding all other laws and codes.

Once the Nurse has disclosed Romeo's identity, Juliet readily admits that 'Prodigious birth of love it is to me that I must love a loathed enemy' (1.5.136–37). The tragic irony of the love Juliet creates together with Romeo out of nothing consists in the fact that it is as unyielding as the hatred of their parents, and, as such, mirrors the very day against which she pits her conviction that they can share a day in night all to themselves. Speaking to him from her balcony after she has retired from her father's feast, Juliet asks Romeo, hidden by the darkness of the night, to 'doff thy name, and for thy name – which is no part of thee – take all myself' and he responds, 'I take thee at thy word. Call me but love and I'll be new

baptized. Henceforth I never will be Romeo' (2.1.89–92). By giving up
their names, and with their names their symbolic positions within their
respective family lineages, both seek not only to contest the diurnal law of
hate which threatens to separate them again: they want no part of the day
at all. Rather, they want to belong to the nocturnal world performed by
their mutual vows of love. Indeed, Juliet, having confessed her 'true love
passion' to the 'dark night' even before Romeo reveals his presence to her,
needs no further exchange of pledges. They would be 'too like the lightning which doth cease to be ere one can say it lightens' (2.1.161–62).
The days that follow unfold a fatal logic of love. Because Romeo and
Juliet can enjoy their transgressive passion only at night, they live only by
night. It would be inaccurate to say their days are now inundated by the
fatal nocturnal law of love. Rather, the other light Juliet embodies, the
light which Romeo repeatedly calls a 'sun of the night', cannot be imported back into the day. If the night functions as a vibrant and resilient
dreamscape where Queen Mab's creative imagination reigns, the day
serves as a rigid temporal zone in which no one can deviate from the
violent quarrel that rules there. Friar Laurence supports Romeo's marriage, hoping that 'this alliance may so happy prove to turn your house-
holds' rancour to pure love' (2.3.90–91). The Nurse successfully carries
Juliet's message to her forbidden lover and thus makes their clandestine
marriage possible. Nevertheless, there is no room for their shape-shifting
love in the day. Its playful power of transformation cannot co-exist with
the cruel logic of a civil war. Because the fantasy of love consumed at
night cannot be sustained in the day, only a radical separation of these two
worlds is possible.

Under the hot afternoon sun, love once more turns into hate, transforming the nocturnal dream of reconciliation into the sobering recognition that there can only be strife between these two houses. During the
day, Tybalt can act out the revenge his kinsman forbade him at night.
Romeo tries to intervene in the fight between Tybalt and Mercutio,
explaining to his former enemy that his name is as dear to him now as his
own. But his interference merely serves to encourage the violence, unwittingly enabling Tybalt successfully to thrust his rapier into his friend's
breast. It was Mercutio who spoke about Queen Mab before he and
Romeo stole into the nocturnal festivities in the house of the Capulets, thus
provoking Tybalt's murderous anger. It was also he who, having warned
Romeo that Tybalt was going to challenge him to a dual, changed the
tone of his speech and began mocking his friend's romantic delusions. Like
Jessica and Lorenzo, he also recalled a series of mythic heroines, so as to
denigrate them all in comparison to Rosaline. Among them was Thisbe,
whose tragic love story is one of the intertextual references for

Shakespeare's tragedy. As the friend whose verbal wit repeatedly vexes Romeo's romantic dreams, revealing the thinness of their substance, Mercutio had thus come to embody the principle of transformation. With his death in the third act of *Romeo and Juliet*, all possibilities that violence might turn into reconciliation and a tragic family grudge into a comedy of marriage are abandoned.

With his last breath Mercutio declares 'A plague o' both your houses' (3.1.87), and in so doing renders visible the fact that these two houses are not only alike in dignity but also alike in their demise. Romeo, who at night was able to dream about relinquishing his bond to the house of Montague so as to acquit himself of this fatal family grudge, recognizes in 'this day's black fate' that he is 'fortune's fool'. In the garish heat of the afternoon sun he finds himself in an impasse. His action is dictated not only by the nocturnal light Juliet embodies for him but also by Mercutio's curse. Ruefully thinking of his secret wife, he confesses that 'Thy beauty hath made me effeminate' (3.1.109) before he takes up his weapon and kills the enemy who, for the last hour, has also been his kinsman. Since with his marriage to Juliet he now is a member of both of the houses, alike in dignity as in hatred, he finds himself compelled to consummate their unrelenting hatred with his own hands, even before performing the amorous rites with which he had hoped to undo all violence. He is fortune's fool, because, by killing his enemy, he strikes himself. The power of transformation, which was able to create true love out of hate in the nocturnal world that had initially unfolded on the dance floor, only to be resumed before Juliet's balcony, produces a very different dissolution of the distinction between enemy and friend in the light of day. If there can be nothing but love in the nocturnal world Romeo and Juliet have created with and for each other, there can, in the lethal economy of 'day's black fate', be nothing but strife.

Once Mercutio, who embodies the force of playful transformation, leaves the stage, Romeo and Juliet's nocturnal world of love loses all transformatory promise. As dawn puts an end to their wedding night, Romeo perceives the first light of day as a sure threat to their happiness: 'more light and light, more dark and dark our woes' (3.5.36). Sunlight is equally lethal to Juliet's gaze, who now sees her husband 'as one dead in the bottom of a tomb / either my eyesight fails, or thou look'st pale' (3.5.56–57). At the same time, her father's insistence that she marry Paris evokes a desire for her own demise, the point of reference for which is an eternal night of death. She begs Friar Laurence to 'hide me nightly in a charnel house … hide me with a dead man in his tomb' (4.2.81–85). The Friar himself has a radical exclusion of the everyday in mind when he proposes that she feign death so as to circumvent her father's marital wishes. In the scenario he depicts to Juliet, she lies dead in her bed when her unwanted bridegroom comes for her on the morning of their wedding day, as though death had beat him to his prize. The following night Romeo will wait for her to awake, so that he can use the protection of darkness, as Lorenzo did with Jessica, to lead her to their new home in Mantua. The tomb thus emerges as the last of the nocturnal love heterotopias, a site which, like the banquet, the balcony and the marital bed, Queen Mab calls forth as vain fantasies as thin of substance as the air.

After the Nurse told Juliet of Tybalt's death, she already had the foreboding: 'I'll to my wedding bed, and death, not Romeo, take my maidenhead' (3.2. 136–37). Accepting the potion from the Friar, Juliet once more shrewdly realizes that her nocturnal love for Romeo can only be sustained in a mutual marriage with death. As though it were the anamorphotic – and in that sense Gothic – inversion of the wedding night she imagined for herself while waiting for her husband to fly to her arms, Juliet now paints a 'dismal scene' in which she awakes in the vault, where night and death reign together, before the time that Romeo will come to redeem her. Just before she drinks the potion, she imagines the horrible night spirits that live in the ancient receptacle where the bones of her ancestors lie. Out of nothing, Juliet creates vain fantasy scenarios, in which she, distraught and gripped by hideous fears, plays madly with her forefathers' joints, plucking the mangled Tybalt from his shroud, and vowing 'with some great kinsman's bone' to 'dash out my desp'rate brains' (4.3.52–53). The force of her imagination, gone awry, is so powerful that she actually believes she already sees Tybalt's ghost. As antidote to this visitation, she appeals to her husband, 'Romeo! Here's drink. I drink to thee' (4.3.57). She privileges a performance of death rather than confront a conflict she cannot resolve, but in so doing, nevertheless embraces its fatal logic. To protect herself from the fantasy that Tybalt, whose death at the hand of her husband has made all reconciliation impossible, has come to haunt her, she chooses a potion that will produce a nocturnal state of death-like stupor.

Juliet will only wake up after Romeo has not only killed his rival Paris but also himself. This scene of closure functions as the realization of Romeo's second prophetic vision at the beginning of the fifth act, in which he dreams that his lady came and found him dead. If Juliet has recourse to the image of birth-giving when, after the nocturnal feast in her father's house, she claims her only love is born from her only hate, Romeo invokes a Gothic inversion of engendering as he approaches the vault of the Capulets. He calls it a 'womb of death', penetrating it violently so as to give birth to himself in the arms of his newly wed wife. One last time he remarks that 'her beauty makes this vault a feasting presence full of light' (5.3.85–86).

As the source of light in the dark, the festive radiance of which surpasses the light of the garish sun, the sleeping Juliet finds her apotheosis. For the rite of death Romeo is about to perform, her beauty suffices as light, as will the light emanating from his body once she follows suit. For the survivors, however, the morning brings only a 'gloomy peace' (5.3.304). The reconciliation following upon the terrible awakening of the parents is without hope. The second wedding night, which Romeo and Juliet (as they had foreseen in their dreams) celebrate with death as the third party, will bring forth no progeny. It engenders instead the golden statue with which the two distraught fathers respond to the judgement of fate the Prince gives voice to by claiming that 'all are punished' (5.3.594).

In the cold, grey light of morning all those who have survived must face the consequences of their hate. They must acknowledge that the world of nocturnal festivities and amorous rites, embraced by their children as the site where hate could turn into love, has irrevocably been abolished. The golden statue, standing in for all the corpses (including Mercutio, Tybalt and Paris), annuls the strife of the parents, yet by commemorating its victims, it also sustains a memory of the consequences of their fatal grudge. But the golden statue is also the answer the gloomy morning and its sobering symbolic laws offer to the body-art Juliet imagined for Romeo's corpse, when in gratitude to the love-performing night, she promised to the 'sober-suited matron all in black' that she could cut her lover's body into little stars to illuminate the heaven so as to outshine the 'garish sun'.

If this gloomy morning insists that those who remain must wake up from the night – as stage and state of mind – it also, however, celebrates the power of love to create a 'misshapen chaos of well-seeming forms'. Called upon by the Prince to 'clear these ambiguities', Friar Laurence summarizes at length – though he claims he will be brief – the passage of the tragic events. This unnecessary reduplication of the play's action in the form of testimony, given by a witness, is justified by virtue of the fact that with his monologue, the Friar ascribes to the dead couple the status of mythic characters, implicitly aligning them with Pyramus and Thisbe. In so doing, he re-iterates belatedly the allegorical status with which the Prologue had endowed them when it declared them to be 'a pair of star-crossed lovers', forced to take their own lives so that their deaths may serve to 'bury their parents' strife' (Prologue 6–8). Their story could find no other closure because 'the fearful passage of their death-marked love' (Prologue 9) was the very precondition for their emergence as *dramatis personae*. The Prologue introduces them not as the children of an 'idle brain, begot of nothing but vain fantasy', but rather as the poetic progeny of Shakespeare's mind, which for two hours will be the 'traffic' of his stage. The dramatic enactment of their story following the Prologue serves to embellish – in the sense of a poetic dream – everything that the rhetorical reduction undertaken by the Prologue could not name. At the end of the five acts the dramatic characters Romeo and Juliet are once more reduced to the formula of the tragic love story which serves as an inscription for their golden statue: 'For never was a story of more woe than this of Juliet and Romeo' (5.3.308–9).

As we awaken from the dream which Shakespeare's language performed before our eyes, a question, however, remains. How much of the stuff of fantasy must again be relinquished, as we, the audience, move from the night into a gloomy morning, from a Prologue and a dramatic enactment of the fearful passage of a death-marked love, to a commemorative statue and its didactic sub-title? After all, the heterotopia of Shakespeare's nocturnal love traffic has also affected our fantasies, leaving traces that resonate beyond the alleged reconciliation that the closure of this tragedy affords.

3

Conceivably *A Midsummer Night's Dream* could also end with a commemorative statue. Like Juliet, Hermia opposes her strict father Egeus, a father who, according to the Athenian law that rendered a daughter the property of her father, can order her to marry a man she does not love. If she does not consent to marry Demetrius, she must either die or live the life of a barren nun, 'chanting faint hymns to the cold fruitless moon' (1.1.73). She, too, seeks the protection of the dark night to flee with her lover Lysander to her aunt, who lives outside the jurisdiction of the Athenian court. Chance will also prevent these lovers from carrying out their plan, and because for them too the events of their sojourn in the nocturnal woods turn their love into strife, they could find a fateful death. In this romantic comedy, however, transgressions do not result in an unyielding nocturnal desire, pitted against the harsh laws of the day. Rather, *A Midsummer Night's Dream* celebrates the triumph of the power of transformation which the lovers encounter in the enchanted woods, although this heterotopia also reflects and contests the diurnal law of rationality and obedience. In Shakespeare's comedy, love also proves to be an 'infection to the eye' which translates its victims into a 'still-waking sleep'. Yet as Helena, Hermia's childhood friend, notes, 'love looks not with the eyes, but with the mind' (1.1.234) – with the faculty of imagination and fantasy, not with the senses.

As in *Romeo and Juliet*, the vain fantasy induced by dreams brings forth confusing shapes, of substance as thin as air, which taunt and torment the night wanderers until, just before the break of dawn, they return to the edge of the woods, utterly exhausted from their visions. But the spirits, who in Juliet's prophetic dream are merely terrifying and lead her to fear she will go mad, enact a far more reversible passage of the imagination in *A Midsummer Night's Dream*. Although their play of magic turns love into hate and violence, it also turns strife into desire and reconciliation. Owing to the power of transformation enacted by the fairies, love objects come to be exchangeable in the nocturnal world of the wood, while desire remains mobile and, as such, not bound to a predetermined trajectory. Furthermore, the nocturnal woods unfold a heterotopic counter-site, a counter-site which offers the lovers not only the possibility of contesting the forbiddances of the day and turning these to their advantage. For the knowledge they win in this nocturnal world, can – even if only in fragments – be transported into the morning after, and thus into all the days and nights that follow.

Even before Hermia and Lysander decide to flee to the woods, the night had served as stage for their forbidden love. In front of the Duke of Athens, the indignant Egeus charges Lysander that he 'by moonlight at her window [did] sing with feigning voices verses of feigning love, and stol'n the impression of her fantasy' (1.1.30–32). According to Hermia's father, Lysander's nocturnal courting stole 'the impression of her fantasy' and came to turn his daughter's obedience to him into a stubborn harshness against his authority. As Hermia herself admits, 'I know not by what power I am made bold' (1.1.59), yet she still insists on determining for herself who her future husband is to be. During the day, and at the Duke's court at that, she thus represents precisely the nocturnal desire, so thoroughly undermining of paternal authority, for which her father is willing to sacrifice her. Like the impetuous young men in *Romeo and Juliet* who play out the relentless grudge of their parents by day on the streets of Verona, Hermia responds to her father's claim to absolute sovereignty with equal obstinacy. At the same time, however, she pits against his mental rigidity her own acknowledgement of the fateful law of love. Precisely because she knows that she cannot avoid love (Cavell 1969), she recognizes in necessity the opportunity for change.

Like Jessica and Lorenzo in *The Merchant of Venice*, Lysander has recourse to the tragic resolution of mythic love stories when imagining the course his true love for Hermia will take. War, death or sickness, he explains, renders it 'swift as a shadow, short as any dream, brief as the lightning in the collied night' (1.1.144–45), only to be devoured by 'the jaws of darkness'. As though she, in turn, had read the Prologue to *Romeo and Juliet*, Hermia shrewdly responds: 'if then true lovers have been ever crossed, / it stands as an edict in destiny. / Then let us teach our trial patience' (1.1.150–51). Against Juliet's impatience, Hermia pits a willingness to persevere, and in so doing shows herself open to any changes of circumstance that she might encounter on her nocturnal journey. Even before entering the nocturnal woods, she wisely assumes that the course of her love will not run smoothly. The transgressions she will encounter there thus involve not only her father's forbiddance, but also precisely those imaginings of the inevitability of mishap, by which both she and her lover believe that true love must necessarily be touched.

As the place and time 'that lovers' sleights doth still conceal' (1.1.212), the night offers both refuge and illumination. In the nocturnal woods, Hermia's worst fantasies of love's woes will come to take shape and confront her with the transformation of love into violence. Not only Demetrius, the bridegroom she rejects, will follow her to this heterotopia, but also Helena, the woman he, in turn, spurns. Even before the fairies begin their magic play, *A Midsummer Night's Dream* enacts the Gothic traffic of these four lovers, who in the light of night suddenly see each other differently than during the day. Helena indulges in her masochistic fantasy of humiliation, asking Demetrius to treat her like his dog: 'Neglect me, lose me', she whimpers, 'only give me leave / Unworthy as I am, to follow you' (2.2.205–6). At the same time, the magic woods serve as the stage for two further performances of the cruel and excessive nocturnal side of love. For one, a small troop of artisans choose this place to rehearse a play they hope to perform at the wedding festivities of the Duke. Its title, *The Most Lamentable Comedy and Most Cruel Death of Pyramus and Thisbe*, explicitly gives voice to the mutual implication of pleasure and cruelty in any enactment of love's delusions. At the same time, their rehearsal offers a grotesque distortion of the mythic story, which like *Romeo and Juliet*, illustrates that the nocturnal side of love may result in the fatal loss of happiness. The moon-lit woods, however, also function as the stage where Oberon and his Fairy Queen fight over a little changeling boy, the boy whom he wants as one of his pages of honour while she seeks to raise him in honour of her friendship with his mother.

Like Mercutio's Queen Mab, Robin intervenes in this tri-fold nocturnal traffic, directing the passage of the diverse lovers. This 'merry wanderer of the night' (2.1.43) is master of a night-rule which celebrates the terrible contingencies, accidents and misfortunes that can befall each and every lover. Under his aegis a play of transformations unfolds, leaving no one untouched. He obeys Oberon's command, and fetches the juice of the magic flower upon which Cupid's arrow fell, 'quenched in the chaste beams of the wat'ry moon' when it missed the 'imperial votress' at which the god of love had taken aim (2.1.162–63). Yet Robin subverts Oberon's command by dropping this magic juice not in the eyes of Demetrius, but rather accidentally – or willingly – on those of Lysander, who has fallen asleep close to his beloved Hermia. Intensifying the infection of the eye, which in the Gothic language of Shakespeare's plays always applies to love, this juice compels the sleeper to dote madly on the first creature he sees when he awakes. Thus the dream of clandestine love transforms into a traumatic enactment of mistaken identities. When Helena finds Lysander sleeping on the ground, she, for a moment, wonders whether he is 'dead, or asleep? I see no blood, no wound' (2.2.107), as though she were expecting the change of tone from romantic comedy to Gothic love tragedy. Yet the cruelty that unfolds once Lysander awakes will take a difference course. Like Romeo, who, upon seeing Juliet at her father's nocturnal festivities, immediately relinquishes Rosaline, the previous object of his desire, so too Lysander declares his true love to Helena in the language of a tragic hero. His transformed gaze, he explains, has led him 'to your eyes, where I o'erlook love's stories written in love's richest book' (2.2.127). This revelation lets him chase after his rival Demetrius, so that the latter may perish on his sword.

In contrast to *Romeo and Juliet*, however, the Gothic magic of love that unfolds is one-sided and partial. Robin only plays with the love-infected gaze of the two young men, as though they were the more fickle of the lovers, while the two women are forced to gaze upon the toxic side-effects of love's madness with their eyes clear. Helena takes Lysander's sudden change as an expression of perfidious mockery, Hermia as an inexplicable experience of abandonment. If she fell asleep thinking her lover was peacefully resting by her side, she wakes up from a terrible dream in which, as she relates to an absent Lysander, she thought 'a serpent ate my heart away, and you sat smiling at his cruel prey' (2.2.155–56). If one follows Freud in his claim that dreams in principle enact wish-fulfilments (Freud 1900), one might ask whether Hermia's vision of her lover, cruelly enjoying her death, dictates to herself the perfect image of the way true lovers are ever crossed. Or does she use this dream vision to give voice – as Juliet does on her balcony – to a Gothic fantasy of self-expenditure in love? Realizing that she has been abandoned, Hermia calls out to Lysander: 'either death or you I'll find immediately' (152). In contrast to Juliet, she will not let chance decide her fate, but rather insists on her own agency. If, in her dream vision, she has acknowledged that Lysander is capable of cruelty towards her, the magical juice will help to enact precisely this disloyalty. Owing to the inexplicable change of circumstances, Lysander, now believing that he hates her, will truly wound her with his words. But the logic of Robin's night rule also undermines the necessity of any tragic resolution to this nocturnal misunderstanding. Because Lysander's inexplicable sudden rebuke of Hermia wounds her emotionally, she does not actually have to die physically. The traumatic experience of her lover's betrayal also makes possible the turn to comedy.

All four Athenians have no choice but to follow Robin's Gothic play, experiencing both the cruel fortuitousness of the choice of love object, as well as the barbaric violence hovering beneath the surface of civility. Hermia believes to recognize in Demetrius the murderer of her love, and pleads with him to kill her as well. He, in turn, accuses her of being a murderer, because it is her stern cruelty which has pierced through his heart. At the same time, he also acknowledges his own proclivity towards cruelty, claiming that he would rather give the carcass of his rival to his hounds than hand him over to Hermia. Oberon intervenes in Robin's night rule, and personally drops the juice of the magic flower on the eyes of Demetrius. However, under the aegis of the merry wanderer of the night who revels precisely in the confusions 'that befall prepost'rously', contingency continues to rule over love in Shakespeare's nocturnal world. Robin's Gothic jest renders visible that even 'true love's sight' can turn into disdain, undermining the certainty that there is a clear difference between true and false love. Still infected by his new vision of Helena, Lysander explicitly names what Hermia saw in her dream. He commands her to 'let loose, or I will shake thee from me like a serpent' (3.2.261–62). The transformation of his gaze, which turns her into an object of hate, forces Hermia to look upon herself with an eye different from that used during the day. If she can no longer trust his love, she can also not be certain who she is. Her question 'Am not I Hermia? Are not you Lysander?' (3.2.274) shifts her dream vision of a serpent, eating at her heart, into an issue of symbolic identity. While Romeo's transformed gaze brings Juliet to ask him to relinquish his family name, wishing for both of them mutually to disavow their symbolic position, Lysander's alteration calls forth in Hermia a disturbing uncertainty about the name connected to her diurnal identity.

Ultimately, all four lovers confront each other in strife. Hermia can only see her former friend Helena as a thief of love: 'come by night and stol'n my love's heart from him' (3.2.284–85). Helena believes the others are all set against her, while the two young men continue to chase each other. But although love has turned into hate, accusation and defamation, the lovers indulge only in an imagined enactment of violence. In contrast to Romeo, who finds himself forced to kill Tybalt even though he has just become his kinsman, Lysander says of Hermia, 'what should I hurt her, strike her, kill her dead? Though I hate her, I'll not harm her' (3.2.270–71). Once more Oberon intervenes in Robin's contingent night-rule, so as to put an end to nocturnal chaos. He seeks to assert a clear division between true love and all magical distortions of love, thus subjecting love to an order compatible with the symbolic laws of the day. In contrast to those spirits who, according to Oberon, are doomed forever to 'consort with black-browed night' (3.2.388), he is not excluded from the world of daylight. 'We are spirits of another sort', he explains, 'I with the morning's

love have oft made sport' (3.2.389.90). He thus commands Robin to conjure up a black fog to cover even the stars, so that in utter darkness the
four lovers will go astray, never meeting each other, until – like Juliet –
exhausted from the Gothic shapes their desire has taken, they fall into a
'death-counterfeiting sleep'.

Because Oberon wishes to transport the new order of love engendered
by his magic into the day, he clears Lysander's eyes just before dawn so
that 'all this derision' will seem to him 'a dream and fruitless vision'
(3.2.371–72) once he awakes. Indeed, in contrast to the star-crossed lovers
in *Romeo and Juliet*, the young Athenians yearn for day to break. Because
the darkness prevents them from ever catching up with each other, the two
young men call for the grey light of day to settle their grudge. So different
from Juliet, Helena calls out at the end of her nocturnal peregrination, 'O
weary night. O long and tedious night, / Abate thy hours' (3.2.431–32), as
though invoking an end to all Gothic magic as well. Darkness does not
appear to her as a protective cloak, but rather as an abyss which has
brought forth terrifying distortions of her familiar world. Yet she follows
Juliet, who drinks the Friar's potion, so as to put an end to her prophetic
vision. For Helena also asks the night to bring her the 'sleep that sometimes shuts up sorrow's eye, / steal me a while from mine own company'
(3.2.435–36). The passage from this magical night into day can only occur
in a state utterly forgetful of all the traumatic knowledge the lovers have
been confronted with in Shakespeare's nocturnal world. Only as distortions, as dreams and fruitless visions can the manifold imaginations of the
nocturnal side of love be brought to bear on the day.

Titania's nightmare, by contrast, sets in once she awakes from the
enchantment of her eyes which brought her the sexual enjoyment of a
mortal. Oberon had sworn to punish her for her unwillingness to subject
herself to his wishes and give up the changeling boy. Functioning as a
Gothic parody of the love at first sight performed in *Romeo and Juliet*,
Titania had, upon seeing the weaver Bottom transformed into a hybrid
between human and ass, immediately fallen passionately in love with him.
Only, however, once Oberon lifts what he designates as a 'hateful imper-
fection of her eyes' (4.1.60) does she see the amorous rites of the previous
night as an act of debasement. Awakening from her nocturnal confusion,
she confesses to Oberon that she had a vision in which she thought she
was enamoured of an ass. In contrast to the serpent Hermia sees in her
dream (re-iterated in Lysander's verbal attacks, but forgotten the next
morning when she awakens), Titania is forced to confront Bottom's distorted visage in a state of wakefulness. As proof that her love-making with
a disfigured mortal actually took place, Oberon points to the grotesque
figure lying next to her and declares, 'there lies your love' (4.1.74). The

recuperation of his sovereignty depends not only on the two-fold correction of his Fairy Queen's eyes (Freedman 1991). Rather, it also requires that, once awoken, Titania is forced to remember her erotic madness. The possibility of repression is not given to her. Bottom does not lose his ass's head until, by the light of dawn, Titania has admitted, 'O, how mine eyes do loathe his visage now' (4.1.76). Owing to her humiliation, she now obediently accepts Oberon's command, agreeing to bless Theseus's house the following night. More importantly, she relinquishes to him the interpretation of the occurrences of the previous night. Taking his hand, she flies away with Oberon, begging him to explain 'how it came this night that I sleeping here was found with these mortals on the ground' (4.1.97–99).

In the grey morning light, Theseus and Hippolyta also ask the lovers, whom they find at the edge of the woods, to explain how it came to be that they were peacefully sleeping next to each other. If Titania is forced not to forget her nocturnal adventure, the young Athenians are blessed with the forgetfulness that not only negotiates between nocturnal dream events and the conscious knowledge of the day, but that also sets a limit to the former. Half sleeping, half waking, Lysander confesses, 'I cannot truly say how I came here' (4.1.145), while Demetrius feels that an inexplicable power has transformed his love for Hermia into a vain memory. At the end of this night he is the only one who is still affected by Oberon's magic juice. This uncanny correction of his love-infected eye has brought him back to Helena, with whom he was in love before he met Hermia. This return to an earlier love, forgotten and now returned, supports Freud's claim that moments of the uncanny call forth an affect which was once familiar and pleasurable, but which repression has rendered loathsome (Freud 1919). The two young women also give voice to the uncanniness that accompanies their awakening. Hermia believes she sees everything 'with parted eye. When everything seems double' (4.1.186–87), while Helena recognizes in Demetrius 'a jewel, mine own and not mine own' (4.1.88–89).

Because upon waking up they, like all mortal dreamers, have forgotten the most traumatic aspects of their nocturnal passage, they retain only fragments of how, in nocturnal woods, hate and violence emerged as the mirror inversion of love. This Gothic experience, however, did not by necessity have to end in death, because the principle of transformation, attributed to Shakespeare's nocturnal world as well as to the dream visions it engenders and unfolds, was never radically excluded from the day. Protected by the cloak of obscurity that forgetting affords, this traumatic knowledge will affect the day without turning it tragic. It is precisely because Hermia came at night to experience the cruel fickleness of her lover that she can endure anything that her marriage to Lysander holds in store for her. Having confronted her worst fantasies in the nocturnal woods, she is well equipped for all contingencies.

To Theseus, who fully inhabits the rational discourse of the day, the stories told to him by the four young Athenians appear to be the shaping fantasies of the seething brains of lovers, who 'apprehend more than cool reason ever comprehends' (5.1.5–6). Hippolyta, in turn, lends her ear patiently to the lovers' story of the night. The fact that all their minds transfigured so together 'is proof that something more than vain fantasy' is at stake, 'something of great constancy / But howsoever, strange and admirable' (5.1.26–27). For the grotesque performance of Bottom and his friends, however, she has only impatience, claiming that 'this is the silliest stuff that ever I heard of' (5.1.207). Yet precisely in its utter lack of imagination, this distorted rendition of a love tragedy, reducing the nocturnal world to empty signifiers, opens up a counter-site in the Duke's court. In the spirit of Gothic parody, Bottom, recalling Juliet's monologue, calls out, 'O night with hue so black, / O night which ever art when day is not! / O night, O night, alack, alack, alack' (5.1.168–70). His performance follows the rhetorical gesture of heterotopia, because it once more turns on the events of the previous night, bringing back into focus that which waking had repressed.

The play Bottom and his friends perform mirrors both the strict law of Athens, from which the four lovers had sought to flee, as well as the violence which inhabits all passionate love. The tragic love story of Thisbe and Pyramus serves as point of reference to both Jessica as well as Mercutio, in *The Merchant of Venice* as homage and in *Romeo and Juliet* as parody. In *A Midsummer Night's Dream*, negotiating the transformation of the tragedy *Romeo and Juliet* into a comedy, the curious performance of this story serves merely as a corrective. To the lovers, who can only imperfectly remember their own nocturnal passage, the sudden transformation of a dream of love into a traumatic loss of life renders visible the consequences of tragic fate which they were successfully able to circumvent. Hermia could have killed herself after Lysander abandoned her. As a result of their tampered vision, the two male rivals could have killed each other. At the same time, this silly performance of a famous tragic love story also points to the enduring correspondence between night and theatricality. The end of this spectacle brings with it the 'iron tongue of midnight', calling all three couples to a different stage where shapes are engendered, namely the marital bed.

Yet what the artisan's performance also heralds is the Epilogue, which the wanderer of the night, Robin, is allowed to speak, because Theseus refused to let Bottom have the last word. With this Epilogue all theatricality is brought to an end. All the actors prove to be shadows and the entire traffic on the stage the vision of a collectively shared dream (Garber

2004). If the artisans, like Shakespeare's players themselves, invoked the night with the help of props, Robin's final monologue declares not only the dreamscape of the nocturnal world but also the day that framed it, which is to say the entire play, as belonging to Queen Mab's realm of spirits whose substance is as thin as air. Theseus had compared the lovers with both madmen and poets, because the imagination of all three gives shape to 'things unknown'. According to the Duke, who has little sympathy for any Gothic stories of the night, the poet undertakes a further transformation, bringing the shapes of fantasy closer to the sensibility of the day. The poet's pen, after all, 'gives to airy nothing / A local habitation and a name' (5.1.15–16). It is precisely this gesture of consistency and emplacement which Robin, true to his night rule, undermines with his Epilogue, reintroducing a Gothic moment into the romantic comedy of marriage. Because he declares all visions to have been 'but a dream' and all the actors to be but shadows, he brings the airy nothing, from which imagination calls forth shapes, back into play. In contrast to the Prince's final words in *Romeo and Juliet*, dismissing us into a gloomy morning 'to have more talk of these sad things' (5.3.306), Robin bids us a good night as well.

If, as Robin claims, everything was only our dream of the dream of four lovers, or Hippolyta's dream of the lovers (Greenblatt 1997), we are left in the position of Bottom, who is forced to recognize that he can only remember fragments of the night he spent with a Fairy Queen. 'I have had a most rare vision', he explains upon waking up. 'I have had a dream past the wit of man to say what dream it was' (4.1.199–201). His attempt to describe what he believes to have seen in his dream exceeds the language of the day: 'The eye of man hath not heard, the ear of man hath not seen, man's hand is not able to taste, his tongue to conceive, nor his heart to report what my dream was' (4.1.204–7). He decides to ask his friend Peter Quince to write a ballad about this dream, which is to be called '"Bottom's Dream," because it hath no bottom' (4.1.208–11). Bottom's bottomless dream serves as a trope for the passage that, leading from dream to waking, necessarily requires forgetting. Ecstatic and traumatic knowledge, won at night, can only be remembered with the help of distortions (Freedman 1991). It is the Gothic turn of waking up, which gives the dreamer ears to see, hands to taste and above all a heart to report, that makes the traumatic knowledge he can only remember in fragments compatible with the ordinary everyday.

The line of demarcation between dream and waking can be transgressed, but only at a price. The dream can only be remembered and reported as a story, much as the poet shapes dark, unknown things by ascribing to them a name and a place. At the same time the dream, told in the light of day, must remain marked by uncanniness; located in the realm of signs but harking back to states which language can never fully grasp. Determined and indeterminate, the dream – and any belated aesthetic representation – has a navel, a point where it straddles, as Freud will have it, the unknown, the unreadable and the unutterable (Freud 1900).

A Midsummer Night's Dream and *Romeo and Juliet* both enact on a public stage the psychic traffic on the intimate stage their players share in the realm of a collective dream. In both plays the night as state of mind can only be made accessible as a theatrical enactment. While giving voice to dangerous nocturnal enjoyment – be it the night of love or the mutual implication of love and hate – both plays protect us from the traumatic knowledge they also invoke by cloaking it in the mantle of poetic form. The Gothic sensibility of Shakespeare may thus ultimately be located in the rhetorical closed circuit that thus unfolds. The nocturnal obscurity reveals and hides, endangers and protects. Yet the actual event, from which all transgressions of love take their shape, remains for the viewer and the reader a 'thing unknown', a 'vain fantasy as thin of substance as the air'. Only belatedly do we come to own it, and own up to its power.

3 Shakespeare Among the Goths

Steven Craig

> This, you see, is a short and commodious philosophy. Yet barbarians have their *own*, such as it is, if they are not enlightened by our reason. Shall we then condemn them unheard, or will it not be fair to let them have the telling of their own story?
>
> (Richard Hurd 1972: 194–95)

Writing in 1762, Bishop Hurd adopts the eighteenth century's most enduring polemic on the topic of historiography: assess the past on its own terms, for there is something inherently lacking in our rational present. As Hurd's *Letters on Chivalry and Romance* progresses, the reader is presented with a feudal chivalric 'Gothic system', histories of tyrannical barons and questing knights which, despite losing cultural currency with the passage of time, retain a certain spirit transmitted through romance literature. Horace Walpole summarizes this 'spirit' in the second preface to *The Castle of Otranto* (1765). Walpole's innovation in blending 'two kinds of romance, the ancient and the modern', widely regarded as the foundational statement of early Gothic writing, is inspired by a sense of present discontent: in the ancient romance, 'all was imagination and improbability'; in the modern romance – what we now know of as the 'novel', itself an example of Hurd's 'short and commodious philosophy' – 'nature is always intended to be, and sometimes has been, copied with success. Invention has not been wanting but the great resources of fancy have been damned up, by a strict adherence to common life' (Walpole 1996b: 9). What is at stake is the well-being of Literature (as we might term it) itself, a greater freedom to 'invent' truly poetical works. As Hurd suggests, the great precedent is William Shakespeare, but this association of the 'Gothic' and the 'Shakespearean' is no arbitrary one. As the inheritor of 'the Gothic system of prodigy and enchantment' (Hurd 1972: 254), Shakespeare's plays demonstrate the operations of a curious agency that supersedes all questions of authorial intention. Hurd then turns to Shakespeare's contemporary,

Ben Jonson, whose witch scenes in *The Masque of Queens* were written 'in emulation' of the three witches in Shakespeare's *Macbeth*, 'but certainly with the view (for so he tells us himself) *of reconciling the practice of antiquity to the Neoteric, and making it familiar with our popular witchcraft*' (Hurd 1972: 258). Jonson's printed text, furthermore, complements his intention to accord due privilege to the 'practice of antiquity' as its sourcing of classic texts attests to his learnedness. For Hurd, however, the agency of 'Gothic enchantments' surpasses even the printed text's learned qualities, for Jonson's emulation of the Gothic Shakespeare already deems it inevitable that the Gothic sway exerts its influence to its fullest. As Hurd concludes:

> And though, as he was an idolater of the antients [*sic*], you will expect him to draw freely from that source, yet from the large use he makes, too, of his other more recent authorities, you will perceive that some of the darkest shades of his picture are owing to hints and circumstances which he had catched, and could only catch, from the *Gothic* enchantments.
>
> (Hurd 1972: 258)

The Gothic, as Shakespeare purportedly conceived it, comprises a set of superstitions and enchantments carried by groups of unspecified migrant barbarians who plunged the civilized world into darkness (Hurd 1972: 254); however, as Hurd's veneration of the Gothic and of Shakespeare has it, this darkness was conducive to the life of the imagination. The Gothic is inherently paradoxical: what is conceived as 'barbarian' is also potentially liberating.

In the eighteenth century, the supernatural 'Gothic enchantments' observed by Hurd become crucial to the sense of Shakespeare as native English 'Original Genius', to the point that Elizabeth Montagu, in her *Essay on the Writings and Genius of Shakespear* [*sic*] (1769), preserves his name under the auspices of 'our Gothic bard' (Clery and Miles 2000: 37). As Jonathan Bate notes in his essay on Shakespeare and 'original genius', supernaturalism became central to the eighteenth-century sense of Shakespeare as an original writer, whose spectres and fairies were created out of nothing (Bate 1989b). And yet, there is much at stake in Montagu's essay: when she writes that 'our Gothic bard employs the potent agency of sacred fable, instead of mere amusive allegory', she locates Shakespeare in an event of parricide, in which the genius of 'Fable' – the raising of the ghosts of national superstition that ought to be contemplated with reverence – is unduly murdered by the 'enlightened' force of 'Allegory', or the tendency to explain away supernatural events as instances of ignorance (Clery and Miles 2000: 37–38). Allegory, or 'Enlightenment', is murderous insofar as it causes Genius to take shelter in the 'groves of philosophy', where the poet's divinities 'evaporate in allegory' (Clery and Miles 2000: 37). As Montagu suggests, poets such as Edmund Spenser, taking shelter in the light of day, wrote *The Faerie Queene*, but true Genius, as exhibited by Shakespeare, continued to walk in the shades of Gothic barbarism, elevating the ghosts of English superstition to the status of spectres to be revered.

But as Walpole's remarks on the 'damning up' of fancy in his own age suggest, eighteenth-century presentations of Shakespeare as 'original Genius' amount to more than mere historical interpretation. The great Gothic past is not discovered in the 1760s; rather, the idea of the Gothic past is created, with Shakespeare at its centre, to attend to present concerns on the state of literature. The post-Reformation 'groves of philosophy', as highlighted by Montagu, are always already the groves of Lockean empiricism, where John Locke's scene of the opening of the senses into the light of day is only superficially the case. In the Lockean paradigm, supernatural scenery is conceived as an effect of the mind's error of 'association'. Joseph Addison, in *The Spectator* (1711–14), approvingly cites Locke's chapter on the 'association of ideas' in his *Essay on Human Understanding* (1690):

> Mr Lock [*sic*] … has very curious remarks to shew how by the prejudice of Education one idea after introduces to the Mind a whole Set that bear no Resemblance to one another in the Nature of Things. Among several Examples of this kind he produces the following instance. *The Ideas of* Goblins and Sprights have really no more to do with Darkness than Light; yet let but a foolish Maid inculcate these often on the Mind of a Child, and raise them together, possibly he shall never be able to separate them again so long as he lives, but Darkness shall ever bring with it those frightful ideas, and they shall be so joined, that he cannot more bear the one than the other.
>
> (Addison 1965: 454)

On the one hand, the word 'Genius' had not yet acquired the cultural currency readily available to Hurd, Montagu and Walpole: when Addison, in *The Spectator* number 419 (1712), defines Shakespeare's 'genius' as a 'noble extravagance of fancy that thoroughly qualified him to touch the 'weak superstitious part of the reader's imagination', his sense of 'genius' is limited to a certain barbarian artlessness that breaks from all obligations of fidelity to the ancient past (Addison 1965: 572–73). In another 1712 essay, John Dennis's 'On the Genius and Writings of Shakespeare', remarkably little is mentioned of Shakespeare's 'genius', vaguely defined here, as it is, as the capacity to exhibit 'noble, generous, easie and natural sentiments' in his tragedies (Smith 1963: 24–25). 'Genius', in fact, is self-undermining, since, for Dennis, the mob scenes in *Julius Caesar* and *Coriolanus* reveal how Shakespeare's artlessness 'offends not only against the Dignity of Tragedy, but against the Truth of History likewise' (Smith 1963: 25). On the other hand, later writers like Bishop Hurd would engage in the task of *present*ing writers such as Addison in order to ensure the success of their *present*ing of Shakespeare as 'our Gothic bard'. In his sixth letter in the *Letters on Chivalry and Romance*, Hurd quotes a passage from *The Spectator*, once more essay 419, in which Addison comments that the vulgarity of English super-naturalism emerged not from great poetry of the ancient past, but from the untamed poetry of 'the darkness and superstition of later ages', from Shakespeare and his contemporaries (Hurd 1972: 259). Addison becomes a character who must concede to his creator's (Hurd's) contention that 'We are on enchanted ground, my friend'. As Hurd concludes, 'the fancies of our modern bards' are 'more sublime, more terrible, more alarming, than those of the ancient fablers' (Hurd 1972: 260). If 'Addison' reads a little closer, he too will see that the modern bards, in their accommodation of superstition, 'are the more poetical for being *Gothic*' (Hurd 1972: 260). By presenting Shakespeare as the preserve of an Englishness, whose ghosts testify to his genius, eighteenth-century Gothic writing engages in the creation of an idea of 'Shakespeare' that satisfies the needs of contemporary litera-ture. This is 'Gothic Shakespeare': the *present*ing of Shakespeare that allows the spectres of the *present*ed past to burst through the 'Enlightened', yet limited, decorum of literature.

Attending the emergence of Bardolatry during mid-century, then, is a commitment to 'dark Genius', where 'Gothic Shakespeare' signals the sense of stepping out of the confines of light to enter the night-time of 'Genius'. As Nathan Drake suggests in *Literary Hours, or Sketches Critical and Narrative* (1798), by the end of the eighteenth century, even 'the most enlightened mind, the mind free from all taint of superstition, involuntarily acknowledges the power of gothic agency' (Drake 1798: 87). As the 'terri-ble' and spectral events of 1790s literature find approval in Drake's *Hours*, his chapter on 'Gothic superstition' is especially noteworthy, not least for the manner in which he holds Shakespeare up to be the Gothic writer *par excellence*: 'The enchanted forest of Tasso, the spectre of Camoens, and the apparitions of Shakespeare, are to this day highly pleasing, striking, and sublime features in these delightful compositions' (Drake 1798: 87). Shakespeare is invoked for more than mere citation. The Gothic gifts to Shakespeare the potential to become *influential*: while, on the one hand, one reads that it is 'Shakespeare, beyond any other poet' who possesses the superior talent of 'raising the most awful, yet the most delightful species of terror', one is also informed that the very writing that is 'formed to influence the people, to surprise, elevate and delight', is under attack from a fashion amongst contemporary literary criticism to discredit it. As Drake responds: 'how shall criticism dare with impunity to expunge them?' (Drake 1798: 93). Gothic Shakespeare addresses not only the cultural celebration of Shakespeare in the eighteenth-century 'present', but cultural anxiety on the part of critics who detect the inseparability of the 'Gothic' from the 'Shakespearean'. To expunge the Gothic mode is also to expunge Shakespeare, and vice versa.

In short, the 'true' story of the Gothic barbarians is one of freedom of imagination, literary excellence and awareness of the biases of history and historiography. Having noted this, however, analysis of one Shakespeare text, *Titus Andronicus*, shows this story up for what it is: a story, an alternative in which the *present*ing of Shakespeare and the Gothic satisfies present needs rather than preserving the purity of the past. I will examine Shakespeare's own sense of the Gothic as it is presented in *Titus Andronicus*, arguing in favour of a malevolent barbarianism that nonetheless offers a critique of the moral readings critics such as Jonathan Bate impose on the play, of a 'Shakespearean Gothic' distinct from 'Gothic Shakespeare'. This essay will examine Bate's Arden edition of the play (1995), which argues unconvincingly that Shakespeare's Goths are harbingers of constitutional reform, a political ideal that is finally realized only later, during the aftermath of the Glorious Revolution of 1688. The trappings of constitutionalism added a further signification to the word 'Gothic' during the eighteenth century. For Joseph Addison, unflinching support for constitutional monarchy is figured as support for the 'Gothick balance': as Addison writes, 'I have often heard of a Senior Alderman in Buckinghamshire, who, at all publick meetings, grows drunk in praise of Aristocracy, and is often encountered by an old Justice of Peace who lives in the neighbourhood, and will talk to you from morning till Night on the Gothick balance' (Addison 1980: 264). Indeed, Bate's anachronism is compounded by the fact that the play itself was widely condemned by eighteenth-century writers and editors of Shakespeare, especially Alexander Pope and Richard Farmer. If, as Bate implies, Shakespeare's Protestant Goths appeal to eighteenth-century sensibilities regarding the Gothic constitution, it is reasonable to suggest that the play might have been adapted to peddle this political ideology, yet its reception history clearly suggests that this was never the case. The essay will also consider eighteenth-century attitudes towards *Titus Andronicus* that favour Shakespeare's authorship of the play: by accepting Shakespeare's authorship, writers such as Elizabeth Griffith, in *The Morality of Shakespeare's Drama Illustrated* (1775), and Ann Radcliffe, in *The Mysteries of Udolpho* (1794), enable a definition of 'Gothic Shakespeare' that involves a *present*ing of Shakespeare that refuses to offer a wholesale endorsement of 'the present'.

In the decades prior to Shakespeare, Renaissance historiography concerning the medieval Gothic past gathered momentum as it contended that the Gothic heritage was not at all liberty loving, but barbarian. In his *Lives of the Artists* (c.1550), Giorgio Vasari outlined the force which he believed to be responsible for the erosion of high art, placing the blame squarely on the doorstep of the Gothic. Although at one point Vasari concedes that Italian art was already on its way out prior to the 'Gothic' invasions of Rome, he nevertheless insists that the barbarian invaders are to be held responsible for its final decline. In a time of great political upheaval, Vasari writes that

> almost all the barbarian nations rose up against the Romans in various parts of the world, and this within a short time led not only to the humbling of their great empire but also to worldwide destruction, notably at Rome itself. This destruction struck equally and decisively at the greatest artists, sculptors, painters and architects: they and their work were left buried and submerged among the sorry ruins and debris of that renowned city.
>
> (Vasari 1978: 35–36)

While Vasari proceeds to savour the triumph of modern Italian art over the barbarian influence, the prospect of a recurrent Gothic influence in writing and in education, for Roger Ascham in the 1560s, had to be avoided by first being addressed in his *The Scholemaster* (published in 1570). In this text, Ascham observes that the unwitting abuse of the Latin tongue taking place in the early modern translation curriculum is proving detrimental to the impressionable school pupil and his future development: 'But, now, commonlie, in the best Scholes in England, for wordes, right choice is smallie regarded, true propriety wholly neglected, confusion is brought in, barbariousnesse is bred up so in yong wittes, as afterward they be, not onelie marde for speaking, but also corrupted in judgement' (Ascham 1967: 2). With the precedent set by Vasari, it comes as no surprise to learn that this corruption is 'Gothic' in origin: Ascham stresses the importance of children learning Latin in a context in which the use of 'Gothic' rhyme in writing is increasing in popularity, to the extent that it has become a saleable commodity. As Ascham writes, 'and shoppes in London should not be so full of lewd and rude rymes, as commonlie they are' (Ascham 1967: 60). If the circulation of rhyme is unenlightened and yet popular in England, the useful myth of Gothic inheritance creates an origin in which the Gothic way in England can be discussed as an aberration, that is, not as something that must be vehemently disavowed, but as an error of nature that can be dismissed with ease.[1] For Ascham, all that is required is an awareness of the inherently virtuous nature of the Latin tongue, for only then is it possible for Englishmen to evaluate their own use of 'rude beggarly ryming'. The preservation of the myth of Gothic inheritance relies on a history of the migration of rhyme: for Ascham, rhyme was first brought into Italy by the 'Gothes' and 'Hunnes', only to migrate to Germany and France, before finally being 'receyved into England by men of excellent wit in deed, but of small learning, and lesse judgement in that behalfe' (Ascham 1967: 60)

As this already suggests, Shakespeare's own sense of 'the Gothic', that is, the Gothic as it is figured in Renaissance historiography, bears little resemblance to late eighteenth-century understandings of the term, with its shades of dark and impending danger often suggestive of Edmund Burke's notion of the sublime. The word 'goth' appears explicitly in two of his plays: *As You Like It* and *Titus Andronicus*. In Act 3, Scene 3 of the former, the pastoral setting of Arden is evoked by Touchstone the clown as an alien space adrift from the realm of civilization, remarking to his betrothed, Audrey, 'I am heere with thee and thy Goats, as the most capricious poet, honest Ouid, was among the Gothes' (3.3.1571–72) [3.3.5–6].[2] In the scene's immediate context, Touchstone is lamenting Audrey's lack of good taste: 'When a mans verses cannot be vnderstood, nor a mans good wit seconded with the forward childe, understanding, it strikes a man more dead than a great reckoning in a little roome … Truly, I would the Gods hadde made thee more poetical' (3.3.1575–79) [3.3.9–13]. Shakespeare's reference to Ovid, moreover, evokes the classical poet's biographical writing as it is presented in his *Tristia*. In this work, Ovid writes of his exile in the 'barbarian' region of Tomis, after circulating the seditious and erotic poem *Ars Amatoria*, expressing his fear of the barbarian Getae populace whose 'Harsh voices, grim faces' and innate violence appear to press too closely on Ovid's sense of his fortunate difference. Although at one point in the text he suggests that his Latin writing has been infected by the metre of 'Getic measure' (Ovid 1988: 157), Ovid reinstates himself as 'a barbarian, understood by nobody', the alien other who is laughed at because of his unfamiliar tongue (Ovid 1988: 249). Ovid's account of the Getic barbarians makes no reference to the terms 'Goth' or 'Gothic', but its references to Getic measure lend themselves well to early modern anxieties concerning the presence of unenlightened sensibilities and writing styles in England, presences that Ascham would term Gothic. In *As You Like It*, Touchstone's appropriation of these barbarians under the name of 'Goth' concurs with the humanist import of Latin texts that stressed the derogation of a race of outsiders identified by the traces of their barbarian Gothic heritage.

It is in *Titus Andronicus*, however, that Shakespeare's position among the Goths is, at once, most pronounced and most contested. In summary, the play begins with the return of the Roman general Titus to his homeland after victory against the barbarous Goths. With the Gothic prisoners Queen Tamora and her sons in tow, Titus duly proceeds to condemn Tamora's son, Alarbus, to sacrifice, in accordance with Roman custom. Upon Tamora's silenced plea – 'A mothers teares in passion for her sonne' (1.1.106) [1.1.106] – the Queen of the Goths, now the bride of the emperor Saturninus, enacts an elaborate revenge that incorporates the murder of Bassianus, brother of the newly crowned emperor Saturninus, as well as the violent rape of the chaste Lavinia at the hands of the Gothic brothers Chiron and Demetrius. While Titus's son Lucius enlists an army of Goths to invade corrupt Rome, Titus's equally spectacular revenge reaches its height as he kills the brothers before proceeding to 'play the Cooke' (5.2.2300) [5.2.203] and serve up an edible 'goth' pie to an unsuspecting Tamora. In this play, the Goths fulfil two important functions. First, Shakespeare's repetition of peculiarly 'Gothic' traits concurs with the textual representation of Goths as presented by Renaissance historiographers and by the pedagogical *Tristia*: Titus returns home after 'weary warres with the barbarous *Gothes*' (1.1.28) [1.1.28]; Demetrius calls for supreme spectacles of violence, recalling a time 'When Gothes were Gothes and *Tamora* was Queene' (l.1.140) [1.1.140], while Tamora plays on Rome's sense of 'Gothic' as 'other' as she accuses Lavinia and Bassianus of calling her 'Laciuious Goth' (2.2.763) [2.2.763]. By the end of the play, however, the Goths are allies of Rome, motivated by Tamora's desertion of them for the sake of her own ambition, while the reader or spectator is treated to one Goth soldier's contemplation of a ruined monastery. For Jonathan Bate, the latter event can be summarized as a 'Goth's meditation upon Henry VIII's dissolution of the monasteries, the most drastic consequence of England's break with Rome' (Bate 1995: 19), a deliberately anachronistic reference to England's break with its dark, Catholic past in the middle of the sixteenth century.

Do the Goths, then, in Shakespearean Gothic, abandon their 'evil' barbarian heritage in their potential to become 'good'? Bate's 'Introduction' to the Arden edition of *Titus Andronicus* (1995) begins by acknowledging the precedents set by Renaissance historiography, and Shakespeare's subsequent collapsing of a variety of Roman epochs onto the site of his drama. As the admired texts of Plutarch and Livy were held as valorizations of Rome's great ancient past, narrating the defeats of the Carthaginians and the Gauls, the word 'Goth' came to denote a general term of denigration of *all* foreign bodies, no matter how close they came to the gates of Rome. Bate recognizes, then, that 'the Goths in the play are not historically specific', that the Goth is distinctly 'other', yet he proceeds to argue that the Goths who come to the aid of Lucius can be located in the Germanic-inspired 'translatio imperii ad Teutonicos' of the late sixteenth century. It becomes clear that the Protestant Goth Bate is intent on preserving in *Titus Andronicus* is relayed through Samuel Kliger's reading of the Goths in England during the seventeenth and eighteenth centuries, as Bate quotes Kliger's famous passage from *The Goths in England* (1952) in which he comments on the 'translatio':

> The translatio suggested forcefully an analogy between the breakup of the Roman empire by the Goths and the demands of the humanist reformers of northern Europe for religious freedom, interpreted as liberation from Roman priestcraft. In other words, the translatio crystallized the idea that humanity was twice ransomed from Roman tyranny and depravity – in antiquity by the Goths, in modern times by their descendants, the German reformers. In their youth, vigor, and moral purity, the Goths destroyed the decadent Roman civilization and brought about a rejuvenation or rebirth of the world. In the same way, the Reformation was interpreted as a second world rejuvenation.
>
> (Bate 1995: 20)

While I do not question Kliger's historiography, Bate's citation of Kliger neglects Kliger's own contention that the 'translatio' as it was inspired by German humanism involved 'not so much political inheritances as racial characteristics', and that the political sense of the word 'Gothic' took hold only in the middle of the seventeenth century. According to Kliger, it was not until anti-Royalist sentiments in 1640s England took hold – against Charles I but also against the Royalist Sir Robert Filmer's political tracts – that the sense of a *political* inheritance was detected (Kliger 1952). While critics such as Edward Jacobs argue for revisionist scholarship concerning the circulation of the word 'Gothic' during the seventeenth and eighteenth centuries, it ought to be conceded that the *naming* of this political inheritance as 'Gothic' becomes the norm only after the 1688 Revolution, and especially following the death of the Protestant William of Orange in 1714, as the example from Addison's *The Freeholder* suggests (Jacobs 2000). In short, it is precisely Bate's overestimation of the influence of the German-inspired 'translation imperii ad Teutonicos' as an *imported* doctrine that leads him to suggest that there is something distinctly Shakespearean about the presence of the benevolent, freedom-loving Goth.

Bate further alerts us to William Lambarde's *Perambulation of Kent* (1570) as a possible source for Shakespeare's portrayal of the Goths who come to the aid of Titus. Bate tells us that Lambarde's text reveals that the names of the numerous tribes that migrated to Britain – Jutes, Getes, Goths and Germans – were interchangeable in Elizabethan times, and that the category of 'Goth' created for Elizabethan culture an ancestry steeped in faith in the values of valour and justice (Bate 1995: 19). If one turns to Lambarde's text, it is evident that there was a sense in which the author is influenced by the translatio: for instance, he evokes the recent Reformation as a time in which 'the glorious and bright shining beames of Gods holy truth and gladsome gospel had pearced the mistie thick cloudes of ignorance' (Lambarde 1970: 169); at the same time, the onset of Enlightenment is not figured as peculiarly 'Germanic' or 'Gothic', as Lambarde adds that this event happened 'not onely to the people of Germanie, but to the inhabitants of this island also' (Lambarde 1970: 169). Even if the Teutonic translation is in operation here, Lambarde is reluctant to concede the fact, preferring instead to frame the imported translatio as merely a shared sense of Protestantism between England and Germany. Furthermore, Bate's use of Kent as a synecdoche for Britain yields further problems when Shakespeare enters the fray. In *2 Henry VI*, Kentish sensibilities, or expressions of valour and of justice, are noted for their absence, as Stafford attempts to crush Jack Cade's rebellion against Henry's claim to the English throne. While Stafford addresses the 'Rebellious hinds, the filth and scum of Kent' (4.2.2283) [4.2.121], Lord Saye laments the inaccuracies of 'the commentaries Caesar writ' on Kent, providing the epitaph of Kent as *'bona terra, mala gens'* ('a good land of bad people') (4.7.2510) [4.7.53]. Even William Lambarde regrets Jack Cade's rebellion against the king, implying a dark period in Kentish history in which Kentishmen temporarily took leave of the freedom-loving traits that confirmed their distinct 'Gothic' heritage (Lambarde 1970: 391). Shakespeare's Gothic is not paradoxical and ambivalent in the sense that Hurd's Gothic is: barbarism is ignorance and violence, without the positive political connotations of liberty and constitutional balance, without the positive literary connotations of dark Genius.

In other words, the absence of the paradox of 'Gothic Shakespeare' marks *Titus Andronicus* as an example of 'Shakespearean Gothic', a category wholly distinct from the former. Because Bate maintains that *Titus Andronicus* prefigures this sense of the Reformation 'as a second world rejuvenation', his reading of the play's bloody spectacles does not, as he suggests, modulate from the Goths as racialized entities to Protestant harbingers of the Reformation; it elides entirely the issues of racial othering that are central to Shakespeare's construction of the Goths, to the extent that the mutilated Lavinia is figured as a martyr worthy of the Protestant John Foxe's *Book of Martyrs* rather than as the victim of the 'laciuious' Goth brothers, Chiron and Demetrius.[3] Moreover, Bate's examination of the 'Protestant Goths' inflects his editorial decisions, as he attempts to explain the presence of the Goths in the final scene of the play ('Ile play the Cooke'). In the final scene, Lucius and the Goths attend Titus's mock-feast, witnessing his killings of Lavinia and Tamora; once Saturninus, in turn, kills Titus, Lucius completes his revenge on the emperor: 'Can the sonnes eie behold his father bleede? / Ther's meede for meede, death for a deathly deede' (5.3.2365–66) [5.3.64–65]. In the same stage direction that requires Lucius to kill Saturninus, the Goths enter the stage, although the significance of this remains questionable. Stanley Wells, in the Oxford edition of *Titus Andronicus* (1986b), inserts the stage direction '*He kills Saturnine. Confusion followes. Enter Gothes. Lucius, Marcus and others goe aloft*'. Here, the presence of the Goths remains passive; they have no bearing on events as they unfold on the stage. In Bate's edition, however, a very different stage direction reads '*He kills Saturninus. Uproar. The Goths protect the Andronici, who go aloft*'.[4] While the Oxford edition endorses mere 'confusion' against a Goth background, Bate inserts the prospect of a kind of violence, or 'uproar', in which the life of Lucius is threatened by virtue of his bloody deed, an uproar that can only be quelled by the Gothic army. But while the Oxford edition retains the Goths' lack of historical specificity, the Arden edition reprints a still from Brook's production, in which the Goths patrol the presumed 'uproar', blocking the passage to Lucius and Marcus Andronicus who speak from aloft. As Bate's moral reading of the play summarizes, 'Where Saturninus went aloft with the "evil" Goths in the first act, Lucius escapes aloft through the offices of the "good" Goths in the last act' (Bate 1995: 14–15). It might be suggested that Bate's edition engages with issues of past and present as outlined in John Drakakis's essay on the problems of editing *The Merchant of Venice*: as Drakakis writes, 'We have become fond of fudging this interplay [of a text printed four centuries ago and of 'present' scholarly ventures to fix the purity of that text], and of emphasising the *difference* between past and present; it is only through recognizing this *difference* as somehow constitutive that we can come to an understanding of ourselves' (Drakakis 2007: 82). While Bate secures the Protestant succession to the throne with the aid of the 'Reformed' Goths, the still from the Brook production reminds the modern reader of the space between our present moment and the lost moment of a text's original literary production, and our inevitable insertion of the present into *all* literary texts. I do not claim that the notion of the 'good Goth' did not exist in Shakespeare's time: rather, I suggest that this notion did not exert the kind of influence upon Elizabethan culture, and certainly upon the works of Shakespeare, that Bate would have the reader believe. The distinction between the benevolent Goth and the barbarous Goth postdates *Titus Andronicus* by nearly a century, and yet, as Bate's analysis suggests, the semantic appropriation of the word 'Gothic' is potentially fraught with dangers that tend towards anachronism. In the case of *Titus Andronicus*, Bate's Gothic Reformation comes at a price: that price is Lavinia.

Bate's reading of the Goths elides the strategy of dissembling that operates in Shakespearean Gothic, within and between the categories of the civilized 'Roman' and the barbarous 'Goth', as the impending rupture of the Roman / Gothic distinction reaches its greatest intensity during the play's central event: the rape of Lavinia. Upon the sacrifice of Alarbus, Lucius returns to the stage with the following triumphant proclamation:

> See Lord and father how we haue performd
> Our Romane rights: *Alarbus* limbs are lopt
> And intrals feede the sacrifising fire,
> Whose smoke like incense doth perfume the skie.
> (1.1.142–45) [1.1.142–45]

The images of 'lopping' and 'hewing' that characterize what Lucius terms 'our Roman rites' proceed to take a sinister turn as Marcus Andronicus discovers the mutilated body of Lavinia:

> Speake gentle Neece, what sterne vngentle hands,
> Hath lopt, and hewed, and made thy body bare,
> Of her two branches those sweet Ornaments,
> Whose cyrcling shadowes, Kings haue sought to sleepe in,
> And might not gaine so great a happines
> As halfe thy loue. Why dost not speake to me?
> (2.4.975–80) [2.4.16–21]

It is only partly through the violence of the play that the binary of Roman/Gothic is brought into disrepute; the transference of the signs of 'lopping' into another realm of signification, the satisfaction of the brothers' lust and the overarching theme of revenge inaugurated by Tamora, shows the Roman principle of justice by sacrifice to be conspicuous in its absence. Instead, sacrifice becomes the site of revenge and is concentrated on the figure of Lucius as much as it is upon Titus: it is Lucius, not Titus, who circulates the imagery of 'lopping' and 'hewing' throughout the first act, just as it is Lucius who finds for his father 'Revenge's cave' to call upon the aid of the Goths: 'But now nor *Lucius* nor *Lauinia* liues/But in obliuion and hatefull greefes … Now will I to the *Gothes* and raise a powre,/To bee reuenged on Rome and *Saturnine*' (3.1.1309–15) [3.1.293–99]. The Goth army serves the double function of securing the 'benevolent' Lucius's claim to Rome while fighting in the shadow of Titus and Lucius's desire for revenge. Roman justice and Gothic violence unwittingly coalesce in the shared desire to brutalize and exhibit tortured bodies. The idea of 'Rome' is itself marked by the tendency to become as Gothic as the barbarian Goths it denounces.

And yet, if 'Rome' is nothing other than the potential to become 'Gothic', does it then follow that 'Gothic' is the potential to become 'good'? If interpreted as a question of morality, then this certainly seems to be the case, but the Romans and Goths in *Titus Andronicus* do not express intrinsic goodness or evil that is then represented in language through the rhetoric of 'justice' or the violence of dismemberment. Rather, Romans (or any arbiters of intrinsic goodness) and Goths share a propensity to inhabit the language of their respective Other. So, while Gothic images of 'lopping' and 'hewing' burst into the Roman delivery of justice, the Goth brothers, Chiron and Demetrius, are able to goad Titus with Latinate quotations that suggest that they have undergone the standard English early modern education. In act four, Titus provokes the brothers into further violence by having young Lucius send a note to them:

DEMETRIUS: What's here? A scrole, and written round about?
     Let's see,
     Integer vitae, scelerisque purus,
     Non eget Mauri iaculis, nec arcu.
CHIRON: O, 'tis a verse in *Horace*, I know it well:
     I read it in the Grammer long agoe.

(4.2.1545–50) [4.2.20–25][5]

Chiron and Demetrius attack the discourse of their 'civilized' counterparts from within, exhibiting the very capacity to learn a language that typically marks early modern man from his counterpart. Chiron and Demetrius do not become 'good' Goths, importing their freedom-loving traits on to a foreign land; instead, their education recalls the Gothic historiography of writers such as Vasari and Roger Ascham, who contended that the misty clouds of Gothic barbarism had been surpassed by an Enlightened sensibility. Such is his cultural currency in the world today that it would appear as if Shakespeare himself had anticipated the arrival of moral readings that limit the potential for deconstructionist critique. In Shakespearean Gothic, what is at stake is not the realization of the good Goth, but the useful myth of Gothic inheritance and its supplementary disavowal.

This is *not* 'Gothic Shakespeare': in Gothic Shakespeare, what is at stake is the preservation of Shakespeare's name, the *present*ing of Shakespeare. It is with this distinction in mind that *Titus Andronicus* illuminates one final irony in Bate's historiography. If *Titus Andronicus* and political Gothicism share so close an affinity, why is it that the play was often excluded from the Shakespearean canon during the late seventeenth and eighteenth centuries? In the published version of his *Titus Andronicus, or the Rape of Lavinia* (1687), the Restoration playwright Edward Ravenscroft suggested that Shakespeare's authorship amounted to little more than 'some Mastertouches to one or two of the Principal Parts or Characters', that the play's lack of refined language made it 'the most incorrect and indigested piece in all his Works ... rather a heap of Rubbish than a Structure' (Ravenscroft 1969: n.p.). Alexander Pope, writing in 1725, contended that *Titus Andronicus*, alongside *The Winter's Tale* and *Love's Labours Lost*, formed a set of plays that was 'produced by unknown authors, or fitted up for the Theatre while it was under his [Shakespeare's] administration: and no owner claiming them, they were adjudged to him, as they give strays to the Lord of the Manor' (Smith 1963: 56). Writing in 1767, Richard Farmer, in his 'Essay on the Learning of Shakespeare', expressed 'not the least doubt that but this *horrible* Piece was originally written by the Author of the *Lines* thrown into the mouth of the *Player* in *Hamlet*, and of the Tragedy of *Locrine*' (Smith 1963: 190). Among those writers who accepted Shakespeare's authorship was Elizabeth Griffith, who, in *The Morality of Shakespeare's Drama Illustrated* (1775), wrote that 'I should suppose the intire [*sic*] Piece to be his ... Because the whole of the fable, as well as the conduct of it, is so very *barbarous*, in every sense of the word, that I think ... he could hardly have adopted it from any other person's composition' (Griffith 1971: 403). Superficially, it seems that Griffith registers the semantic shift that the word 'barbarous' takes during the late eighteenth century. First, Griffith likens the play's violent spectacles to the execution of the regicides D'Aveiro and Tavora in Portugal in 1759:

> I should imagine, from the very shocking spectacles exhibited in this Play, that it could never have been represented on any theatre, except the Lisbon scaffold, where the duke d'Aveiro, the Marquis of Tavora, *cum suis*, were so barbarously massacred, for the supposed Jesuit's plot against the present King of Portugal.
>
> (Griffith 1971: 403–4)

Second, although Griffith expresses surprise that the play could ever have been popular on the English stage – 'The different humours and tastes of times! It would not only be hissed, but driven off the stage at present' (404) – the word 'barbarous' also denotes Shakespeare's originality, since 'he could hardly have adopted it from any other person's composition'. But as the example of D'Aveiro reveals, the semantic shifts in the terms 'Gothic' and 'barbarous' do not merely privilege their present meanings, but carry with them that which must be rejected: the 'barbarous', that is, violent, spectacles of *Titus Andronicus* do not belong to the past, or to a 'past text', because they are still present, and are made, in Griffith's analysis at least, to coincide with the eighteenth century's sense of Shakespeare as 'original Genius'. If 'originality' is but one sense of the word 'barbarous', the Gothic *present*ing of Shakespeare evokes its other, darker implications.

By the 1790s, the Gothic appropriation of Shakespeare moves closer to Drake's notion of 'gothic agency', an agency that shows itself in Ann Radcliffe's endorsement of her present, in the form of the bourgeois doctrine of sensibility. The subtitle of Ravenscroft's adaptation of *Titus Andronicus*, 'The Rape of Lavinia', is telling, as Lavinia's rape proves crucial to Radcliffe's revision of the narrow definition of 'Gothic' as univocally 'barbarian' at the end of the eighteenth century. In the penultimate chapter of *The Mysteries of Udolpho* (1794), the pastoral Languedoc landscape 'conspires' with the melody played by Emily St. Aubert on her lute, lulling 'her mind into a state of gentle sadness' as the remembrance of past times affects tears in the fashion of sensibility (Radcliffe 1998: 666). Emily's emotional susceptibility is introduced by the following epigraph, taken from *Titus Andronicus*: 'Then, fresh tears / Stood on her cheeks, as doth the honey-dew / Upon a gather'd lily almost withered', including the signature 'SHAKESPEARE'. The source of Radcliffe's epigraph superficially appears problematic, not only by recalling Titus's response to the mutilated body of his daughter, but also by unequivocally accepting and asserting Shakespeare's authorship of the play:

> Thou hast no hands to wipe away thy teares,
> Nor tongue to tell me who hath martred thee:
> Thy husband he is dead, and for his death
> Thy brothers are condemnde, and dead by this.
> Look, *Marcus*, ah, sonne *Lucius*, looke on her!
> When I did name her brothers, then fresh teares
> Stood on her cheeks, as doth the honie dew
> Vpon a gathred Lillie almost withered.
> (3.1.1122–29) [3.1.106–13]

What is the dialogue between Shakespeare's text and Radcliffe's appropriation? As Radcliffe begins her epigraph with the adverb 'Then', it seems plausible to suggest that the reader of *The Mysteries of Udolpho* ought to be familiar with the context of rape that precedes it. It might then be

suggested that the early modern scene of sexual violation undermines
Radcliffe's scene of sensibility, but this explanation proves unsatisfactory if
one considers that the female characters in *Udolpho* face little or no threat
of rape. As Mary Poovey and Robert Miles have suggested, threats to the
female characters, in particular Emily herself, are economic and not
sexual, as the villainous Signor Montoni chases Emily's signature, a signature that will guarantee him her inheritance (Poovey 1979; Miles 1995:
129–49). The diminution of the sexual threat attests to the semantic shift
that the term 'Gothic' had undergone by the 1790s, as the overtly violent
sexualities of the Goth brothers, Chiron and Demetrius, are contained in
the play through their murder by Titus, and by Radcliffe in her retelling
of tears for the ends of an amiable sensibility. Emily is not the only tearful
character in *Udolpho*: in the same chapter, Emily is reunited with
Valancourt and, as both declare their love for each other, the latter
'pressed her hand to his lips, the tears, that fell over it, spoke a language,
which could not be mistaken, and to which words were inadequate'
(Radcliffe 1998: 668). While sexual violence dictates that Titus has no
control over the fate of his daughter, the decidedly asexual union of Emily
and Valancourt honours the memory of Emily's late father:

> St. Aubert, as he sometimes lingered to examine the wild plants in his
> path, often looked forward with pleasure to Emily and Valancourt …
> he, with a countenance of animated delight, pointing to her attention
> some grand feature of the scene; and she, listening and observing with
> a look of tender seriousness, that spoke the elevation of her mind.
> They appeared like two lovers who had never strayed beyond these
> their native mountains; whose situation had secluded them from the
> frivolities of common life, whose ideas were simple and grand, like the
> landscapes among which they moved, and who knew no other happi-
> ness, than in the union of pure and affectionate hearts. St. Aubert
> smiled, and sighed at the romantic picture of felicity his fancy drew;
> and sighed again to think, that nature and simplicity were so little
> known to the world, as that their pleasures were thought romantic.
>
> (Radcliffe 1998: 49)

The difference between *Titus Andronicus* and *The Mysteries of Udolpho* is the
difference between shaming the father and honouring him. Lavinia's rape
brings impossible feelings of shame upon Titus – 'Die, die, *Lavinia*, and thy
shame with thee, / And with thy shame thy Father's sorrow die' (lines
2346–47) – while in *The Mysteries of Udolpho* the preservation of the
memory of St Aubert is never in doubt because Radcliffe's appropriation/
repetition disperses the sexual violence that is at the heart of Titus's sense of

shame. And yet, Radcliffe's appropriation of Shakespeare is not verbatim repetition, but a creative repetition that, in order to be creative, must make present that which it seeks to discard, a point that might be made of the very nature of Gothic writing itself. Poovey's comment that Radcliffe's fiction 'merely reassserts an idealized – and insulated – paternalism and relegates the issues she cannot resolve to the background of her narrative' (Poovey 1979: 311) does not hold up to Radcliffe's appropriation of *Titus Andronicus* in *Udolpho*: although Emily has learned from the threats of excesses in her own sensibility, both she and Lavinia shed their tears at the same time. Sensibility can only become the sign of benevolence when it runs concurrently with threats to its stability. Sensibility is not undermined by the horrors of the 'prior' text; those horrors enable sensibility to exist as such in the first place.

Both eighteenth-century Gothic and 'appropriation', then, share a concern with assigning privilege to 'the present'. Adopting Stephen Greenblatt's notion of 'self-fashioning', Jerrold E. Hogle suggests that Gothic fictions 'oscillate between different discourses of self-definition in the eighteenth century by being later and more uprooted signifiers of the conflicts in modes of symbol-making and beliefs about "self-fashioning" that arose in fifteenth to sixteenth century Europe' (Hogle 2001: 296). On the one hand, Hogle's comment expresses the problem of assigning privilege to the present, as the curious agency of the 'Gothic ghost of the counterfeit' continues to pull back towards the past. However, by adapting Greenblatt verbatim, the possibility of dialogue with prior literary works is obviated in favour of a mechanical repetition forever haunted by 'the ghost of the counterfeit', that sense of 'betwixt-and-betweenness' that is encoded in both Renaissance and eighteenth-century assertions of middle-class integrity (296). To think of the problem of 'the present' in terms of literary appropriation instead of 'blocks' of self-fashioning is to acknowledge the force of those intentional and creative repetitions that flow through Nathan Drake's sense of 'gothic agency'. We can say this, because just as, say, Ann Radcliffe's sense of the past lends itself especially well to the task of *present*ing Shakespeare, so too will our own present become a past to be appropriated in the future.

Notes

1 My use of the term 'useful myth' is taken from Mark Madoff's essay 'The Useful Myth of Gothic Ancestry', which suggests that variant definitions of the word 'Gothic' uncover one common thesis: 'the gothic is *ancestral*' (Madoff 2004: 28).

2 In every Shakespeare quotation in this essay, I have provided two references. In the first set of parentheses, I have cited Stanley Wells and Gary Taylor's *The Complete Works: Original Spelling Edition* (1986b). All references in square parenthesis refer to Wells and Taylor's modern spelling edition of *The Complete Works* (1986a). By including old spellings in the essay, I hope to gauge a sense

of the difference between Shakespeare's 'Gothic' and later eighteenth-century Gothic appropriations of Shakespeare.

3 More recently, Francesca T. Royster has questioned the racialized white/black binary opposition, figured in the play as the difference between civilization and Moorish barbarism (Aaron), observing that Shakespeare's Goths are racially marked by their extreme whiteness. As Royster argues, this impacts significantly on the Roman/Goth binary, as it becomes difficult to identify racial differences between the Romans and their Gothic counterparts (Royster 2000).

4 For a brief analysis of Bate's stage direction, see Anthony Brian Taylor's review in *Notes and Queries*, which argues against Bate's reading of the play by identifying Lucius's supposed allegiance to Roman Catholicism (Taylor 1996).

5 Bate's translation, attributed to Horace, reads thus: 'the man of upright life and free from crime does not need the javelins or bows of the Moor' (Bate 1995: 219).

4 Gothic and the ghost of *Hamlet*

Dale Townshend

'A masterpiece always moves, by definition, in the manner of a ghost.'

(Jacques Derrida 1994: 18)

1

'Shakespeare's Ghost', an anonymous poem published in *The London Magazine* in June 1750, conjured up the scene of an imperious cultural haunting.[1] In a canny reworking of the spectral visitation of the murdered father in *Hamlet*, the ghost of Shakespeare returns in the poem not from the purgatorial 'prison-house (1.4.14) of Shakespeare's play, but 'From fields of bliss, and that Elysian grove, / Where bards' and heroes' souls, departed, rove' (1–2).[2] His destination, too, is more a mythologized rural England than the castellated battlements of Elsinore, for this is a spectre, we are told, who 'seeks his native isle once more', viewing with 'filial eyes the parent shore' (3–4). It is not long before the ghost of Shakespeare, at once the fountainhead and offspring, father and son of his native country proceeds to speak, apostrophizing Britain from beyond the grave as that place 'Where first, in humble state my lyre I strung; / Where first the tragick muse unloos'd my tongue' (9–10). His fame, the ghost insists, cannot be shackled to his original cultural moment, and in what reads as a defiance of what some eighteenth-century critics took to be Shakespeare's controversial disregard for the Aristotelian unities of time, place and action in *Hamlet*, the Bard's renown is described as radiating outwards across historical time and cultural space: 'Nor was the pow'r to draw a nation's tears / Fixt to one circle of revolving years: / Nor cou'd so short a space my fame confine, / The present hours, nay, those to come, are mine' (15–18). It would seem that, within the poem's mid-eighteenth-century context, the original spectral injunction to 'Remember me' (1.5.91) has become curiously redundant. What this ghostly father does require of 'ye Britons'

(22), though, is protection, a defence against the numerous acts of editing, adaptation and revision to which the Bard and his texts had been subjected in earlier decades by the 'idly busy bookworm' (25) – meddlesome textual interventions, the ghost maintains, which have invariably served to alienate his 'true genius' in language (28). Performance, Shakespeare's spectre insists, is the only viable means of mourning, honouring and commemorating the dead (30–33). In what appears now to be a predictable gesture, the ghostly father finds in David Garrick, Shakespearean actor *par excellence* and eventual manager of the Drury Lane theatre, a Hamlet-like son, a figure who, like his tragic counterpart, will dutifully restore his father's wounded legacy through passionate and inspired performance of his dramatic roles:

> To thee, my great restorer, must belong
> The task to vindicate my injur'd song,
> To place each character in proper light,
> To speak my words and do my meaning right,
> To save me from a dire impending fate,
> Nor yield me up to Cibber and to Tate: [...]
> (83–88)

Issuing from an historical moment characterized by a profound cultural veneration of Shakespeare, the poem's references to the destructive textual interventions of writers the likes of Colley Cibber and Nahum Tate assume a particular urgency. Playwright, actor and Poet Laureate Colley Cibber, one of the maligned objects of Pope's satire in the four-book version of *The Dunciad* (1743), was, by 1750, notorious for his tasteless adaptations of Shakespeare's plays.[3] Nahum Tate, the other textual meddler from whom the ghost of Shakespeare seeks protection in the poem, had wreaked havoc with the tragic ending of Shakespeare's play in his version of *The History of King Lear* in 1680.[4] As Robert D. Hume has argued, these and other such appropriations, reworkings and plagiarisms of Shakespeare were common practice in Britain until as late as the 1740s, that is, before the rise of Bardology and its subsequent apogee in such significant cultural events as the Shakespeare Jubilee in Stratford in 1769, Edmond Malone's supplementary edition of Shakespeare in 1780, and the opening of Boydell's Shakespeare Gallery in 1789 (Hume 1997). By 1750, the interventions of Cibber, Tate and others could be poetically figured in 'Shakespeare's Ghost' as forms of attack upon the Bard which could only be rectified through the specific performative instructions of a spectral father. The irony here, of course, is that, as Hume has pointed out, Garrick would turn out to be anything but a textual purist, the actor-turned-playwright himself taking great liberties with Shakespeare's *Hamlet* in his adaptation of the play in late 1772 (Hume 1997: 47).

And yet, the poem's appropriation of the script of *Hamlet* in the defence of Shakespeare was anything but an isolated example. In 1772, Arthur Murphy, though not without mildly satirical effect, would rework significant portions of *Hamlet* in order to replay the scene of a father's ghostly visitation of his son as a dialogue between the spectre of Shakespeare and the Hamlet-like Garrick: 'I am Shakespeare's Ghost, / For my foul sins, done in my days of nature, / Doom'd for a certain term to leave my works / Obscure and uncorrected' (Vickers 1979: 466, 1–4).

Though forbidden 'to tell the pangs, / Which Genius feels from ev'ry blockhead's pen' (11–12), the chilling tale that the spectre of Shakespeare here unfolds is rather more specific than that recounted in the earlier poem 'Shakespeare's Ghost'. The blood of Shakespeare stains the hands of one French assailant in particular:

> 'Tis giv'n out, that in a barb'rous age
> Shakespeare arose, and made th'unskilful stare
> At monstrous farces; so the ear of Europe
> Is by the forged process of a Frenchman
> Rankly abus'd. But know, ungrateful man!
> The serpent that did sting thy poet's fame
> Has made his fortune by him.
>
> (37–43)

As in the earlier poem, Garrick is urged by the spectral father to 'Revenge his foul and most unnatural murder' (26), and it is evidently upon references such as these that the myth of David Garrick as the primary force behind the revival of interest in Shakespeare in mid-eighteenth-century England came to base itself.[5] Though the perpetrators in 'Shakespeare's Ghost' and Arthur Murphy's poem are different, both texts share a sense in which Shakespeare, the venerable Father of English culture and letters, has been murdered. Whether it be at the hands of native British editors and adaptors or foreign French critics, Shakespeare, like the old King in *Hamlet*, has fallen unfortunate victim to violent assault and assassination.

Murphy's allusions to the national identity of Shakespeare's murderer take us closer to the identification of a particular historical suspect than does the earlier anonymous poem, although 'Shakespeare's Ghost', too, is haunted by a culprit larger and more threatening than the destructive powers of both Colley Cibber and Nahum Tate combined. What informs the scene of assassination in both texts, in fact, is the criticism to which Shakespeare had been subjected by French Enlightenment wit, essayist and philosopher François Marie Arouet, better known by his *nom-de-plume* Voltaire. As Thomas Lounsbury's now classic study *Shakespeare and Voltaire* (1902) presents it, Voltaire's expressed views on Shakespeare, though marked by a certain consistency across time, fall roughly into three periods. The first period, spanning the years 1727–53, saw the expression of Voltaire's impressions of Shakespeare across a number of publications, including the discourse on tragedy prefixed to the printed script of *Brutus*, Voltaire's play that premiered in Paris in December 1730; an essay on epic poetry translated into English in 1727 and Voltaire's 'Letters Concerning the English Nation' of 1733, later published in France as *Lettres Philosophiques*. Voltaire's early views on Shakespeare were nothing if not ambivalent. As the *Essai sur la poésie Épique* put it, 'monstrous tragedies' were most frequently the work of the 'divine' Shakespeare (cit., Bailey 1964: 3); while holding that 'His genius was at once strong and abundant, natural and sublime', Shakespeare was also 'without the smallest spark of taste, and devoid of the remotest ideas of the rules' (cit., Lounsbury 1902: 63). This reference to aesthetic rules is significant, for what seems most to have perturbed Voltaire about Shakespeare was what he took to be the playwright's patent disregard for the Aristotelian unities of time, place and action, the aesthetic principles informing so much French neoclassical art and criticism during the period. In fact, so marked was Shakespeare's failure to conform to neoclassical standards in a play such as *Hamlet* that, as Helen Bailey has pointed out, the French critic denied it all tragic status, repeatedly referring to it instead as a 'monstrous farce' (Bailey 1964: 23). Despite these shortcomings, Voltaire was struck by the aesthetic powers of the ghost scenes in *Hamlet* – so struck, in fact, that he undertook to imitate them, with a few significant alterations, first in his tragedy *Eriphyle* in 1732, and then later in his *Sémiramis* of 1748. In the *Dissertation sur la tragédie ancienne et moderne*, Voltaire defended the supernaturalism of *Sémiramis* through illustrative recourse to *Hamlet*, though making it quite clear that his enthusiasm for this aspect of the play, along with a few other 'beauties' such as the 'To be, or not to be' soliloquy, did not compensate for its overall crudeness and barbarity (Bailey 1964: 11–12). And yet, if, as Murphy's poetic adaptation of *Hamlet* had claimed, 'The serpent that did sting thy poet's fame/Has made his fortune by him' (42–43), this was because Voltaire, in seeking to rework the Shakespearean model in accordance with French neoclassical strictures, had appropriated *Julius Caesar*, *Hamlet* and *Othello* as the basis for his own tragedies *La Mort de César* (1743), *Zaïre* (1732) and *Sémiramis* (1748) respectively. Shakespeare's greatest critic was also his greatest popularizer, at least on the continent. However, for culturally patriotic Britons, these somewhat positive sides to Voltaire's Shakespearean endeavours went almost unnoticed, and as Alice

Clark points out, Voltaire rapidly came to embody 'a hostile French classicism to generations of patriotic English bardolaters' (Clark 2005: 514).
Though failing to acknowledge Shakespeare in the preface to *Eriphyle*,
Voltaire would begrudgingly mention his debt to Shakespeare in the preface to *Sémiramis*, though only as a preamble to asserting Shakespeare's
ultimate inferiority to Corneille and Racine and the provision of the first
of several inaccurate paraphrases of *Hamlet* in an attempt at arguing his
point: when compared with the superior productions of Corneille and
Racine, the English Bard was nothing short of barbarous.

The second phase of Voltaire's attack on Shakespeare and English letters in general spanned the years 1755–69, a period of crucial importance
for the rise of the Gothic aesthetic from 1764 onwards. Voltaire reiterated
his impressions of Shakespeare in his preface to the *Orphelin de la Chine*
(1755). Meanwhile, the French nation in general had steadily been gaining
more exposure to Shakespeare and his works through Pierre Antoine de la
Place's multi-volume French translations. Although La Place's endeavours
were not without echoes of Voltaire's criticisms – when not audaciously
mixing the fate of the mighty with that of several low-life characters,
Shakespearean drama, for La Place as for Voltaire, was replete with scenes
of horror, bloodshed and violence – his work nonetheless betrayed a latent
sympathy for the English playwright. La Place's translations also coincided
with two positive assessments of Shakespeare published in the *Journal
Encyclopédique* in 1760.[6] Though the possibility remained that the authors of
these two reports were English rather than French, Voltaire was prompted
into urgent action, seeking in his *Appel à toutes les nations de l'Europe* (1761) to
counteract what he perceived to be the further spread of evil into French
society. As if in order to prove the superiority of Corneille and Racine to
the work of the upstart Englishman, Voltaire provided another inaccurate
translation and paraphrase of *Hamlet*; without wholly retracting his early
admiration of *Hamlet*'s ghost scenes, he here regarded the supernaturalism
of Shakespeare's plays as a form of barbaric entertainment akin to duels,
bull-fights and acts of sorcery. Much of this work continued in Voltaire's
Commentaries on Corneille (1764), in which he commended Shakespeare for
his ability to amuse and interest his audience, while still arguing ultimately
for the superiority of the works of Corneille over the barbaric works of the
English Bard. In a second appeal to the French nation, Voltaire appended
to an edition of Corneille's *Cinna* a rather wooden translation of the first
three acts of *Julius Caesar*, apparently as a means of inviting invidious
comparisons between the two dramatists.

The third and final stage of Voltaire's attack, a period characterized
more by an increasingly vociferous tone than any significant variation in
content, spans the period 1769 until his death in May 1778. Seemingly

self-conscious about the role that he had unwittingly played in introducing Shakespeare to continental Europe, Voltaire, prompted by an adaptation of *Hamlet* by Jean-François Ducis in Paris, expressed his anxieties about the enthusiastic French embrace of theatrical supernaturalism in a letter to d'Argental on 13 October 1769: 'The spectres are going to become the fashion. I have opened the course modestly; they are now going to run at full speed. I have wished to enliven the stage somewhat by more action; and everything has become absolutely action and pantomime. Nothing is so sacred that it is not abused' (cit., Lounsbury 1902: 327). Voltaire's cultural authority was further undermined by Le Tourneur's translations of Shakespeare into French, and the positive impact this had upon Shakespeare's French reputation: having first introduced the French to Shakespeare, Voltaire also demanded the right to set the terms of his critical reception. In his 'Letter to the Academy' written in 1776, Voltaire's tone was at its most vehement. As many of his private letters of the time indicate, what was at stake for Voltaire was a matter no less serious than engaged cultural warfare, an aesthetic equivalent to the Seven Years' War that had waged between England and France not too many years before. But As Horace Walpole's response to Voltaire's 'Letter to the Academy' in a letter to Mann on 1 December 1776 indicates, Voltaire had, by this time, become little more than a parody of himself: 'Voltaire, who first brought us into fashion in France, is stark mad at his own success. Out of envy to writers of his own nation, he cried up Shakespeare; and is now distracted at the just encomiums bestowed on that first genius of the world in the new translation. He sent to the French Adademy an invective that bears all the marks of passionate dotage' (Lewis 1944: 267). Shakespeare's reputation seems to have been sufficiently consolidated by the mid-1770s so as to require fewer and considerably less urgent forms of cultural response.

In earlier years, however, things had seemed considerably different. The proliferation of published defences of Shakespeare by such culturally significant figures as Lord Kames, Horace Walpole and Elizabeth Montagu during the period 1755–69 attests to the sense of urgency with which the nation initially responded to the French assault upon one who, at this very time, was being constructed as its cultural figurehead.[7] English culture galvanized its responses to the French attack with the ideologically charged construction that was 'The Gothic Bard'. As Lounsbury has argued, Voltaire, though occasionally describing Shakespeare as 'Gothic', was more likely to use the terms *Allobroge* or *Velches* when referring to what he took to be the Bard's barbarian excesses. By '*Velches*' Voltaire would have meant the descendants of the barbarous Celtic tribes which inhabited ancient Gaul, a native French term which, partly like the term 'Gothic' in

England, signified 'the enemies of light and learning' (Lounsbury 1902: 321). But in the work of English defence, the notion of a 'Gothic Shakespeare' was heavily dependent upon the numerous, often paradoxical meanings that the term 'Gothic' had come to signify by the middle of the century. Historically, of course, the term referred to the ancient Germanic invaders of Rome, and through this, a certain untamed barbarity or at least anti-Roman impulse in politics, art and cultural life. This would segue seamlessly with the significations that the term had absorbed in the work of Renaissance historiographers, especially in their tendency to denounce the darkness of the medieval Catholic past as 'Gothic'. But if Gothic was barbaric and medieval, it was also the origin of all that Whiggish English politicians and cultural theorists of the Enlightenment embraced, valued and admired, not least of all the in-built protection against absolute monarchy that the political structures of the ancient Gothic tribe were purported to contain. Consequently, by the mid-eighteenth-century, 'Gothic' came also to signify all things traditional, familiar and native to enlightened, Whiggish England. As Samuel Kliger has pointed out, the actual links between the Gothic invaders of Rome, and the Angles, Saxons and Jutes as the aboriginal inhabitants of England, are tenuous at best; through however many sleights of hand, Gothic had come somewhat inaccurately to denote all invading Barbarian tribes (Kliger 1952). Nonetheless, what Mark Madoff describes as this 'useful myth of Gothic ancestry' was pervasive throughout the period, featuring prominently in historiographic enquiries such as Edward Gibbon's monumental *The Decline and Fall of the Roman Empire* (1776) and Aikin's translation of Tacitus's *Germania* in 1777 (Madoff 2004). Gothic signified, at once, the barbaric, the anti-classical, the medieval, the unenlightened and the natively English, although attempts at isolating one or more particular meanings within this rather broad range of semantic possibilities were not uncommon.

The polyvalence of the term 'Gothic' was put to particularly good effect in the national defence of Shakespeare. The fact that, for the anonymous author of *Miscellaneous Observations on the Tragedy of Hamlet* (1752), Shakespeare was to be hailed as the very *antithesis* of the Gothic spirit attests more to the rich, often contradictory significations of the term 'Gothic' during the period than a notable exception to what, by consensus, was deemed to be Shakespeare's quintessentially Gothic status.[8] John Upton, in his *Critical Observations on Shakespeare* (1748), sketched out a familiar literary-historical narrative concerning the ways in which French taste had come to dominate English culture since the reign of 'our frenchified king' James II, rendering everything, 'unless of French extraction … aukward and antiquated' (Vickers 1975: 291). It is hardly surprising that, in this state of aesthetic affairs, 'the masculine and nervous Shakespeare and Milton should so little please our effeminate taste' (Vickers 1975: 292). Gothic, however, serves Upton well as a bulwark against these rather enervating French influences, even if the term implies, in part, a regression to an original state of barbarism: 'the more liberal sciences and humane letters are not the natural growth of these Gothic and northern regions. We are little better than sons and successors of the Gothic, ever and anon in danger of relapsing into our original barbarity' (Vickers 1975: 292). For Richard Hurd in the second edition of *Letters on Chivalry and Romance* (1765), Milton and Shakespeare alike were to be conceptualized as 'Gothic', and in the course of his discussion, the term comes to signify, at once, the ancient Northern tribe; the magic, superstition and enchantments of, say, the witches in *Macbeth*; as well as a native and original English tradition in art, politics and cultural existence in general. For Hurd, Shakespeare is at his most sublime when he foregoes formal classicism in favour of his native Gothic traditions: 'even he is greater when he uses *Gothic* manners and machinery than when he employs classical: which brings us again to the same point, that the former have by their nature and genius, the advantage of the latter in producing the *sublime*' (Hurd 1972: 266). In his embodiment of all the delightful mystery and superstition of his native England, Gothic Shakespeare mobilizes a stubborn resistance to the measured and regulated cadences of an imported neoclassical aesthetic.

A similar sense pertains to Elizabeth Montagu's *An Essay on the Writings and Genius of Shakespeare, Compared with the Greek and French Dramatic Poets, with Some Remarks Upon the Misrepresentations of Mons. de Voltaire* (1769). As in Samuel Johnson's earlier preface to his edition of *The Plays of William Shakespeare, in Eight Volumes* […] (1765), the memory of Voltaire's assassination of Shakespeare for Montagu is green. Momentarily conceding along with Voltaire that there was, indeed, something barbaric about Shakespeare's theatre, Montagu swiftly changes rhetorical direction in order to claim that, if these may be described as faults at all, they are more the product of the dark and unenlightened Gothic age in which Shakespeare lived and wrote than any sign of a lack of genius. This is especially the case when Montagu turns to her assessment of Shakespeare's supernaturalism in her chapter in *An Essay* entitled 'On the Praeternatural Beings':

> Shakespear [*sic*], in the dark shades of Gothic barbarism, had no resources but in the very phantoms that walked the night of ignorance and superstition: or in touching the latent passions of civil rage and discord; sure to please best his fierce and barbarous audience, when

he raised the bloody ghost, or reared the warlike standard. His choice of these subjects was judicious, if we consider the times in which he lived; his management of them so mastery, that he will be admired in all times.

(Montagu 1769: 150–51)

Shakespeare for Montagu is 'our Gothic bard' in the sense that he represents and epitomizes a native English literary tradition that, for all its residual traces of pre-enlightenment barbarity, is nonetheless worthy of protection, preservation and celebration (Montagu 1769: 147). Here, as elsewhere, the negative connotations accreting around Voltaire's sense of *Velches* or the barbarian Goth are offset and counteracted by a range of positive significations. While serving, as for Hurd, as a sure illustration of Shakespeare's sublimity, the supernaturalism of his plays is attributable for Montagu to an English tradition of 'national superstitions' that is far superior to the classical supernaturalism of Aeschylus (Montagu 1769: 158).

For Samuel Johnson and those who, like him, adopted a more sceptical attitude towards the supernatural, it was precisely the fact that the Bard lived and wrote in Gothic times that rendered the supernaturalism of his plays both aesthetically and morally acceptable. While approving of the emotional effects of Hamlet's ghost in his 1765 edition of Shakespeare's plays, Johnson's endnote to his edition of *Hamlet* expressed a sense in which the spectre's return was largely extraneous to the remainder of the action. But earlier, in his *Miscellaneous Observations on the Tragedy of 'Macbeth': with Remarks on Sir T. H.'s Edition of Shakespeare* (1745), Johnson had remarked that Shakespeare's supernaturalism was to be vindicated from the charge of implausibility primarily because such beliefs were current in the playwright's own day (Vickers 1975: 165). For those opposed to the sheer incredulity of the supernatural, the ghost in Shakespeare was a residual trace of a certain Gothic quaintness. As Thomas Seward put it in his preface to his edition of *The Works of Mr Francis Beaumont, and Mr John Fletcher* (1750), 'the Banks of the *Avon* were then *haunted* on every side' (Vickers 1975: 387). Shakespeare's superiority to his contemporaries Beaumont and Fletcher lay in the fact that, unlike them, his native Gothic superstitions had not been crushed by the weight of a classical education – a point frequently invoked in defences of Shakespeare throughout the eighteenth century. Although Alfred E. Longueil has argued that it was only in the late 1790s that the term 'Gothic' came to assume its modern, commonplace associations with the 'grotesque, ghastly, and violently superhuman' (Longueil 1923: 459), it is clear to see that, as early as the 1740s, 'Gothic' is already a synonym for a native English tradition of sublime supernaturalism, or what Johnson in 1765 refers to as 'the

Gothick mythology of fairies' (Vickers 1979: 66). It was Shakespeare, in other words, who introduced, via the interventions of his numerous defenders, a sense of the ghostly to the already overdetermined signifier 'Gothic' during the middle decades of the eighteenth century. When Horace Walpole adds the subtitle 'A Gothic Story' to the second edition of *The Castle of Otranto* in 1765, he is conscripting the supernatural into the cultural task of Shakespearean defence. Inextricably bound up in the work of cultural patriotism, Gothic appropriations of Shakespeare are inherently political from the start.

In his own account of his endeavours in the preface to the second edition of *Otranto*, Walpole is concerned more with defending Shakespeare from Voltaire's objection to the inappropriate formal intermingling of the comic and the tragic in the graveyard scene in *Hamlet* than he is with any defiant representation of a native Gothic supernaturalism.[9] Choosing to repeat rather than redress the curious formal suturing of Shakespeare's mode, Walpole in *Otranto* audaciously couples not only the ancient romance and the modern novel but also the 'high' tragedy of Manfred's fate with the 'lowly' comic elements generated by the 'deportment of the domestics' – elements, Walpole claims, which 'at first seem not consonant to the serious cast of the work' (Walpole 1968: 44). However, his model throughout, he declares, was 'That great master of nature, Shakespeare' (Walpole 1968: 45). The often-remarked-upon hybridity of *The Castle of Otranto* resides, in part, in Walpole's defiance of the terms of Voltaire's formal critique of *Hamlet*. Against this, Garrick's decision to excise the grave diggers from his version of *Hamlet* seems somewhat craven. While pointing out, in an extended footnote, the inaccuracies in Voltaire's sense of English history – in his preface to Thomas Corneille's *Essex*, Voltaire was evidently not aware of the fact that the Earl of Leicester and Dudley were the same person – Walpole's second preface to *Otranto* outrageously courted controversy with the observation that 'Voltaire is a genius – but not of Shakespeare's magnitude' (Walpole 1968: 45). Having learned of Walpole's published response in the second preface, Voltaire, much to Walpole's embarrassment, requested a copy. An extensive system of three-way correspondence between Walpole, Madame du Deffand and Voltaire himself ensued, in which Voltaire, though ostensibly in response to Walpole's *Historic Doubts on the Reign of Richard III*, replied to each of Walpole's criticisms in the second preface to *Otranto* while asserting his role as Shakespeare's greatest promoter on the Continent.[10]

In his deliberate suturing of the high and the low, the resistance that Walpole stages to Voltaire in *Otranto* is primarily formal. But in by far the majority of cases, the cultural work of defending the Bard from the slings and arrows of outrageous French fortune centred upon the ghost of the old King in Shakespeare's tragedy. Voltaire, to be sure, had remained remarkably consistent in his enthusiasm for the ghost in *Hamlet*, only slightly revising his general approbation in the private letter to d'Argental in mid-October 1769 (Bailey 1964: 14). As Bailey's study of the fate of *Hamlet* in France has demonstrated, the French reception of the ghost, if only through the general critical ascendancy of the views of Voltaire, was invariably positive (Bailey 1964: 12). French critics and writers such as Abbé Jean-Bernard Le Blanc; Abbé Prevost; Bacular d'Arnaud; and La Harpe had variously responded to the spectre of the old King in the most positive, even occasionally rapturous of terms. However, what seems to have developed alongside this general sense of French approbation was a view of the ghost that, if not overly critical, was decidedly more measured in its assessment and considerably more withholding in its praise. This tendency had manifested itself as early as La Place's translation of the play, and its expressed sense that, though remarkable, Shakespeare's handling of the ghostly scenes would have been considerably stronger if he had lived long enough to have fallen under the influence of French neoclassical aesthetics. La Place's version of the play had even rewritten Hamlet's encounter with his father's spirit in the alexandrine metrical form favoured by French writers such as Corneille and Racine (Bailey 1964: 8). Furthermore, despite his general admiration for Shakespeare, Jean-François Ducis had wholly elided the ghost from his production of the play that opened on 20 September 1769 – a production that was itself based upon the neoclassical text of La Place – on the grounds that it was 'absolutely inadmissible' (cit., Bailey 1964: 15).[11] Despite what appears to be the intensification of its vengeful aims in its insistence that Hamlet also kill his mother, the spectre that continues to hold sway over the outcome of events in Ducis's *Hamlet* appears exclusively in the mind's eye of the son. In his critique of Ducis's *Hamlet*, Denis Diderot, one of the most public exponents of French Enlightenment thinking, found it absurd that the entire play turned upon the authority of a tale told by a non-present supernatural agent: 'If ghosts inspired terror [and] spoke true in Shakespeare's time, they do not frighten [people] and are not believed in ours' (cit., Bailey 1964: 18). Still, if a ghost was necessary to the action, Diderot preferred the Shakespearean original to Ducis's pastiche. Though Le Tourneur's translation of *Hamlet* restored the ghost to its central position within the play, there were sufficiently anti-supernatural prejudices in circulation in France during the 1760s for De Jaucourt to give the ghost in *Hamlet* a measured, even slightly critical review in his entry on tragedy in the *Encyclopédie* of d'Alembert and Diderot. Deeming phantoms, supernatural forces and chimerical personages in general as little more than 'superstitious foibles', Shakespeare's handling of the supernatural in *Hamlet* was, according to the *Encyclopédie*, to be excused only on the grounds that these beliefs were current in his day.

These and other such qualifications were enough to mobilize the English into a position of supernatural defence. Maintaining that 'the French wits have often mentioned Hamlet's ghost as an instance of the barbarism of our theatre' (Montagu 1769: 158–59), Elizabeth Montagu's *Essay* was particularly keen to demonstrate the genius of its dramatic execution. And despite his reticence on matters pertaining to the supernatural in the 1765 preface, Walpole, while repeating his determination to mix high and low elements, would later restore the ghost in *Hamlet* to its central position in the task of patriotic Shakespearean defence in his musings upon Voltaire's critique in his *Book of Materials* (1779–80):

> Compare Ben Jonson's *Catiline* with *Hamlet*. The former is all pedantry and bombast. Are the royal dignities of the Ghost, of the Queen or of Hamlet lowered by the veracity of familiar incidents taken from common life that are introduced into the tragedy? The rules of Aristotle, of Bossu, are ridiculous and senseless if they prohibit such conduct and operations of the passions.
>
> (Vickers 1981: 213).

This was a rhetorical gesture that had become prevalent in critical accounts of Shakespeare since the 1740s. As William Smith opined in his translation of Longinus's treatise on the sublime, ghosts, so quintessentially English, are 'the peculiar Province of *Shakespeare*. In such Circles none but he could move with Dignity' (Vickers 1975: 100). The ghost in *Hamlet*, he continues, is introduced 'with the utmost Solemnity, awful throughout and majestic', while Banquo's ghost in *Macbeth* strikes 'the Imagination with high degrees of Horror' (Vickers 1975: 100). For the anonymous author of a pamphlet entitled *Miscellaneous Observations on the Tragedy of Hamlet* (1752), Shakespeare's manipulation of the ghost in the tragedy, though regrettably the object of much second-rate imitation, was the stuff of genius: 'The most artful and spirited Recital could never have raised the Terror that possesses the Spectators at the Appearance of the Phantom, who from first to last is grand and majestick, and maintains an equal Character' (Vickers 1975: 456). William Duff would draw a similar link between Shakespeare's genius and the supernaturalism of his plays in his *Critical Observations on the Writings of the Most Celebrated Original Geniuses in Poetry* in 1770. To defend Shakespeare was to embrace his ghosts; of all the Bard's supernatural beings, it was the spectre in *Hamlet* that was the most warmly received. As Robert P. Reno has argued, a ghostless version of *Macbeth* was produced for John Philip Kemble's inauguration of the new Theatre Royal in Drury

Lane in 1794 (Reno 1984: 97). But where *Hamlet* was concerned, a similar excision of the supernatural, at least in Britain, was unthinkable. Continuously cited as the touchstone of Shakespeare's original genius, the ghost in *Hamlet* reduced to silence even those critics who were otherwise utterly opposed to dramatic renditions of the supernatural.[12]

As E. J. Clery has argued, Walpole's introduction of the spectre to the pages of popular romance in *The Castle of Otranto* was contingent upon the ghost's loss of weighty theological import (Clery 1995). Though once central to polemical Christian accounts of the afterlife in the apparition narratives of Glanville, Defoe and others, the ghost in Gothic is emptied out of spiritual meaning and handed over to the commercial economies of spectacle and popular entertainment. Its definitive presence in Gothic writing, though, is also deeply indebted to the energies that Walpole and his contemporaries expended upon defending Shakespeare from the cultural hegemony of French neoclassicism. The Gothic revival and the renewal of interest in Shakespeare are two manifestations of the same cultural impulse. Called, like David Garrick, to avenge their father's symbolic assassination through engaged critical activity (editorship; commentary; critical treatise) and repeated acts of symbolic remembrance (performance; pictorial illustration; national celebration), the primary exponents of the Gothic revival occupied in relation to Shakespeare the position of the aggrieved son Hamlet. As Paul de Man's reading of prosopopoeia argues, the voice that proceeds from beyond the grave latently carries with it the danger of vexing the living to stony silence.[13] But where Shakespeare during the latter part of the eighteenth century in England is concerned, prosopopoeia incites intense cultural loquaciousness. Indeed, like Hamlet, at least in his early resolve, Gothic sons are more inspired to urgent action than paralysed by terror at the approach of their father's spectre. At least where Shakespeare is concerned, ghosts are more frequently invoked than they are exorcized. If only in principle, Gothic discourse welcomes the spectre as the remainder of a venerable Gothic past and the promise of a progressively Whiggish future. In fact, the Shakespearean father's ghostly return in Gothic writing inspires action considerably different from the Oedipal repudiations and parricidal disavowals theorized by Harold Bloom in *The Anxiety of Influence* between, say, Milton and those writing in his wake. As Jonathan Bate has argued, Romantic-era writing is more intent upon seeking protection from Shakespeare than subjecting the Bard to a wilful act of misreading or misinterpretation, however fruitful it might prove to be (Bate 1989a: 2). In the second preface to *Otranto*, Bate reminds us, Walpole seeks 'to shelter [his] own daring under the cannon of the brightest genius this country, at least, has produced' (Walpole 1968: 48). But coupled with the protection and aesthetic credibility that Shakespearean affiliation affords the lowly turns of popular romance is the pose of protectiveness assumed by the early writers of Gothic themselves. In relation to Gothic, Shakespeare is, at once, the revered subject and object of protection. Through incessant acts of citation, appropriation and allusion, Shakespeare provides the dominant mode through which Gothic fictions seek to establish their aesthetic credibility, as well as their legitimate position within a native or distinctly 'Gothick' literary genealogy that runs from Chaucer, through Spenser and Shakespeare, and into Milton and beyond. Strictly speaking, of course, Gothic writing as we understand it today does not exist until Walpole adds the subtitle 'A Gothic Story' to the second edition of *The Castle of Otranto* in 1765. But in a backward-looking gesture of double causality, the early writers and theorists of the Gothic defensively project back onto the Shakespearean text an origin for their own aesthetic practices. Freud's term for this is *Nachträglichkeit*. The protection the Bard affords Gothic is offset by the protection that the Gothic itself offers up in turn – an energized, culturally organized spirit of Shakespearean defence without which the rise and development of Gothic writing may not have taken quite the turns it did.

2

Hamlet would continue to exert its ghostly presence over Gothic writing well beyond the mid-century Gothic revival and its literary culmination in *The Castle of Otranto*. In works after *Otranto*, *Hamlet* serves the writers of Gothic romance and drama as a blueprint or set of dramatic instructions pertaining specifically to the appropriate treatment of the dead. Out of the carnage of Shakespeare's tragedy Gothic writers retrieve two invaluable lessons, and in appropriating them to the formally divergent ends of romance and Gothic melodrama, narrowly avert the bloody catastrophes of the fifth act of *Hamlet* through highly conventionalized endings reminiscent more of Shakespearean comedy than tragedy. The lessons in death that the Gothic extracts from Shakespeare's play are two-fold. First, death, however resistant, must be drawn into an intimate and enduring relation with truth. That is, the situations that led up to any particular death – its origins and its causes – as well as the physical embodiment of that death – in the form of a corpse or, more frequently in Gothic, a mere skeletal remainder – must be disclosed in their full immediacy, giving themselves over to the workings of verifiable knowledge and empirical truth in the process. As Derrida's reading of *Hamlet* in *The Specters of Marx* has argued, mourning in the West is contingent upon the interrelated functions of knowledge and truth:

It consists always in attempting to ontologize remains, to make them present, in the first place by *identifying* the bodily remains and by *localizing* the dead … One has to know. *One has to know it. One has to have knowledge* [Il faut le savoir]. Now, to know is to know *who* and *where*, to know whose body it really is and what place it occupies – for it must stay in its place, in a safe place. … Nothing could be worse, for the work of mourning, than confusion or doubt: one *has to know* who is buried where – and *it is necessary* (to know – to make certain) that, in what remains of him, *he remains there.* Let him stay there and move no more!

(Derrida 1994: 9)

The ghost of old King Hamlet initiates this impulse towards deathly veracity in Shakespeare's play through his account of how 'the whole ear of Denmark' has been 'Rankly abus'd' by the 'forged process' of his death (1.5.36–38). In the course of the action, forgery and dissimulation are replaced by narrative accounts of death which, though subjected by the sceptical son to the crucible of authentification during the play-within-the-play, eventually assume the status of truth: 'O good Horatio, I'll take the ghost's word for a thousand pound' (3.2.280–81). In Gothic, similarly, the space of deception, conjecture and mystery that surrounds the dead must, in the course of the narrative, eventually be submitted to the rigours of empirical proof, even if this amounts to the rendering of death and the dead, decaying body as a horrid spectacle. Again, *Hamlet* epitomizes this process. Horatio will assure not only the transmission of his friend's story into posterity, but also manage under the authority of Fortinbras the memorialization of the dead through handing over their bodies to the didactic powers of the tragic gaze: 'give order that these bodies / High on a stage be placed to the view, / And let me speak to th'yet unknowing world / How these things came about' (5.2.380–85). Against the backdrop of early modern Reformation debates, these and other similar dramatic renditions of the corpse as spectacle are highly ideologically inflected. As Susan Zimmerman has argued, the corpse of medieval Christianity was organically mobile and generative in nature, the putrefying body often taken as evidence of its eventual transfiguration in the afterlife (Zimmerman 2005: 33–34). Critiquing the corporeal materiality of Catholicism while emphasizing the morbid nature of all corporeal matter, the Reformers asserted the triumphant resurrection of the spirit to the utter exclusion of the body (Zimmerman 2005: 45–47). In line with much early Protestant thought, the spectacle of the corpse in early modern drama illustrates that the dead body remains, after all, fundamentally dead, utterly incapable of undertaking any mystical process of change. Though divested of its original theological meanings, the eventual spectacular disclosure of the corpse in Gothic is bound up in the assertion of death's sublime truth.

Second, having had their stories taken up by the workings of verisimilitude, the dead in Gothic need to be adequately remembered, memorialized and mourned. Whether it take the form of a proper burial or the informal remembrance of the dead through their continuous recollection on behalf of the living, death in Gothic necessitates an often lengthy process of deliberate and considered grieving. Mourning, in other words, is the fundamental obligation in Gothic writing. *Hamlet*, of course, is marked by a profound inadequacy where matters of ritualized grief are concerned: Polonius is buried without ceremony, and Hamlet describes Ophelia's partial Christian burial as an instance of 'maimed rites' (5.1.212). But the primary example of thwarted mourning in the text must surely be the inappropriate responses to the death of the old King performed and sanctioned by the leaders of the Danish state themselves. Claudius's slippery chiasmic rhetoric early in the play formally demonstrates the extent to which the sombre memorialization of the dead has been inappropriately mixed with the joyful celebrations of the living (1.2.1–7). Funerals have been turned into marital celebrations, with mirth accompanying the former and dirges the latter (1.2.12). In all respects, 'heavy-headed revel east and west' (1.4.17) has usurped the place of solemn remembrance at Elsinore. Gertrude implores her son to abandon his mourning dress prematurely, while Claudius dismisses Hamlet's commitment to the work of mourning as a sign of 'unmanly grief' (1.2.94). A son's mourning of his father for any extended period is, for Gertrude as for Claudius, at once 'a fault to heaven, / A fault against the dead, a fault to nature, / To reason most absurd' (1.2.101–3). Thrift, thrift indeed! In the context of a King who is 'But two months dead – nay, not so much, not two' (1.2.138), these and other aspects of the play read as the severe proscriptions against the thorough mourning of the dead that they are.

Like the spectacle of the corpse, this aspect of the play is, as recent scholarship has stressed, the product of its early modern historical provenance. For Stephen Greenblatt, the sense of curtailed funeral rites in *Hamlet* is directly related to contemporary anxieties pertaining to the appropriate means of mourning the dead generated by the Protestant critique and dismantling of Catholic notions of purgatory (Greenblatt 2001). To be sure, the concept of purgatory facilitated lengthy and ongoing relations between the living and the dead, not least of all in the elaborate clerical rituals – alms; liturgies; masses; fasting; prayers – necessitated by the soul in its purgatorial state. Central to late-medieval conceptualizations of mourning, notions of purgatory invariably served to enable the bereaved 'to work though, with less psychological distress than they otherwise might experience, their feelings of abandonment and anger at the dead' (Greenblatt 2001: 103). To dismantle purgatory was thus also to impose an abrupt ending upon frequently drawn-out grieving practices. Where matters of death were concerned, the Protestant Reformation was experienced by its opponents as an inappropriate interruption at the heart of mourning. Issuing forth from its purgatorial prison-house, old Hamlet's ghostly injunction to 'Remember me' (1.5.91) registers for Greenblatt the anxieties attendant upon the Reformists' abolishment of purgatory, and the related fear that, as a Catholic such as Thomas More had stressed, the dead would henceforth be consigned to a state of utter oblivion. In his elaboration upon Greenblatt's thesis, Tobias Döring has shown just how culturally traumatic the Protestant reorganization of grieving rituals was (Döring 2006). Cut short, curtailed, diminished and thoroughly reconfigured, the already performative aspects of early modern mourning turned to the stage for theatrical performances of grief not otherwise culturally sanctioned (Döring 2006: 18).

Eighteenth-century commentators were all too aware of the extent to which Shakespeare's tragedy, in its accounts of the ghost's purgatorial origins, entertained traces of the culturally denigrated Catholicism. For one K. L. in the article 'Shakespeare and Milton Compared' published in the *British Magazine* in July 1763, Shakespeare's patent dabbling in Catholicism in *Hamlet* constituted the play's only weakness: 'The poet, as a Protestant, was, however, guilty of an absurdity in making a ghost talk of purgatory' (Vickers 1976: 535). Commenting upon Hamlet's interaction with the ghost, Francis Gentleman, in *The Dramatic Censor; or, Critical Companion* (1770), opined that 'The Roman catholic opinion of purgatory is inculcated through the whole of this interview; and funeral rites, or preparatives thereto, particularly mentioned in this line: "Unhousel'd, unanointed, unaneal'd"' (Vickers 1979: 376). Although he ultimately side-steps the issue, the matter of Shakespeare's Catholic affiliations remains for Gentleman a conceivable possibility. The possibility of Shakespeare's Catholicism constituted a particular difficulty for those intent upon recuperating him as the national Bard. For Gothic, however, the matter is more secular than theological, the anti-Catholic biases of the form notwithstanding. For irrespective of the ideological, religious leanings to which the thwarted grieving practices in the play might attest, *Hamlet* serves the Gothic, in a decidedly more modern and psychological sense, as horrific testament to the ghosts and spectres that issue forth when any failed, curtailed or prohibited act of mourning is at stake.

As Manfred's curious lack of affective response to the death of his son Conrad in *The Castle of Otranto* attests, the mode would be given over to the exploration of pathological forms of grief and mourning from its inception.

More precisely, Gothic writing, almost as a preamble to its application of *Hamlet*'s two deathly lessons, explores the perversion of these very ideals – that is, what transpires when truth does not superimpose itself upon death, and through this, when the process of mourning the dead has been halted, blocked or even entirely neglected. Here, Gothic writing is at its most characteristic, for almost without exception, the consequences attendant upon the interruption of death-rites accrete around one of the Gothic's most definitive elements: the ghost. Even when issuing forth only as a spectral murmur that is subsequently explained by the turns of the explained supernatural, the ghost in Gothic is frequently placed in causal relation to a fundamental disruption at the heart of mourning. In Gothic, that which has not been adequately mourned is likely to return as a ghost. The account of the true history of Beatrice de las Cisternas, better known in her assumed form of the Bleeding Nun in Matthew Lewis's *The Monk* (1796), encapsulates this Gothic truism in one pithy sentence: 'The bones of Beatrice continued to lie unburied, and her Ghost continued to haunt the Castle' (Lewis 1973: 175). Here again, the script of *Hamlet* is central.

Gothic, in fact, deduces from *Hamlet* precisely the same lesson that the psychoanalysis of Jacques Lacan extracted from the play almost three-and-a-half centuries later. As Lacan's reading of the play in the essay 'Desire and the Interpretation of Desire in *Hamlet*' observes, mourning in *Hamlet* is blocked, interrupted or prematurely curtailed in almost every respect: 'Nor can we fail to be struck by the fact that in all the instances of mourning in *Hamlet*, one element is always present: the rites have been cut short and performed in secret' (Lacan 1977: 40).[14] The direct result is the return of old King Hamlet in the symptomatic form of a ghost. As Lacan continues, death occasions a traumatic rupture in the symbolic fabric of everyday life, a hole in the real that can only be mended, patched or darned through the needle-like interventions of the work of mourning: 'The work of mourning is first of all performed to satisfy the disorder that is produced by the inadequacy of signifying elements to cope with the hole that has been created in existence, for it is the system of signifiers in their totality which is impeached by the least instance of mourning' (Lacan 1977: 38). When the hole in the real remains exposed, it draws towards itself a psychotic swarm of images, numerous phantasmagorical simulacra of the dead which, in the absence of adequate mourning rites, attempt to stitch up the gaping hole of the real in and of their own accord. 'This', continues Lacan, 'explains the belief we find in folklore in the very close association of the lack, skipping, or refusal of something in the satisfaction of the dead, with the appearance of ghosts and spectres in the gap left by the omission of the significant rite' (Lacan 1977: 39) Of course, what is at work here is Lacan's reformulation of the emphasis which Freud had brought to bear upon the salutary effects of mourning in his 1917 essay 'Mourning and Melancholia'. While mourning for Freud is necessary, vital and even life-affirming, any disturbance of its field occasions the pathological symptoms of melancholia. In Lacan's version, the symptom is replaced by the spectre: that which we do not properly mourn is likely to return as a ghost – precisely the psychoanalytic point to which *Hamlet*, as cultural artefact, attests.

Admittedly, Lacan's reading of the play is already an appropriation, a form of twentieth-century 'Hamletism' such as that identified by R. A. Foakes, for certain aspects of the script admit of no easy correlation between inappropriately curtailed acts of mourning and the appearance of the spectre (Foakes 1993).[15] Lacan's reading of the ghost in *Hamlet* also offers little by way of a means of conceptualizing the appearance of ghosts at other moments in the Shakespearean *oeuvre*.[16] One of the few exceptions is the understanding of the cause of supernatural occurrence implicit in Robin Goodfellow's description of the approaching dawn in *A Midsummer Night's Dream*:

> My fairy lord, this must be done with haste,
> For night's swift dragons cut the clouds full fast,
> And yonder shines Aurora's harbinger,
> At whose approach ghosts wandering here and there
> Troop home to churchyards. Damnèd spirits all
> That in crossways and floods have burial
> Already to their wormy beds are gone.
>   (Shakespeare 1967: 3.2.378–84)

As Greenblatt observes, ghostly activity here is tied directly into the curtailed forms of mourning that officially pertained during the early modern period to suicides, and unofficially to those victims of natural disaster who, due to the very nature of their death, were not afforded proper burials (Greenblatt 2001: 162). This explanation of the aetiology of the ghost is that by which the Gothic sets the most store. Lacanian psychoanalysis and late eighteenth-century Gothic writing are bound by the same version of 'Hamletism', for in both discourses, spectres roam the battlements when mourning falters or fails. In Gothic, as in psychoanalysis, spectrality threatens whenever the dead remain unsatisfied, whenever the time of grief is even slightly out of joint. Jerrold E. Hogle has pointed out the centrality of Hamlet's invocation of 'The counterfeit presentment of two brothers' (3.4.55) to the spirit of forgery that permeates the early Gothic aesthetic (Hogle 2001). What was already in Shakespeare's play an anxiety pertaining to the reliability of signs becomes, by the end of the eighteenth century, the 'ghosting' of already spectral signifiers, resulting in an intense

Baudrillardian alienation in a world of increasingly faked and counterfeited images. As apposite as this observation is, it has perhaps served to
obscure the importance of another fragment from Shakespeare's tragedy
to early Gothic writing, namely the sense of curtailed mourning encapsu-
lated in Hamlet's caustic observation that 'The funeral bak'd meats / Did
coldly furnish forth the marriage tables' (1.2.180–81). Etched deeply into
the unconscious of Gothic discourse, these lines condense the reality of
thwarted mourning and the inevitable return of the ghostly dead. The
inappropriate intermingling of death and sex, grief and marriage that they
encode also serves as the substance against which the formal requirements
of romance, in seeking somehow to avert the horrors of Shakespeare's
tragedy and set the ghost and its terrors permanently to rest, will work
their effects.

Clara Reeve's *The Old English Baron* (1778), for instance, replays the
central dramatic occurrences in *Hamlet*, ostensibly in the interests of
restoring to Gothic romance the sense of high sublimity that, at least for
Reeve, had been compromised by the ludicrous, laughter-inducing
extremes of *The Castle of Otranto*. Approximately twenty-one years prior to
the commencement of the narrative, Sir Walter Lovel had commissioned
the assassination of Sir Arthur Lovel, his brother and rightful heir of the
Lovel castle and dynasty. Like Claudius, Sir Walter's crime has 'the primal
eldest curse upon't – A brother's murder' (3.3.37–38). This 'primal eldest
curse' provides the basis for much of the action in Ann Radcliffe's *The
Romance of the Forest* (1791) too. Here, the noble Marquis Henry de
Montalt, the father of the hero Adeline, occupies the place of old King
Hamlet, murdered, as he is, according to the designs of his Claudius-like
brother, Phillipe de Montalt. In *The Old English Baron*, as in *Hamlet*, the act
of fratricide is partly motivated by Sir Walter's incestuous attractions to his
sister-in-law, although in a swift alteration of Shakespeare's play, Reeve's
Gertrude-like figure dies prior to the actual consummation of her wooer's
incestuous intentions. A similar elision of a brother's incestuous approach
upon his sister-in-law is effected in *The Romance of the Forest*: Adeline's
mother died when her daughter was still an infant, leaving her uncle free
to covet only the fortune that his brother had accessed through his wife,
'the heiress of an illustrious family' (Radcliffe 1986: 343). In Shakespeare's
drama, Claudius's claim that his acts had been fuelled by 'My crown, mine
own ambition, and my queen' (3.3.55) locates the action firmly within
tragedy's higher social reaches; in Reeve and Radcliffe, the trappings of a
residual aristocracy are scant disguise for the bourgeois values that
permeate both texts in their entirety.

Despite these differences, the plot-structures of *The Old English Baron* and
The Romance of the Forest rely upon the same perversion of death-rites that

Lacan had identified in his reading of *Hamlet*. Recalling Claudius's circulation of a fallacious account of old Hamlet's death, Reeve's Sir Arthur perpetuates the false narrative of his brother's demise in battle against the Welsh. Bundling his corpse into a trunk and hastily concealing it beneath the apartments in the East wing of the castle, the murdered Sir Walter remains as officially unmourned and unmemorialized as Hamlet's father. A similar fate befalls the heroine's father in *The Romance of the Forest*. Seeking also to occlude the truth of Lady Lovel's escape, Reeve's villain stages for the absent woman an elaborate but faked funeral. As Oswald later informs the hero Edmund, this ritual, far from serving as a legitimate social expression of grief, was little more than 'a fiction, … the work of the present Lord, to secure his title and fortune' (Reeve 1977: 63). With the bones of both Sir Arthur and his wife buried 'out of consecrated ground' (Reeve 1977: 116), the social rites that should accompany the mourning of the dead in *The Old English Baron* and *The Romance of the Forest* have been cut short, counterfeited, neglected and denied. In both narratives, the dead exist for the most part in a state of continuous dissatisfaction.

As in Shakespeare's play, the consequence of this neglect is a number of spectral visitations, if not of the mother of Edmund in Reeve's text, then certainly of his father, the murdered Baron. Although Gertrude during the closet scene fails to see the ghost of the old King, the father's ghost returns to Lady Lovel in *The Old English Baron* during several moments of distraction that are mistaken by those in her attendance for madness (Reeve 1977: 34). Rumours concerning supernatural activity at Castle Lovel circulate freely among the servants, and in a replaying of the appearance of old Hamlet's spectre before the guards Marcellus and Barnardo, the reader of *The Old English Baron* is afforded first-hand exposure to Sir Arthur's ghost only when he appears before the terrified servants Wenlock and Markham (Reeve 1977: 78). In Radcliffe's romance, the dead father returns more as a series of spectral murmurings than as a fully actualized ghost. However, in James Boaden's dramatic adaptation of Radcliffe's romance in *Fontainville Forest* (1794), the murdered father appears to his daughter Adeline in the form of a fully realized ghost while she reads the account of his death in the manuscript towards the end of Act III, an inclusion which concretizes Radcliffe's indebtedness to *Hamlet* throughout *The Romance of the Forest* in general. Though initially featuring merely as a chilling voice that is heard off-stage, the phantom in Boaden's play makes himself 'faintly visible' prior to effecting a complete materialization (Boaden 1794). The ghost will also pursue his guilty brother in Act IV. It is upon the basis of this that Boaden's heroine Adeline, in a regendering of Shakespeare's script, will assume her Hamlet-like guise, while foregoing the need for vengeance by attributing its workings to some greater quasi-

Divine power: 'My boding spirit tells me that a great, / A mighty vengeance works to punish guilt? / Shall my weak fears prevent or thwart its aim?' (Boaden 1794: 4.1.25–25). The closing lines of the play set equal store by a form of revenge that is emphatically not exercised by human agency:

> The great Avenger of perverted nature
> Before us has display'd a solemn lesson,
> How he dispels the cloud of mystery,
> With which the sinful man surrounds his crimes;
> It calls us to adore in awful wonder,
> And reccommend [*sic*] ourselves by humble virtue.
>   (Boaden 1794: 5.2)

The formal transition from tragedy to Gothic melodrama brings with it the suspension of Hamlet's injunction to avenge his father's murder. Though his namesake is another Shakespearean son, Reeve's Edmund will unwittingly assume the mandate of the young Hamlet in swearing to avenge the death of this as-yet-unknown victim: 'He vowed solemnly to devote himself to the discovery of this secret, and the avenging the death of the person there buried' (Reeve 1977: 54). But nothing comes of this initial desire once the truth of his parents' death has been disclosed. In its insistence upon idealized endings that involve forgiveness, restitution and the imposition of Divine justice, Gothic romance strenuously avoids the bloody consequences attendant upon the tragic revenge motif. As if the key to his identity as the aggrieved Hamlet lies in the internal and external signs that he must subsequently learn to interpret, Edmund, while spending the night in the haunted East wing of the castle, will be subjected to a nightmarish vision in which his dramatic precursor's sense of the funeral bak'd meats coldly furnishing forth the marriage tables achieves graphic realization: 'After this, he followed a funeral as chief mourner; he saw the whole procession, and heard the ceremonies performed. He was snatched away from this mournful scene to one of a contrary kind, a stately feast, at which he presided; and he heard himself congratulated as a husband and a father' (Reeve 1977: 45). Though this dream has a happy conclusion, Edmund, having assumed his true identity as the son Hamlet, will come to learn just how dire the consequences of neglecting the work of mourning have been.

Setting the ghost to rest in *The Old English Baron* and *The Romance of the Forest* relies upon the application of the lessons in death afforded the Gothic aesthetic by the negative example of *Hamlet*. In Shakespeare's play, the problem that the supernatural poses is not resolved so much as it is excluded, marginalized or even forgotten in the implacable descent into chaos and violence in the last three acts. As a dramatic mode, tragedy depends more upon the spectacle of human suffering than a sustained theological enquiry into the nature and provenance of ghosts. In Gothic, by contrast, the idealized endings attendant upon fictional romance demand that tragedy, though initially courted, be ultimately averted, that horror be expunged, and that the terrors of spectral activity be either explained away, resolved or thoroughly exorcized. Here again, the formal requirements of romance in *The Old English Baron* and *The Romance of the Forest* take the script of *Hamlet* in other directions. Reeve's Sir Walter confesses the truth of his murderous designs against his brother, and Sir Philip Harclay publishes the truth of Sir Arthur Lovel's death after the Tournament. Laying the father's spectre to rest, too, depends upon the two-fold processes of mourning outlined above. Death hands itself over to the workings of empirical, visually verifiable truth as the corpse of the father – or at least his skeletal remainder – is eventually disclosed as an 'awful spectacle' (Reeve 1977: 131) to all those concerned:

> They proceeded till they discovered a large trunk, which with some difficulty they drew out. It had been corded round, but the cords were rotted to dust. They opened it, and found a skeleton which appeared to have been tied neck and heels together, and forced into the trunk. Behold, said Edmund, the bones of him to whom I owe my birth!
>
> (Reeve 1977: 131)

Wishing to inter the bones of both his parents 'all together in consecrated ground' (Reeve 1977: 132), Edmund subsequently presides over the exhuming of his mother's skeleton. The fakery at the heart of the mother's earlier burial is exposed, and placed in a 'stately coffin' alongside one another (Reeve 1977: 133), the hero's dead parents in *The Old English Baron* are eventually afforded a proper interment. Restored to its deathly truth and monumentalized in the inscriptions of Sir Philip Harclay, the ghost of the father is content to disappear. Exorcism in *The Old English Baron* depends upon the interrelated processes of truthful death and the work of proper mourning. Adeline's undertakings in *The Romance of the Forest* are equally efficacious in banishing the terrors of ghostly superstition. The disclosure of the morbid truth of her father's skeleton in the chest buried beneath the Abbey is followed by a salutary, life-affirming period of deep mourning (Radcliffe 1986: 354–55). As Adeline learns from La Luc's determination to mourn and remember, through the erection of an inscribed monument, his dead wife Clara, virtue consists partly in the living subject's commitment to the ongoing memorialization of the dead.

In what reads as a pointed avoidance of the state of affairs invoked in Hamlet's observations concerning the funeral bak'd meats, Reeve's Edmund, attired in 'deep mourning' (Reeve 1977: 145), is insistent that the time of grieving be respected, even though the deaths of the particular individuals concerned occurred as long as twenty-one years in the past. The passage of time is no excuse for the short-circuiting of grief. Only once a period of official grieving has passed will Edmund, of his own accord, cast off his inky cloak of mourning, and dressing himself in clothes more expressive of his happy state, celebrate his nuptials with Lady Emma. Adeline insists upon a similar period of sustained mourning before she will even consider a marriage to her keen suitor Theodore at the end of *The Romance of the Forest*. Relishing the time of grieving that Hamlet is so painfully denied, Adeline will eventually throw off 'the mourning habit which filial piety had required her to assume' and give 'her hand to Theodore' (Radcliffe 1986: 357). In Gothic, the dead must be appeased and satisfied before ordinary life may resume.

As the case of Adeline's assumption of a Hamlet-like identity in *The Romance of the Forest* attests, the script of Shakespeare's tragedy was often subjected by the early writers of Gothic to concerted acts of regendering. In a contemporary theatrical culture presided over by such renowned Shakespearean actresses as Sarah Siddons, this feminizing of an otherwise masculine Shakespearean text is perhaps unsurprising. As E. J. Clery has pointed out, Siddons's influence during the last two decades of the eighteenth century was sufficiently strong to guide, influence and inspire the self-fashioning of most of the prominent female writers of Gothic fiction during the period (Clery 2000). As Tony Howard in *Women as Hamlet* has recently shown, Siddons herself would play the part of Hamlet in Dublin in July 1802, but even earlier on in the eighteenth century, Shakespeare's tragic prince had been performed by such prominent actresses as Charlotte Charke (the youngest daughter of poet Laureate Colley Cibber), Fanny Furnival, Elizabeth Inchbald, Jane Powell and Julia Glover (Howard 2007: 36–43). In most instances, this amounted to little more than a form of dramatic cross-dressing. Somewhat more radically, though, Matthew Lewis undertakes both a fundamental regendering and a teasing rewrite of *Hamlet* in *The Castle Spectre*, the notorious Gothic melodrama which opened in Drury Lane in December 1797. As if in defiance of Voltaire's formal critique of the play so many years before, Lewis's Prologue announces that his mixture of tragedy and comedy, 'high' and 'low' dramatic elements is guided by the example of Shakespeare (Lewis 1992: 36–37). It is not long into the action before the ghost of *Hamlet* makes its presence felt. As Motley the Fool explains to Percy, Conway Castle, the site of the action in Wales, is rumoured by the servants to be haunted by the ghost of its previous owner Reginald, a spectral Earl who apparently effects his return in a form identical to that of old King Hamlet: 'since the late Earl's death the Castle is thought to be haunted: the servants are fully persuaded that his ghost wanders every night through the long galleries, and parades the old towers and dreary halls which abound in this melancholy mansion. He is supposed to be drest in compleat armour' (Lewis 1992: 2.1). Having gestured thus towards the primal crime of fratricide, the play continues to invoke *Hamlet* in its account of the ruling Count Osmond's incestuous attraction to Evelina, the wife of his late brother. In a merging of the conventions of romance with those of Shakespeare's tragedy, Angela, the daughter of the late Reginald and Evelina, occupies, at once, the place of the conventionally orphaned Gothic heroine and the position of the aggrieved son *Hamlet*, subjected, as she is, to the corrupt authority of her Claudius-like uncle. As in *The Romance of the Forest*, it is the Gothic heroine, and not the hero, who assumes the position of Shakespeare's tragic Prince.

As if this regendering were not radical enough, *The Castle Spectre*, having conjured up *Hamlet*'s tragic intertext, rapidly dispenses with it, largely through the eventual revelation that it was not the brother Reginald who was killed at the hands of Osmond's incestuous ambitions so much as his wife, the Gertrude-like Evelina, who intercepted herself in her husband's place. Consequently, when Reginald does eventually return in the play, it is not as a spectre but in the form of another living Shakespearean father, King Lear, restored in a flood of tears to his reason and his daughter simultaneously. Consequently, the ghost to which the title of the play refers is not the anticipated ghost of old King Hamlet but the restless spirit of his murdered wife. The paternal ghost in *Hamlet*, in fact, is subjected in the play to a playful and comic counterfeiting when Percy, in a turn that recalls the performed haunting during the Bleeding Nun episode in *The Monk*, disguises himself as the armoured ghost of Reginald in order to effect his amorous designs at the castle. In a play that admits of so many different versions of the supernatural, true supernaturalism is reserved for the appearance of the ghost of the mother Evelina at the end of Act 4, while the ghost of old Hamlet becomes the stuff of pantomimic farce. Even the spectre's earlier purported appearances to the guilt-stricken Osmond are more a reworking of Macbeth's guilty projections that culminate in the ghost of Banquo than any simple appropriation of *Hamlet*:

> When I wake, I find in every object some cause for distrust – reward the dread charge in every eye, 'Thou art a murderer!' – and tremble lest the agents of my guilt should work its punishment. – And see where he walks, the chief object of my fears! – He shall not be so

long! – His anxiety to leave me, his later mysterious threats – No, no!
I will not live in fear. – Soft! – he advances.

(Lewis 1992: 3.2)

Not even Hamlet's anxieties around the portrait's potential for fakeness
can escape Lewis's impulse to rewrite Shakespeare in *The Castle Spectre*.
Instead, they are inverted when Osmond presents before his niece a painted representation of Ferdinand during his outlining of the terms of her
false choice between incest and parricide: Angela must either consent to a
relationship with her uncle or be complicit in the murder of her father.
Osmond's powers of manipulation in this scene depend upon the fact that
the portrait of Ferdinand is emphatically not the 'counterfeit presentment'
of one dead brother but an accurate rendition of a living yet 'Unhousel'd,
disappointed, unanel'd' father:

> Look upon this picture! Mark, what a noble form! How sweet, how
> commanding the expression of his full dark eye! – Then fancy that he
> lies in some damp solitary dungeon, writhing in death's agonies, his
> limbs distorted, his eye-strings breaking, his soul burthened with
> crimes from which no priest has absolved him, his last words curses on
> his unnatural child, who could have saved him, but who would not!

(Lewis 1992: 4.2)

Signs in *The Castle Spectre* are more evocative of living presences than
ghostliness. In fact, the only two aspects of *Hamlet* that the play seems to
conserve are the tragic dimensions of the revenge motif, and the lessons in
ghostliness inscribed in Hamlet's observations concerning the unsettling
presence of the 'funeral bak'd meats' upon the 'marriage tables' (1.2.180–
81). Unlike characters such as Reeve's Edmund, Radcliffe's Adeline and
even Hamlet himself, Lewis's heroine Angela successfully fulfils the
injunction to avenge a death when she pierces Osmond's breast with a
dagger during the play's closing moments. But even here, the mass devas-
tation and bloodshed of tragedy are averted as Osmond's injury proves not
to be fatal. Second, and more pointedly, the supernatural activity inscribed
in the play's title is attributable, as in *Hamlet*, to the marked absence of
truthful death and appropriate mourning that has plagued Oswald's illegitimate regime from the start. False stories concerning the death of
Reginald and Evelina at the hands of banditti had been in regular circulation, while what the maid Alice describes as the absence of any dead
body has prevented the proper operations of grief. As of old in Gothic, the
work of legitimate mourning may only get under way once the corpse has
been exposed in all its horrid yet necessary truth. With death and

mourning in the play drawn by villainy into a worrying state of neglect, the dissatisfied dead have no option but to effect a spectral return.

Although the main title of Richard Sickelmore's *Edgar; Or, The Phantom of the Castle* (1798) conjures up the predicament of another Shakespearean son, this Minerva Press romance, like so many other Gothic fictions of the 1790s, derives its central narrative dynamics from *Hamlet*. Deep in mourning for his father Sir Edgar Fitz-Elmar, Edgar occupies the place of Shakespeare's tragic Prince. Not even the passage of three full years is sufficient to quell the hero's grief, and after hearing again Bardolph's account of his father Sir Edgar's death, 'the tears of sad remembrance, which had collected in his eyes' are still to be seen 'trickling down his face in mournful succession' (Sickelmore 2005: 13). Like Hamlet, Edgar is 'buffeted by the wayward gales of outrageous fortune' (Sickelmore 2005: 52), resisting all the while the invidious position of being passion's slave. Although he is as yet consciously unaware of the Claudius-like role that his usurping uncle the Baron Armine Fitz-Elmar has played in his father's death, Edgar appoints himself as the avenger of his father at the hands of banditti, the 'instrument of thy divine vengeance to punish this diabolical act of villany [*sic*]' (Sickelmore 2005: 13). Although Sickelmore's reworking of *Hamlet*, like *The Romance of the Forest*, elides the Baron Armine's incestuous motives – his sister-in-law, Lady Emma Fitz-Elmar, had died when Edgar was only 15, and Armine, we are told, acted 'with no other motive than to secure his brother's wealth to himself' (Sickelmore 2005: 65) – Armine's founding act of fratricide turns out to be just as significant. Even in life, Sir Edgar and the Baron Armine constitute nothing if not the 'counterfeit presentment of two brothers' (3.4.55): 'The present Baron Fitz-Elmar, and our hero's father Sir Edgar Fitz-Elmar, were two brothers; but as different in principles and disposition as the extremes of good and bad could possibly be delineated' (Sickelmore 2005: 16). While Sir Armine, in marrying a lady of noble lineage 'soon after the decease of his father' (Sickelmore 2005: 16) had failed to respect the differences between death and marriage, his brother married his own 'amiable lady of good family and large fortune' a full 'two years preceding his father's death' (Sickelmore 2005: 18). Where the noble brother is concerned, there is no danger of the vestiges of deathly preparation turning up in the midst of marital celebrations. However, circulating in the fallacious account of his brother's death at the hands of banditti, death in *The Phantom of the Castle* is as initially resistant to exposure by the workings of truth as it is in Shakespeare's play. But what makes Sickelmore's novel distinctive is that the ghost of the father never effects a real spectral return. Given the links between thwarted mourning and ghostly activity established, via *Hamlet*, in Gothic fictions since Clara Reeve, this is perhaps unsurprising: the father in Sickelmore's text has been properly mourned, at least within the parameters allowed by the prevailing false account of the cause of his demise. Although Armine duplicitously stages 'some well-feigned heart-breaking sobs' (Sickelmore 2005: 29) when hearing of his brother's death, he is nonetheless interred 'with great funeral pomp' (Sickelmore 2005: 31). Sir Edgar is also the subject of continuous mourning on his son Edgar's behalf. Even the retreat of night in the fiction is described as being 'as if in mourning for the god's departure' (Sickelmore 2005: 11). Continuously mourned, grieved for and remembered, the dead father in Sickelmore's text need not effect a spectral return.

And yet, with the true cause of his death remaining, as yet, undisclosed, Sir Edgar will continue to assert his presence through a series of ghostly symptoms. On several occasions, the guilt-stricken conscience of his fraternal assassin projects, like Macbeth, the ghost of his victim onto his external surroundings: 'thrice had his guilty mind conjured up to his tortured fancy, the bleeding image of his murdered brother, as he lay convulsed in fear, and shivering with apprehension, lest every crash of thunder, which seemed bursting over his head, was winged from Heaven to hurl his guilty soul into everlasting perdition' (Sickelmore 2005: 75). When Edgar dresses himself in his father's suit of armour that had been concealed behind the portrait in the old Priory, both Armine and Bernardine mistake him for the ghost of the murdered Sir Edgar. When the ghost of *Hamlet* walks in *The Phantom of the Castle*, it is only in the form of a disguise that is guiltily mistaken by others for true supernatural activity. But all spectral symptoms in the text disappear once the part that Armine has had to play in his brother's murder has been disclosed. Dragged by the confession of Bernardine into a relation with truth, the truthful death is an effective means of banishing all spectral symptoms. The death of Baron Armine must, itself, be rendered an empirical reality, or what the text elsewhere refers to as an 'ocular [*sic*] demonstration of the fact' (Sickelmore 2005: 73): 'Edgar, followed by Helen, soon reached the apartment where Sir Armine lay stretched upon the couch of death; a spectacle, from the convulsive agonies of his last moments, dreadful to behold' (Sickelmore 2005: 99). As if to underline its insistence upon the importance of proper mourning – Lady Emma Fitz-Elmar, for one, is grieved for intensely by her husband (Sickelmore 2005: 20) – not even the villainous Baron might leave this life unmourned. As Helen's determination to grieve the hideous Lucretia demonstrates, the necessity of mourning remains unaltered by consideration of the deceased's moral stature. In Gothic, even the evil have to be lamented, for nothing but ritualized grief can provide any insurance against their spectral return.

Routinely conjuring up the ghost only in order to exorcize it, Gothic writing is characterized by what Derrida in *The Specters of Marx* terms a

'Specular circle: one chases after in order to chase away, one pursues, sets off in pursuit of someone to make him flee, but one makes him flee, distances him, expulses him so as to go after him again and remain in pursuit' (Derrida 1994: 140). Invited, though the medium of Shakespeare, into the pages of popular romance, ghosts in Gothic are the object of a concerted cultural conjuring. But once admitted, they rapidly become, as in *Hamlet*, the object of a conjuration, especially if by this term, we mean an exorcism via the act of swearing together, the making of a league, by common oath, against the uncomfortable presence of a superior power (*OED*): 'Swear by my sword / Never to speak of this that you have heard' (1.5.167–68).

In Radcliffe's *The Mysteries of Udolpho*, the ghost eventually figures more as a series of horrid mispresumptions and terrifying misrecognitions on the heroine Emily St. Aubert's behalf than it does as a fully actualized presence. The first scene of psychic spectral conjuring in Radcliffe's narrative concerns Emily's unintentional but no less illicit reading of her late father's letters and documents. As Robert Miles has argued, the undisclosed secrets of the dead father lay down in the heroine from this pivotal moment onwards a range of horrid, spectre-like imaginings, not least of all in relation to the legitimacy of Emily's own birth (Miles 2002b). The second and equally momentous scene of psychic spectral conjuring concerns that which is thought to lie behind the veil in the castle of Udolpho itself. As in the earlier scene, Emily is plagued by spectre-like imaginings of ghastly import, albeit this time in relation to what she believes to be the gruesome fate of the Signora Laurentini. It is at this point in particular that *The Mysteries of Udolpho* reveals its indebtedness to *Hamlet*, for what the veil actually hides is an object of thwarted mourning not unlike those repeatedly figured in Shakespeare's play: no actual corpse but merely a wax effigy of a decrepit body that had once been used as a *memento mori* in a lengthy ritual of atonement. As Terry Castle has observed, *Udolpho* is replete with similar scenes, each of which promises a certain deathly immediacy only in order to disappoint readerly expectations with bathos and emptiness: a pile of clothes in place of the anticipated corpse of Emily's aunt; an empty grave in Udolpho's crypt; the fugitive pirate in the apartments of the dead Marchioness de Villeroi, and so on (Castle 1987: 243). In the absence of a dead body, the work of mourning at Udolpho is perpetually in abeyance. In seeking to account for this historically, Castle's reading of the text invokes Philippe Aries's cultural history of death in late eighteenth-century Europe in his influential study *The Hour of Our Death*: the prioritizing of the so-called Beautiful Death amounted to a concerted repression of death's corporeal reality, the far-reaching consequences of which Castle convincingly reads into the numerous maskings, veilings and sublimations of death that punctuate Radcliffe's narrative. Following this line of argument, the late eighteenth-century heyday of Gothic writing and the early modernity of the Shakespearean text are characterized by at least one remarkable parallel, for both are cultures in which the work of mourning, though once considerably more elaborate, has been shortened, pared down and cut short. This accords well with Coral Ann Howells's account of the so-called 'Gothic way of death': for Howells, early Gothic writing is to be conceived as the repressed underbelly of a neo-classical tradition in mourning, a tradition in which death has been all too neatly rendered under the sign of euphemism and religious platitude (Howells 1982). In place of the placatory epitaphs, the stylized Grecian urns, the picturesque broken colums and the draped female figures of neoclassical funereal iconography, Gothic foregrounds the more macabre realities of corporeal decomposition and religious insecurity. Gothic writing thus serves late-eighteenth-century culture as a place for the expression of negated grief, the form functioning as a socially symbolic site of mourning in much the same way that the Renaissance stage, following Döring, served the early modern period. The differences between the two cultures are, at once, relative and substantial: what Greenblatt and Döring read as the effects of Reformation theology is reworked in arguably less intense a fashion through Howells's neoclassical death-culture of euphemism and the death-defying turns of Aries's Beautiful Death. But the over-riding connection between them – a link only implicit in Castle's argument – remains: as Lacan's reading of *Hamlet* makes clear, spectres roam when the work of mourning falters.

In *The Mysteries of Udolpho*, Radcliffe directly enlists *Hamlet* in the work of mourning when she begins Chapter Two, the account of the funeral of Madame St. Aubert, with the epigraph 'I could a tale unfold whose lightest word / Would harrow up thy soul' (1.5.15–16). Unsurprisingly, Radcliffe's description of the proceedings at La Vallée after her mother's funeral are not without references to the soul in its purgatorial afterlife: 'St. Aubert read, in a low and solemn voice, the evening service, and added a prayer for the soul of the departed' (Radcliffe 1966: 20). But despite what appears to be Radcliffe's affinities with Catholic mourning rites in *Udolpho*, Madame St. Aubert's funeral, with its self-conscious modesty and pared-down sense of ceremony, is decidedly Protestant in nature.[17] Even more tellingly, St. Aubert's actual descriptions of the afterlife elsewhere in the text are as distinctly Protestant as those which Greenblatt identifies in the young Hamlet, confronted, as he is, with the spectral and historical remainder of his father's Catholic conceptualization of purgatory. La Voisin prompts St. Aubert's musings on the afterlife with a teasingly direct question: 'Do you believe, monsieur, that we shall be permitted to revisit the earth, after we have quitted the body?' (Radcliffe 1966: 67). St. Aubert's reply, in questioning the likelihood of a ghostly return from any purgatorial space between the heaven and earthly existence set so starkly apart by La Voisin, strikes at the heart of Radcliffe's Protestant conceptualization of the afterlife:

> 'I hope we shall be permitted to look down on those we have left on the earth, but I can only hope it. Futurity is much veiled from our eyes, and faith and hope are our only guides concerning it. We are not enjoined to believe, that disembodied spirits watch over the friends they have loved, but we may innocently hope it. It is a hope which I will never resign ... '
>
> (Radcliffe 1966: 67–68)

Unlike the space between the Protestant extremes of 'airs from heaven' and 'blasts from hell' (1.4.41) that Hamlet is forced to negotiate, there are, emphatically, *no* 'more things in heaven and earth' than are dreamt of in Radcliffe's philosophy. However, Radcliffe's Protestantism does not bring with it a decidedly religious way of mourning. Rather, true mourning in *The Mysteries of Udolpho*, though attended by the Catholic rituals of Radcliffe's southern European setting, occurs in a realm that is primarily secular and subjective in nature. The death of Emily's father St. Aubert is the best case in point. Buried in the Church of the Convent of St. Clair near the ancient tomb of the Villerois, St. Aubert's funeral is notionally Catholic in its external ritualized elements: a sad procession, a venerable priest, a procession of nuns, the solemn chants of anthems, and the peal of the organ (Radcliffe 1966: 87). Still, the physical fact of his interment is plain, modest and understated, distinctly lacking in the more elaborate finishes of Catholic funerary furniture: 'St. Aubert was buried beneath a plain marble, bearing little more than his name and the date of his birth and death, near the foot of the stately monument of the Villerois' (Radcliffe 1966: 91). More pointedly, Emily's loud sobbing during the official requiem for her dead father unearths a private scene of mourning, a personal and intensely sentimental experience of death that, far from being soothed by the external sights and sounds of Catholic ceremony, severely disrupts it from within:

> Emily drew the veil entirely over her face, and, in a momentary pause, between the anthem and the rest of the service, *her sobs were distinctly audible.* The holy father began the service, and Emily again commanded her feelings, till the coffin was let down, and she heard the earth rattle on its lid. Then, as she shuddered, *a groan burst*

from her heart, and she leaned for support on the person who stood next to her.

(Radcliffe 1966: 88; emphasis added)

True grief in Radcliffe occurs in clandestine isolation, and not in Catholicism's socially theatrical funerary practice nor solely in the consolations of a Protestant conceptualization of the afterlife. Radcliffe, we might say, secularizes and psychologizes the process of grieving, for as Emily's actions in relation to her dead father throughout the remainder of *The Mysteries of Udolpho* attest, the work of mourning consists more of memory, tears and deliberately commemorative acts than anything approaching the religious. Though *Hamlet* has been appropriated by the Gothic as a lesson in the appropriate treatment of the dead, the religious discourses attendant upon constructions of mourning in the play, both Catholic and Protestant, have been repressed by the processes of cultural secularization. In place of mourning's socially binding effects, grieving, for Emily in *Udolpho* as for La Luc in *The Romance of the Forest*, is a private, even solitary activity, a labour that is contingent more upon the internal processes of memory than the trappings of ritual and externalized woe. Its only external manifestation is weeping, the tears that are occasioned by the painful process of de-cathecting the grieving subject not only from the dead love-object itself, but as Emily's responses to La Vallée indicate, from any external objects that evoke memories of the deceased too (Radcliffe 1966: 92). These responses will still be in place several years later when Emily returns to La Vallée at the romance's end. Despite its pains, the effects of sustained mourning in Radcliffe are invariably salutary. After her 'hour of melancholy indulgence', Emily is 'refreshed by a deeper sleep' than she had experienced for a long time; upon awakening, 'her mind was more tranquil and resigned, than it had been since St. Aubert's death' (Radcliffe 1966: 91). La Luc enjoys similar relief from the pressing symptoms of grief when he returns from his numerous solitary walks in the mountains, thickly wrapped in the mantle of memories of his dead wife (Radcliffe 1986: 246). Proper mourning in Gothic relieves the symptoms of melancholia.

Certainly, we are conceptually within the same discursive territory occupied by psychoanalysis approximately one hundred years later. For Freud, the work of mourning, when successfully undertaken, entails the painful decathexis of the subject from the lost love object through the workings of memory. Any interruption of its path occasions the all-consuming blackness that is melancholia. In their elaboration upon the Freudian differences between mourning and melancholia, Nicolas Abraham and Maria Torok in *The Shell and the Kernel* have served to emphasize mourning's positive effects. Like successful mourning in Freud, introjection involves a broadening of the ego through the eventual accommodation of the loss of the love-object. Incorporation, by contrast, is characterized by a marked refusal of the slow and painful process of mourning that is introjection, the 'refusal to acknowledge the full import of the loss, a loss that, if recognized as such, would effectively transform us' (Abraham and Torok 1994: 127). As Abraham and Torok describe them, the consequences of failed or refused acts of mourning are dire, laying down in the subject psychic crypts or intrapsychic tombs. Those love-objects incarcerated and hermetically sealed within the psyche of those who refuse to mourn them exist in a state that is tantamount to live burial: 'Inexpressible mourning erects a secret tomb inside the subject. Reconstituted from the memories of words, scenes, and affects, the objectal correlative of the loss is buried alive in the crypt as a full-fledged person, complete with its own topography' (Abraham and Torok 1994: 130). So watertight, in fact, is this act of live psychic entombment that the subject of refused mourning does not even experience the symptoms of melancholia as such; only occasionally, in fact, does the subject of incorporation become anything like the haunted subject that is Shakespeare's tragic Prince of Denmark: 'Sometimes in the dead of night, when libidinal fulfillments have their way, the ghost of the crypt comes back to haunt the cemetery guard, giving him strange and incomprehensible signals, making him perform bizarre acts, or subjecting him to unexpected sensations' (Abraham and Torok 1994: 130). As Lacan's musings on the ghost in *Hamlet* indicate, failed mourning in psychoanalysis is, quite simply, Gothic, issuing forth in the symptomatics of spectres, tombs, crypts and live burials – the latter, as Sedgwick reminds us, being the very 'master–trope' of Gothic writing (Sedgwick 1986). A similar sense applies to Julia Kristeva's conceptualization of the mourning process in *Black Sun: Depression and Melancholia*. As for Freud, Lacan and Abraham and Torok, mourning, the acceptance of the fundamental lack at the heart of symbolically determined subjectivity, is, for Kristeva, vital, salutary and life-affirming. Partially placated by the symbol, the subject of symbolic loss is, for Kristeva, a Heideggerian form of *being-unto-death*, a subject reconciled to the inevitability of sacrifice and the ongoing work of grieving the absent mother or Thing. But the refusal of the symbol, or what Kristeva refers to as the denial of symbolic negation, brings with it a regressive fixation in a form of impossible mourning, with the subject either pathologically refusing to relinquish its grasp on the Thing, or cannibalizing it in an equally ghastly version of Abraham and Torok's act of incorporation. Like the subject of incorporation, the subject of denied negation is also the subject in which the maternal Thing is buried alive:

They have lost the meaning – the value – of their mother tongue for want of losing the mother. The dead language they speak, which foreshadows their suicide, conceals a Thing buried alive. The latter, however, will not be translated in order that it not be betrayed; it shall remain walled up within the *crypt* of the inexpressible affect, anally harnessed, with no way out.

(Kristeva 1989: 53)

The life of the depressive, consequently, is the life of the 'living dead' (Kristeva 1989: 82), the putrefying corpse of the mother either consumed in a filthy act of cannibalism or walled up internally within the subject's internal crypt. Psychoanalysis is at its most Gothic when pathologies of mourning are at stake; in both discourses, ghosts, spectres, tombs and crypts are the foreseeable consequences of failed acts of grief.

And yet, in its insistence upon the work of mourning that, contrary to Freud, is never finally completed, in its preoccupations with spectres which are not explained away so much as reconfigured as the phantasmagorical supplements of consciousness (Castle 1987), has not Radcliffean Gothic already moved beyond the psychoanalytic paradigm in order to negotiate an ethical form of mourning that, in a Derridean more than a Kristevan sense, is ultimately impossible? In both *The Romance of the Forest* and *The Mysteries of Udolpho*, mourning appears to have an end: Adeline consoles Monsieur Amand with the adage that "'Time will blunt the sharpest edge of sorrow,' said she; 'I know it from experience'" (Radcliffe 1986: 290). In *Udolpho*, too, Emily's time of grieving for her father seems teleologically to develop into a comfortable psychic state in which the rawness of bereavement changes, over time, into the bearable, even pleasurable symptoms of melancholy or luxurious grief (Radcliffe 1966: 99). In Radcliffe, as in Freud, mourning has a beginning, a middle and a conceivable termination. And yet, even at the end of the novel, Emily is still given over to the symptoms of a wound that, however vehement her assertions, has not healed over by the passage of time: 'she could not think of her approaching return to La Vallée, without tears, and seemed to mourn again the death of her father, as if it had been an event of yesterday' (Radcliffe 1966: 590); even in the narrative's closing moments, Emily wishes to return 'once more to weep over the spot, where [St. Aubert's] remains were buried' even at the end (Radcliffe 1966: 642). La Luc in *The Romance of the Forest*, too, is a subject in perpetual mourning. Enjoying the 'luxury of grief' even after so many years after his wife's death, he clings to the work of continuous mourning as if it were a matter of ethical principle (Radcliffe 1986: 247). Contrary to the neatness of Freud's psychoanalytic model, mourning the dead in Radcliffean Gothic is never completed. This is, in a certain sense, evidence of the overwhelming melancholia that Angela Wright has identified in texts of the female Gothic tradition (Wright 2004). But it also attests to a process of mourning which, by dint of its incompleteness alone, is based upon far more ethical a relationship between the subject of grief and the lost love object. While the ghost of the other might well be subject to a process of psychic internalization in the course of Radcliffe's narrative, the persistence of mourning in the text points to an unassimilated residue or remainder of this process, an obdurate excess to the dead other that continuously defies the grieving subject's powers of assimilation. Perhaps Derrida's notion of impossible mourning is the best means of describing it.

Unsettled by the narcissistic tendencies of psychoanalysis, its tendencies to internalize the dead through the violent objectifications of introjection, Derrida's alternative of impossible mourning is ethically driven by the commitment to leave the other to his alterity, 'respecting thus his infinite remove' by either refusing or being unable to take 'the other within oneself, as in the tomb or vault of some narcissism' (Derrida 1986: 6). For Derrida, as for Kristeva, mourning is the condition of being: invariably haunted by the other even long before his actual death, the subject exists as such only through the perpetual work of grief. But while Kristeva's sense of impossible mourning is, in effect, a refusal of this very condition, impossible mourning, for Derrida, succeeds in the very failure of internalization, that is, in the respectful acknowledgment of the insurmountable otherness of the dead: 'an aborted interiorization is at the same time a respect for the other as other, a sort of tender rejection, a movement of renunciation which leaves the other alone, outside, over there, in his death, outside of us' (Derrida 1986: 35). Impossible mourning is prosopopoeia, elegy and grief to infinity; it is the sublimity 'of a mourning without sublimation and without the obsessive triumph of which Freud speaks' (Derrida 1986: 38). As *Specters of Marx* puts it, impossible mourning 'always defers the work of mourning, mourning itself and narcissism' (Derrida 1994: 131); it is 'A mourning in fact and by right interminable, without possible normality, without reliable limit, in its reality or in its concept, between introjection and incorporation' (Derrida 1994: 97). As this essay has shown, early Gothic writing finds it hard to live with ghosts. At its most characteristic, it eradicates and exorcizes them as the objects of unbearable horror and terror. But if, in these very gestures, Gothic writing in the West has failed to acknowledge the ethical role that the spectre might play as the *arrivant* – the harbinger of what Derrida in *Specters of Marx* gestures towards variously as an experience of the impossible; the messianic without messianism; the religion without a content; the alterity of the future that cannot be fully anticipated – it perhaps recovers its ethical commitment in the visions of its subjects, permanently engaged in the task of mourning impossible lost objects, to which it gives such graphic realization.

Notes

1 This poem is reprinted in Brian Vickers's edited collection *Shakespeare: The Critical Heritage Volume 3, 1733–1752* (Vickers 1975: 382). Line references will appear in parenthesis in the text. All other material from Vickers's multi-volume edition of contemporary material utlized in this essay will be indicated parenthetically by date, page and line number.

2 All references to *Hamlet* in this chapter are taken from Harold Jenkins's Arden edition of the play (Shakespeare 1989). Act, line and scene references will appear parenthetically in the text.

3 Perhaps more crucially for the writer of 'Shakespeare's Ghost', Cibber had dared in his biography *An Apology for the Life of Mr. Colley Cibber, Comedian, and Late Patentee of the Theatre-Royal […]* (1740) to interrogate an unnamed actor's overly passionate performance of Hamlet's encounter with his father's ghost – a sure slight upon the emotionally engaged forms of 'method acting' for which Garrick was so renowned (Vickers 1975: 106).

4 For a good account of the political sides to Tate's Shakespearean endeavours, see Nancy Klein Maguire's argument in 'Nahum Tate's *King Lear*: "the king's blest restoration"' (Maguire 1991).

5 See Arthur H. Scouten's explosion of this myth of Garrick in the article 'Shakespeare's Plays in the Theatrical Repertory When Garrick Came to London' (Scouten 1945). In view of Scouten's findings, Garrick was as much a pro-duct of mid-eighteenth-century Bardolatry as he was one of its primary agents.

6 The first of these praised the ghost scenes in *Hamlet* in language steeped in the discourse of the sublime, eventually concluding that Shakespeare's abilities far surpassed those of the French Corneille; the second article contained some equally unflattering observations on Racine.

7 See Michael Dobson's argument in *The Making of the National Poet: Shakespeare, Adaptation and Authorship, 1660–1769* (Dobson 1994).

8 The anonymous writer makes the following claim: 'Shakespeare, who first revived, or more properly form'd the Stage, was the greatest Dramatic Author this Country ever produced. By the Force of a sound Judgment, most lively Imagination, and a perfect knowledge of human Nature, without the least Assistance from Art, *he dispell'd those condense Clouds of Gothic Ignorance* which at that Time obscured us, and first caused Britain to appear a formidable Rival to her learned Neighbours' (Vickers 1975: 452; emphasis added).

9 Voltaire had expressed his dissatisfaction with the 'monstrosity' of the grave-diggers' scene throughout his career, including *Lettres philosophiques*; the *Dissertation sur la tragédie ancienne et moderne*; *Appel à toutes les nations de l'Europe*; as well as the later *Lettre à l'Académie*. As the second preface notes, Walpole is responding in parti-cular to the accusations levied in Voltaire's preface to *The Prodigal Son*.

10 For an account of the correspondence between Walpole and Voltaire, see M. B. Finch and E. Allison Peers's article 'Walpole's Relations with Voltaire' (Finch and Peers 1920).

11 For an excellent account of Ducis's alteration of Shakespeare's play in his ver-sion of *Hamlet*, see J. D. Golder's article '"Hamlet" in France 200 Years Ago' (Golder 1971).

12 Although Bonnell Thornton in *Have At You all, or The Drury Lane Journal* (1752) would 'willingly confine all dumb ghosts beneath the trap-doors' of contemporary stage craft, the spectre in *Hamlet* marks his only exception 'as he is an interesting character, and not only speaks but is a principal engine in carrying on the fable: – otherwise their mealy faces, white shirts, and red rags stuck on in imitation of blood are rather the objects of ridicule than terror' (Vickers 1975: 463). Though elsewhere vehemently denouncing a belief in the supernatural as the mark of benighted, antediluvian superstition, Arthur Murphy, like Thornton, commended the ghost in *Hamlet* as a marker of Shakespeare's originality, particularly since it did not feature in the account provided by Saxo Grammaticus: 'The Ghost is entirely his own Invention, nothing of this Sort being in the History. How nobly is that imaginary Personage introduced! And what a Solemnity of Ideas the Poet has assigned him!' (Vickers 1976: 277). Henry Mackenzie, writing in the Edinburgh magazine *The Mirror* in 1779, had also argued that Shakespeare's originality lay in his having introduced to Saxo Grammaticus's account of the story of Amleth the avenging spirit of the tragic hero's father. The Enlightenment's widespread cultural resistance to ghosts met its comeuppance in *Hamlet*: as Francis Gentleman opined in 1779, 'even those who laugh at the idea of ghosts as old women's' tales cannot avoid lending an eye and ear of serious attention to this of Hamlet's father' (Vickers 1979: 375).

13 See Paul de Man's account of prosopopoeia in the essay 'Autobiography as De-Facement' (de Man 1984).

14 Lacan further addresses notions of thwarted mourning in *Hamlet* in *The Four Fundamental Concepts of Psycho-Analysis* (Lacan 1981: 38).

15 Shortly after the ghost's appearance, for instance, Horatio recalls another scene of historical haunting as a means of conceptualizing the appearance of the spirit of old Hamlet: 'In the most high and palmy state of Rome, / A little ere the mightiest Julius fell, / The graves stood tenantless and the sheeted dead / Did squeak and gibber in the Roman streets' (1.1.116–19). Here, the ghost is more the harbinger of gross civic disturbance than the consequence of failed mourning. More trenchantly, *Hamlet*, far from unequivocally emphasizing the importance of ritualized grief, seems keen in places to dispense with the formalized signs of mourning – the inky cloak; the customary suits of black; the sighing; the tears; the dejected facial expressions invoked by Hamlet in 1.2.77–85 – as merely 'the trappings and the suits of woe' (1.2.86), the external paraphernalia of 'That monster, custom' (3.4.163) which in no way captures the unrepresentable excesses of internalized loss and anguish. Indeed, by Hamlet's own reckoning, it is more his father's inadequate preparation for death *during* his lifetime than the inadequacy of mourning *after* his demise that seems to result in his spectral return: Claudius, he tells us, killed Hamlet when he was 'full of bread, / With all his crimes broad blown, as flush as May' (3.3.80–81), a version of the ghost's earlier description of himself at the moment of death as 'Unhousel'd, disappointed, unanel'd' (1.5.77). Moreover, not everyone in the play who has not been properly mourned is condemned to a path of spectral return. As Laertes claims, Polonius's death has passed without even the most rudimentary forms of memorialization: his was an 'obscure funeral', an occasion with 'No trophy, sword, nor hatchment o'er his bones, / No noble rite, nor formal ostentation' (4.6.210–14). And yet, unlike his double the old King, he never returns as a supernatural agent. As even Ophelia in her madness

knows, Polonius is a father who will never come again, for 'he is dead, / Go to thy death-bed, / He never will come again' (4.6.187–91). At certain moments in the play, death marks the place of an absolute limit, an inviolable boundary that neither the living nor the dead themselves may ever successfully cross. Even Prince Hamlet himself unwittingly legislates against the ghostly return of the dead when he figures death as 'The undiscover'd country, from whose bourn / No traveller returns' (3.1.79–80).

16 As Greenblatt has argued, Shakespearean spectres – or at least the spectral effects in some of the plays – emanate variously from a nightmarish sense of history (*Richard III* and *Julius Caesar*); from deep psychological disturbance (*King Lear* and *Macbeth*); or through the effects of false surmise (*Comedy of Errors* and *Twelfth Night*). Whatever their provenance, the ghosts in Shakespeare, Greenblatt argues, are always highly theatrical, the stuff of dramatic entertainment more than the products of deep theological debate or failed and curtailed acts of mourning.

17 Medieval Catholic funerals were elaborate affairs, costly utilizations of incense and candles over a number of pre- and post-burial requiem masses, extended masses and liturgies, the anniversary obit and, in some cases, annual masses of remembrance in perpetuity (Litten 2002: 6). Frequently through drawing attention to the extortionate economies of Catholic mourning rites, the Reformation sought to cut off the spectacular ceremonies of Catholic funerary practice at their roots (Litten 2002: 156).

5 The scene of a crime

Fictions of authority in Walpole's 'Gothic Shakespeare'

Sue Chaplin

Through Shakespeare, Horace Walpole's *The Castle of Otranto* (1764) – the faked 'Gothic Story' that dubiously initiates Gothicism[1] – exemplifies the operation of a literary and juridical mimesis that simultaneously instantiates and derives its authority from a fiction of authority that essentially fabricates a crime-scene. Within this economy, the emergence and development of the Gothic (a genre uniquely concerned with crime-scenes, of course) is both legitimized and problematized with reference to a certain literary re-presentation of 'Shakespeare': the Gothic consolidates and contests a national literary archive that constructs 'Shakespeare' as its most authoritative precedent. This archive can be construed in the Derridean sense as a place of 'commencement' *and* 'command' (Derrida 1995: 2); it is the place of origin of a chain of precedents, of juridical citations that reproduce within each generation the symbolic and material power of 'family' and 'lineage'. This power is presented as pure, as sacred, in so far as it has its origin in pure presence, in the self-sufficient 'being' of the *logos*. As Pierre Legendre has argued, however, the abject truth about power is that it has no origin in anything outside of its own economy of signs (Legendre 1985); the law exists only in and through an endless re-citation of narratives that produce what might be termed 'the false appearance of a presence' (Derrida 2000a: 200).[2] To historicize this point and to orient it towards my concerns in this essay, the institution in the eighteenth century of an authoritative English literary tradition is inseparable from the contemporary formulation of a uniquely English juridical tradition – a system of national precedents that depends abjectly upon a contingent, self-referential narrativity that affirms/effaces *logos*. This juridical and literary economy ensures continuity for the living through a deathly order of mimesis – a compulsive 'repetition, reproduction, re-impression' of the past (Derrida 1995: 11). This compulsive monumentalization and repetition of the past, this maddening evocation of spectres, of the 'oldest names'[3] ('I am the spirit of thy father' announces the most famous of

Shakespearean ghost) is ultimately 'indissociable from the death drive' (Derrida 1995: 12). The literary archive that obsessively reproduces 'Shakespeare' as its point of paternal origin and the legitimate source of its 'commands' ('Swear!' says the spectre: 'I am the spirit of the father') is a spectral juridico-literary space. It also re-presents a crime scene. I will return to it.

This essay begins with a consideration of the emergence of the Gothic in the eighteenth century as a highly ambivalent literary *and* juridical category. I examine the Blackstonian formulation of English law as a 'Gothic castle' that is authenticated by virtue of its Gothicism, but which requires 'modernization' if it is to reflect and serve the new national interest effectively (Blackstone [1765] 1966). This historical and theoretical Gothicization of English law by eighteenth-century jurists served a specific and pressing ideological function (as I shall discuss) and it is inseparable from the simultaneous development of an authorized *literary* tradition with a similarly vital yet ambivalent relation to the Gothic. The emergence of a certain eighteenth-century construction of 'Shakespeare', and Walpole's utilization of it as an authoritative precedent for his work, will be set within the context of the uneasy relation between law, literature and the Gothic in the mid-eighteenth century. Through its own appropriation and re-presentation of Shakespeare, *Otranto* comes to exist within this early modern juridico-literary economy as a site of power in itself, a point of 'commencement' and 'command' in respect of texts to follow. The novel is also a site of transgression, however; it is the (in)authentic Gothic 'original' that plays with its own origins and that institutes a genre so susceptible to mutation that it comes to resist the very drive towards archivization which constitutes it as 'Gothic'. Gothic textuality (and, I will argue, 'Shakespearean' textuality as it was re-ordered and re-presented by critics in the eighteenth century) appears to repudiate the very possibility of textual authenticity. The second section of the essay broadens out this analysis by means of a return to the scene of a crime. I seek here to interrogate, through Derrida, the relation between law, literature and 'a certain interpretation of mimesis' within the Western tradition. The initial focus of this section is, perhaps rather eccentrically, Derrida's playful reading of Mallarmé's *Mimique*, a text which is ostensibly neither 'Gothic' nor 'Shakespearean'. Like Shakespeare's *Hamlet* and Walpole's *Otranto*, however, *Mimique* turns upon the commission of a hidden crime, a crime which can only be re-presented uncannily as 'the false appearance of a presence'. I argue finally that *Otranto's* re-presentation of the spectral *appearance* of a crime allows the text obliquely to reproduce and subvert contemporary national juridical and literary discourses that worked to conceal the absence of proper legal and literary origin through their 'reproduction, re-impression' of precedents, of paternal 'names' that compel allegiance to spectres. According to Walpole's re-ordering of Shakespeare's economy of ghosts, there is no authentic 'commencement'/'command' signified by the father's return, or 're-impression' – there is *only* the compulsive, uncanny, spectral 're-impression' that is always-already a pathological, death-driven fiction.

Gothic 'origins'

Alexandra Warwick has recently addressed the tendency within contemporary criticism of the Gothic to expand the category of the Gothic almost indefinitely so as to include texts that 'fifteen years ago would routinely have been described as science fiction or feminist or Victorian' (Warwick 2007: 6). It is within the context of this wide-ranging critical re-evaluation of the Gothic that it has perhaps become possible now to speak of and to interrogate 'Gothic Shakespeares'. This critical enterprise is problematized, however, by this extreme flexibility of taxonomy. It has become almost impossible to account consistently for the generic properties of the Gothic, to the extent that it appears necessary to abandon the concept of 'genre' altogether if Gothic criticism is to remain coherent. As Warwick observes, 'if there is any consensus, it seems to be that the Gothic is a mode rather than a genre, that it is a loose tradition and even that its defining characteristics are its mobility and its continued capacity for reinvention' (Warwick 2007: 6). The Gothic becomes, then, the 'category' that 'defies the very concept of category' (Williams 1995: 14); it emerges out of this criticism almost as a Derridean *trace* that simultaneously affirms and erases the 'presence' of something that is (but only provisionally and equivocally) 'Gothic'. Indeed, it can be argued that the Gothic is that which exposes most insistently and traumatically within literature and law the illegality and inauthenticity of any stable origin – including its own (Chaplin 2007). To invoke Blanchot, it is *Gothic* textuality in the modern period that may be posited as 'the enemy of all relationships of presence, of all legality' (Blanchot 1981: 156). The Gothic reveals the illusion of a 'presence' that can exist only in and through an abyssal order of mimesis.

Warwick's analysis, moreover, suggests the importance to Gothic criticism of a principle of exemplarity that the Gothic problematizes: 'What compounds the difficulty [of defining the Gothic] is the permanently problematic status of the example. How does an example manifest its exemplarity, especially when many examples of Gothic appear to be categorized by their departure from the genre?' (Warwick 2007: 6). The problem of 'the exemplarity of the example' is one of the foci of Derrida's *Sauf le Nom*. To summarize Derrida's argument, the 'Idea' that is meant to be exemplified through the citation of some specific instance or allegorization of it – the 'example' – cannot be seen to exist anywhere independently of the chain of citations that 'presents' it. Western thought depends upon a 'logic of exemplarity' that defeats the very idea of 'presence' (Derrida 1995: 18). If this analysis is combined with Derrida's study of the 'mark' of genre as that which simultaneously announces and effaces the 'presence' of genre according to this logic of exemplarity (Derrida 1992: 230–31), then the generic trangressions that appear paradoxically to define the Gothic do indeed become theorizable in terms of the 'problematic status of the example', precisely as Warwick suggests. The Gothic – as that which, if we *are* to define it, seems through its mutability to confound the very principle of genre – is *exemplary* of the 'mark' of genre as Derrida theorizes it. By means of the seemingly endless examples of itself that 'the Gothic' generates, it endlessly defers its 'presence'. And thus it bears the most abject and the most 'truthful' relation to the law. There is no 'mark' of pure juridical presence that exists independently of the law's citation and re-citation of itself; if the law has a 'genre', it is Gothic.

(To re-iterate – the spectre 'appears', opaque in his armour, to re-present a crime. He announces his presence – authentically? What precedent exists for this? – 'I am the spirit of thy father.' 'Swear!')

This theoretical understanding of Gothicism opens up a means of conceptualizing the Gothic's uneasy re-presentations, appropriations and misappropriations of the 'presence' or 'example' of Shakespeare within an emerging national literary tradition in the eighteenth century – a tradition closely bound up with contemporary juridical re-presentations, appropriations and misappropriations of the Gothic. In this period, the question of the origin of national law assumed a certain urgency as legal and political theorists sought to divorce the common and constitutional laws of England from the traumas of seventeenth-century civil war and regicide. This juridical trauma, to paraphrase Slavoj Žižek, had to be *narrated over*, concealed by a 'symbolic fiction' of the founding moments of national law (Žižek 2001: 52). This 'fiction' took the form of a Gothic romance of English law historicized and theorized most famously in William Blackstone's *Commentaries on the Laws of England*. Law was authenticated here with reference to a form of juridical folklore – the labyrinthine narratives of English common law reaching back to a fictive 'Gothick' past. Simultaneously, though, Blackstone sought to validate the law according to what he perceived as its essential rationality, its derivation from a divinely ordained Law of Nature which the *Commentaries* discusses in its Preface. Within a modern Enlightenment context, this innate rationality of law effects the transformation of a range of authentic, authoritative, but also somewhat disorganized and primitive juridical narratives into a juridical 'science' (Blackstone [1765] 1966: 2). Blackstone's 'Gothic castle' of English law undergoes its necessary Enlightenment 'modernisation' through this process of transformation of legal romance into legal reason.

For Blackstone, eighteenth-century English law represents the culmination of a historical process that had managed to blend the ancient customs and practices of the 'Gothick' constitution with a modern, scientific, transparent rule of law. I would argue that, within literary discourse in the eighteenth century, Shakespeare functions ideologically in precisely the same way. The eighteenth-century 'Shakespeare' emerged into and consolidated an economy of representation that sought to affirm and reform a national literary and juridical archive with reference to a certain conceptualization of legal and literary Gothicism. A certain nostalgia for Gothic primitivism accompanied the nation's attempts to narrate its origins to itself and what Shakespeare was seen to inherit and perfect was an English-Gothic romance tradition that (like the English-Gothic constitution) could be said to have its origin 'in the woods'.[4] This national tradition possessed a primitive genius that received its essential 'modernization' through the writings of the great national poet – 'our Gothic bard', as Elizabeth Montagu termed Shakespeare.[5] The notion of the 'Gothic' at work within these discourses was highly contrived and exceptionally ambivalent, however. Even as its historical, political and cultural value was affirmed, Gothicism in literature and law was at the same time acknowledged as the very antithesis of the modernizing and rationalizing spirit of the Enlightenment: it constituted, more often than not, an abject textuality given to the fraudulent manufacturing of 'lost' legal and literary origins. From the moment of its inception, a highly artificial conceptualization of 'the Gothic' in legal and literary terms exposed the 'fantasy-construction' that was the English nation, its origins, its laws (Dean 2004: 3). It was within this context that Walpole's Gothic experiment took shape in 1764 as a 'Shakespearean' negotiation of juridical and literary traumas.

Horace Walpole's *The Castle of Otranto* was, of course, initially published under a pseudonym. Moreover, it was prefaced by an 'editor's' note presenting the text as a Gothic 'original' – a medieval manuscript from southern Italy found by the editor in a library in the North of England. Following the initial success of that first addition, Walpole re-published the work with a further Preface claiming authorship of the text and attempting to justify its publication according to certain standards of mid-eighteenth-century literary propriety. This second Preface demonstrates a keen awareness of the political importance of a literary tradition capable of conferring upon the nation a unique cultural identity distinct in particular from Catholic Europe and, even more specifically, from France. Walpole compares Shakespeare's literary innovations favourably with the conservatism of the French national poets and uses Shakespeare to justify his own literary experimentation – an innovation comprised of the blending of ancient romance with the modern principle of literary realism. I have suggested that an analogous process was underway within juridical discourse at the same moment: the eighteenth-century English constitution was seen to rationalize and perfect an older juridical tradition; an authentic national legal romance tradition was transformed into an enlightened modern rule of law. In Walpole's second Preface, Shakespeare functions to mediate between the primitivism of the popular romance tradition and a more disciplined, realist mode of writing. Like Samuel Johnson's almost contemporaneous writing on Shakespeare, Walpole praises Shakespeare's capacity to re-shape older dramatic conventions so as to produce a new, more sophisticated mode of dramatic representation that combines the fertile imaginative invention of old romance with an adherence to what Johnson and Walpole term 'life'. Johnson's *Preface* to Shakespeare and Walpole's Preface to *Otranto* both conceptualize the 'Gothic bard' as *the* national genius in whose works an essential synthesis is achieved between old and new: 'Shakespeare is, above all writers, at least above all modern writers, the poet of nature, the poet that holds up to his readers a faithful mirror of manners and of life', writes Johnson (Greene 1984: 421). 'Shakespeare,' he goes on to say, 'approximates the remote, and familiarises the wonderful; the event which he represents will not happen, but, if it were possible, its effects would probably be such as he has assigned; and it may be said that he has not only shown human nature as it acts in real exigencies, but as it would be found in trials to which it cannot be exposed' (422). It is precisely this desire to emulate Shakespeare in 'familiarizing the wonderful' that Walpole cites as his primary motive for producing his 'Gothic Story'. The second Preface concludes with the explicit citation of Shakespeare as the 'model' for Otranto: 'The result of all that I have said is to shelter my own daring under the cannon of the brightest genius this country, at least, has produced' (Walpole [1764], 1991: 12). Shakespeare is the Gothic 'original' behind the slippery literary tradition which Walpole's (in)authentic text (first a 'fake', then vindicated as a Shakespearean experimentation) inaugurates. The publication of this precedent-text for literary Gothicism, a text that cites Shakespeare as *its* authority, thus anticipated the tendency of the Gothic ever since to problematize the very notion of a lawful, authentic national literature. Gothic fictions from Walpole onwards were denounced for, amongst other things, their literary trickery – their plagiarisms and outright forgeries. Walpole's faked 'Gothic' sets a precedent for later Gothic writings, then, not least in so far as it 'exposes the bad faith of literary forgery in the manner Kristeva allots to aesthetic abjection: [Walpole] turns aside, misleads, corrupts a "prohibition," or "rule"; he is a "trickster who draws attention to the fragility of law'" (Miles 2001: 61). The first edition of *Otranto*, and many subsequent Gothic fictions which duplicated Walpole's abject (de)authenticating gesture, tapped into eighteenth-century anxieties concerning the circulation of literary forgeries that threatened the integrity of the national literary archive, particularly when, later in the century, such literary 'bad faith' was to strike at the very heart of the literary canon through the production of forgeries attributed to Shakespeare himself.[6]

Indeed, there was, even in Johnson's work in the 1760s, an acknowledgement of just how problematic an enterprise the authentication of the Shakespeare canon was. Johnson observes that it was not the practice in Shakespeare's time necessarily to authenticate a text with reference to a signature; moreover, even those texts that do 'bear the name of Shakespeare' have undergone a range of alterations, additions and effacements at the hands of various editors (Greene 1984: 441). Johnson presents himself as one such editor of the Shakespeare corpus concerned to present to his culture the 'authentic' version of the work of a poet who, through this process of 'authentication', problematically achieves the status of the national 'Gothic bard' – the (absent) father of the literary tradition his editors and critics inaugurate. The problem for Johnson, and for all subsequent editors who re-present 'Shakespeare', is that this authentication-through-revision exposes precisely the ficticiousness of 'Shakespeare' as the proper point of origin of the national canon. From a wider theoretical perspective, these (de)-authenticating gestures reveal the illegality of textuality per se: through processes of 'repetition, reproduction, re-impression' (Derrida 1995: 11), textuality manufactures a fiction of its origin in a pure presence (the proper name of the father-author) outside of the text. This 'outside' is the phantasmal space of law mythologized as *logos*. It is also *the* crime scene.

Mimesis: staging a crime

Textuality functions in Derrida's analysis as the essential, yet disavowed supplement of a *logos* that perpetually, and impossibly, sets itself *against* the necessary interventions of writing. Derrida conceptualizes textuality as the double-edged trickster-*pharmakon* that has the capacity to act as both a poison *and* a cure (Derrida 2000b: 65–73). The 'cure' that textuality offers to the law pertains to the law's inability to establish its own permanence, or presence, without some literary intervention: only once it is 'put into writing' does the law remain 'on record', its permanence 'ensured [by the text] with the vigilance of a guardian' (Derrida 2000b: 113). At the same time, however, textuality could be said to commit a kind of crime against the *logos*: it improperly appropriates the 'presence' of the law, steals it and substitutes itself for it. Writing is, to invoke Blanchot once more, 'the enemy of all relationships of presence, of all legality' (Blanchot 1981: 156). The law nevertheless has no 'presence' whatsoever without this criminal narrativity. In particular, the emergence of law requires the emergence of a narrative capable of resolving the trauma that attends the inception of communal and individual subjectivity: the law acquires its 'presence' only after a certain violent communal fantasy has established a vital untruth about the law's origins. The founding moment of Western law is a representation of a fictive transgression that serves to account for the terrifying, symbolically *unrepresentable* rupture that separates the individual and the community from the pre-symbolic void. In order for the law to take its place, it is necessary to stage a 'crime' and then to re-present it as the law's sure foundation. This crime is parricide and Derrida links it explicitly to the advent of narrativity as the law's uncanny, necessary condition of being:

> […] this quasi-event bears the marks of fictive narrativity (fiction *of* narration as well as fiction *as* narration: fictive narration as the simulacrum of narration and not only as the narration of an imaginary history). It is the origin of literature as well as the origin of law – like the dead father, a story told, a spreading rumour, without author or end, but an ineluctable and unforgettable story.
>
> (Derrida 1992: 199)

The question of the law's origin thus becomes a question of *mimesis*: a quasi-event, a murder, is staged just outside of the order of representation it is said to institute and it is narrated thereafter as the 'legitimate' origin of all authority.

In 'The Double Session', Derrida's essay on Mallarmé (Derrida 2000a), he turns to the question: 'What is literature?' This question, he contends, can be answered only at the interface between 'literature' and 'truth', and this relation has been defined within the Western tradition by means of a 'certain interpretation of mimesis' (Derrida 2000a: 183). According to this interpretation, mimesis produces a double of some original to which the double is inferior. More than this, the double is posited as 'worth nothing in itself'; whatever value it might have comes only from its model, such that the copy 'is in itself negative' (Derrida 2000a: 187). Nevertheless, this double possesses a certain kind of 'presence', if only by virtue of its resemblance to its original, and thus it has a subversive form of inauthentic 'being'. It is on account of the untruthful existence of the double generated by mimesis that mimesis ultimately becomes 'an evil' within this order of representation. To imitate 'is bad in itself', and this *in itself* is vital. The 'presence' that comes dubiously into being through mimesis *is* untruthful *in itself*, and its 'evil' lies not in the fact that it doubles a more authentic original that remains apart from it, but in its re-presentation of this 'original' *as* untruth. Mimesis sets in motion a chain of 'repetition, resemblance, doubling, duplication' according to which the copy substitutes for the original, disseminates it and finally, necessarily, displaces it (Derrida 2000a: 188). The original requires the intervention of mimesis to 'ensure its permanence', to put it 'on record', and yet this essential intervention is always already a *supervention* of the 'truth' it purports to 'copy': '[the] image *supervenes* upon reality, the representation upon the present in presentation, the imitation upon the thing, the imitator upon the imitated' (Derrida 2000a: 191). The order of mimesis becomes 'the order of all appearances: it is the order of truth' (Derrida 2000a: 192). Juridical and literary authority is reliant upon this 'truth' that achieves its only possible presence through mimesis. Mimesis is the abject ordering principle of literature and law.

(A group of players in a play-within-a-play mime the murder of a king. The King absents himself. What does this signify?)

To reiterate, the law's 'origin' exists only in and through the fabrication of a crime – the 'spreading rumour, without author or end' of a murder. This is a 'crime', though, that must be staged just outside of the juridical order that it institutes; it takes place as an absence, an abyssal re-presentation of death that reproduces the law as a copy of the authority of an imaginary, murdered Father. In Mallarmé's *Mimique*, a murder is simulated by the mime, Pierrot. Conventional readings of this work (which proceed according to that 'interpretation of mimesis' which Derrida critiques) tend to emphasize the apparent tension in the narrative between 'representation' and 'reality', between the mime-show and the 'authentic' event. These readings have been seen to be authorized, as it were, by Mallarmé's *own* intervention into the narrative: he inserts into the text a quotation – 'The scene illustrates but an idea, not any actual action' (Derrida 2000a: 194). The twist, as Derrida points out, is that this 'quotation' is in fact fictive and Derrida's own approach to the text resists the Platonic Idealist interpretation that this fake 'quotation' appears to demand. Derrida reads *Mimique* according to 'the specular process and play of reflections' that mimesis initiates (Derrida 2000a: 188). The 'crime', or 'idea', that the text reproduces emerges for Derrida not merely as an absence, but as a series of absences endlessly deferred by the aberrant textuality of Mallarmé's work. *Mimique* challenges that interpretation of mimesis which places representation secondary to a 'presence' that supposedly precedes and authorizes the image (and, subversively, Mallarmé's text calls attention to the very philosophy it repudiates by means of that inauthentic citation placed at the very centre of the narrative). Mallarmé's ghostly Pierrot silently reproduces a 'crime' that has no existence beyond the ambiguous moments in which it is recited by the gestures of the mime, by the text of *Mimique* itself and by the mysterious 'original' narrative upon which Mallarmé purports to base his fiction ('the suggestive and truly rare booklet that opens in my hands') (Derrida 2000a: 198). The 'crime', the 'idea' (which is not to be confused with 'any actual action'), takes place only through these multiple stagings of it, and through these abyssal re-presentations of no actual *event* it assumes (as Mallarmé puts it) 'the false appearance of a presence' (Derrida 2000a: 200).

(To reiterate – 'The dumb-show enters: Enter a King and a Queen very lovingly; the Queen embracing him, and he her. She kneels, and makes show of protestation unto him. He takes her up, and declines his head upon her neck: lays him down upon a bank of flowers: she, seeing him asleep, leaves him. Anon comes in a fellow, takes off his crown, kisses it, and pours poison in the King's ears, and exits. The Queen returns; finds the King dead, and makes passionate action. The Poisoner, with some two or three Mutes, comes in again, seeming to lament with her. The dead body is carried away. The Poisoner wooes the Queen with gifts: she seems loath and unwilling awhile, but in the end accepts his love. Exeunt.' *Hamlet*, Act 3, Scene 2.)

The play-within-a-play that Hamlet stages to catch the conscience of his uncle re-presents a 'crime' that makes its only appearance in *Hamlet* through this mime-show. The 'crime' has taken place (if it has taken place at all, and that is the question) off-stage as the inaugural event of Claudius's (mis)rule. It also re-presents, as does the mime show in *Mimique*, a crisis of interpretation pertaining to a 'certain order of mimesis'. Hamlet wishes to invest in this order of mimesis: he wishes to establish an authentic relation between the mimetic and the real, between his play and an actual event – the murder as narrated to him by the spectre that presents itself as 'the spirit of thy father.' This attempt to guarantee the truth of the spectre's narrative produces in Claudius what Hamlet interprets as a sign of guilt: Claudius flees from the 'crime' scene. Still, though, Hamlet does not act and this failure of action is an abject and inevitable failure of juridical interpretation. As Goodrich observes, the 'symbolisation of authority' that functions to present the authentic, original principle of governance is 'no more than a massive simulation, revealing only that the so-called "authentic truth" of law is unrepresentable save by means of the detour of metaphors' (Goodrich 1990: 252). The ultimate sign of 'truth' within this system, Goodrich argues, is the family tree, which posits as the foundation of juridical authority 'an ancestor, or oldest name' (Goodrich 1990: 252). At the commencement of *Hamlet*, there is a demand for vengeance that appears to emanate out of the very being of the law itself, from the body of the Father, this 'oldest name' appearing in 'spirit' to require the restitution of proper paternal rule. The law, however, can only present itself to the son as the appearance / apparition of a presence, as the spectral copy of a father whose command can only be authenticated with reference to the narration of a crime and the miming of the narration of a crime. *Hamlet* symbolizes the trauma of a juridical subject, the legitimacy of whose action depends upon an impossible appeal to 'truth' beyond re-presentation: it is thus an exemplary Gothic text.

Hamlet is *Otranto*'s precedent text in terms of Walpole's re-presentation of an abject juridical economy of spectral 'presences'. *Otranto*'s re-citation of *Hamlet*, though, complicates this economy of ghosts even further and in so doing sets the scene, as it were, for the Gothic's future re-presentations of the problematics of paternal juridical power. Significantly, the one moment in the text that most unequivocally evokes *Hamlet* is the very point at which Manfred *does* confront a sign that promises to reveal to him the nature of the circumstances in which he finds himself; this spectral appearance, however, is one that again fails to deliver any possibility of interpretation to the traumatized son. Acting as if to support the ghost of Alfonso in impressing upon Manfred the peril he is in, the portrait of Manfred's grandfather breaks free of its frame; in spite of Manfred's protestations, however, it refuses to speak. This apparition reveals nothing to Manfred beyond the fact of its own spectral presence which – given that Manfred's grandfather was the usurper of Alfonso's throne – functions as an uncanny supplement to Alfonso's haunting of his former seat of power. The apparition is otherwise an opaque sign: it gestures to Manfred to follow it only to shut him out of the chamber into which it disappears. Manfred is left, once more, frantic and unknowing. He begs the spectre to reveal whatever secret it holds; the apparition, however, will not even allow Manfred to name the crime for which it was responsible and which now condemns Manfred to rule Otranto in fear and guilt:

> Do I dream? cried Manfred returning, or are the devils themselves in league against me? Speak, infernal spectre! Or, if thou art my grandsire, why dost thou too conspire against thy wretched descendant, who too dearly pays for – Ere he could finish the sentence the vision sighed again, and made a sign to Manfred to follow him. Lead on! cried Manfred; I will follow thee to the gulph of perdition. The spectre marched sedately, but dejected, to the end of the gallery, and turned into a chamber on the right hand. The prince, collecting courage from this delay, would have forcibly burst open the door with his foot, but found that it resisted his utmost efforts. Since hell will not satisfy

my curiosity, said Manfred, I will use the human means in my power for preserving my race; Isabella shall not escape me.

(Walpole 1996b: 24)

The animation of the portraits of ancestors – of visual re-presentations of the law's 'oldest names' that break out of their frames and out of the past usually to announce guilt – becomes a key trope of the Gothic, one that uncannily symbolizes and contests the fictions of authority that are the essential supplements of law and literature. The spectre that presents as the ghost of Hamlet's father breaks the physical and symbolic frame of Elsinore by beckoning the son on to the castle walls, to the very margins of juridical/domestic space (the archive, home of the Father and his law), to narrate a dreadful 'truth' about the law; the spectre's crime-story and its subsequent re-presentation at the behest of Hamlet himself fatally complicates Hamlet's already tenuous grip on a juridical 'reality' that is always already the 'false appearance of a presence'. Moreover, as I have suggested, there is an analogy between Hamlet's interrogation of juridical appearances and the 'appearance' of Shakespeare as the legitimate father of the English literary tradition. As even Johnson acknowledged, the Shakespeare canon is not truly capable of proper authentication; even those texts which do 'bear the name of Shakespeare' (Greene 1984: 441) require textual re-workings before they can properly be presented as 'Shakespeare'. The construction of the Shakespearean precedent is simultaneously an authenticating and a de-authenticating gesture and similar gestures are repeated, along with the breaking of symbolic, textual and generic frames, as exemplary Gothic devices after the first Gothic story originated in 1764. The Shakespearean precedent produces this exemplary Gothicism in the Derridean sense that the transgression of borders and the problematization of textual-juridical authority has come simultaneously to re-present 'the Gothic' as a genre whilst also complicating and deferring the 'presence' of the Gothic within any given text. Walpole's 'Gothic Shakespeare', framed initially as a fake and then as a 'proper' literary experimentation, equivocally inaugurates a mode of textuality that stalls the operation of literary and juridical fictions of authority.

Conclusion – a nostalgia for the law

In relation to the place of Shakespeare within the canon and the humanities curriculum, Marjorie Garber asks the following question: 'What is it about the humanities in general and Shakespeare in particular that calls up this nostalgia for the certainties of truth and beauty – a nostalgia that, like all nostalgias, is really a nostalgia for what never was?' (Garber 1990:

243). According to Linda Hutcheon, nostalgia depends 'precisely on the irrecoverability of the past' (Hutcheon 2000: 180); for Susan Stewart, it is no less than a 'social dis-ease […] the repetition that mourns the inauthenticity of all repetition' (Stewart 1984: 23). If this 'dis-ease' characterizes a certain yearning for a 'true' Shakespeare, moreover, it also constitutes a necessary response to law within the Western tradition. The law's founding moment takes place always uncannily outside of the scheme of re-presentation that it institutes. The law's point of origin necessarily exists somewhere 'off-stage', somewhere outside of what Plato terms the 'law pure and simple', and the juridical subject thus stands before the law in a condition of dis-ease, homesickness, mourning. This dis-ease is the product of an economy of mimesis that insists (impossibly) upon the sort of juridical 'truth' in representation that constructs Shakespeare as the authoritative moment of origin of the modern English literary archive.

Derrida refers to *Mimique* as a 'handbook of literature' (Derrida 2000a: 223). I would argue that so is *Hamlet* and so is *Otranto*: all of these texts present an example of *Gothic* textuality, where this is understood to signify an abyssal, inauthentic narrativity that paradoxically constitutes narrative in its 'truest' (most spectral, most monstrous) form. One could argue further that this 'Gothic' text brings before the law the 'philosophical problem with literature itself' (Douzinas and Greary 2005: 337), the problem of a mimesis that simultaneously sets the law in place (copying it, disseminating it) and effaces its claim to original presence. The law here (the 'idea' that *Mimique* alludes to, one might say) is the *logos* as a copy derived from the staging of an imaginary point of origin. This fiction generates a homesickness, a nostalgia for some point of return to what Garber terms 'the certainties of truth and beauty'; to Law 'pure and simple'; to 'Shakespeare'.

Notes

1 See Miles (2002b), Clery (1995)
2 Derrida in the essay 'The double Session' quotes Mallarmé's *Mimique* on the dumb-show (and the various 'texts' of *Mimique* itself) as reproducing the 'false appearance of a presence'.
3 As Peter Goodrich argues, juridical narratives reproduce the 'ancestor' or 'oldest name' as the legitimate origin of juridical power (Goodrich 1990).
4 Montesquieu, 'Spirit of the Laws' (1750) (Clery and Miles 2000: 63).
5 See Elizabeth Montagu's 'On the Praeternatural Beings' (1769) (Clery and Miles 2000: 32).
6 Miles analyses one of the most notorious literary forgeries of the late eighteenth century – the 'discovery' in 1795 of an extensive Shakespearean archive. One interesting feature of the presentation of this 'discovery' is the extent to which it seems to mimic the Gothic device of the discovered manuscript (Miles 2005).

6   In search of Arden

Ann Radcliffe's William Shakespeare[1]

Angela Wright

> In the productions of Mrs. Radcliffe, the Shakspeare of Romance Writers, and who to the wild landscape of Salvator Rosa has added the softer graces of a Claude, may be found many scenes truly terrific in their conception, yet so softened down, and the mind so much relieved, by the intermixture of beautiful description, or pathetic incident, that the impression of the whole never becomes too strong, never degenerates into horror, but pleasurable emotion is ever the predominating result.
>
> (Nathan Drake 1798: 249)

In 1798, Nathan Drake in *Literary Hours* made a brief reference to the reputation of Ann Radcliffe, hailing her as 'the Shakspeare of Romance writers' (Drake 1798: 249). He did not, however, pause to justify the terms of his praise, nor to explain what he meant by forging this intimate connection between Shakespeare and the writer of romance. Earlier in the same work, Drake grouped together the works of Horace Walpole, Clara Reeve and Ann Radcliffe, amongst others, in order to argue that while their romances 'still powerfully arrest attention, and keep an ardent curiosity alive, yet is their machinery, by no means, an object of popular belief' (Drake 1798: 37–38). Whereas 'in the times of Tasso, Shakspeare and even Milton, witches and wizards, spectres and fairies, were nearly as important subjects of faith as the most serious doctrines of religion', Drake was satisfied that 'In the present century when science and literature have spread so extensively, the heavy clouds of superstition have dispersed, and have assumed a lighter, and less formidable hue' (Drake 1798: 37–38). For Drake, then, an admiration of romance writers such as Radcliffe seemed to be contingent upon the levity of their engagement with 'terrific' incident. Drake's celebration of Ann Radcliffe as 'the Shakspeare of Romance writers' suggests that romance writing at its best should sanitize the horror and superstition that characterized Shakespeare's tragedies. Such a use of Shakespeare, removing the terrifying aspect of his supernatural characters, becomes conservatively synonymous with Radcliffe's nomination as 'the Shakspeare of Romance writers'.

Without doubt, the terms of Drake's praise for Radcliffe were generated by the first recognized attempt at Gothic romance, Horace Walpole's *The Castle of Otranto* of 1764. Walpole's self-confessed 'attempt to blend the two kinds of romance, the ancient and the modern' led him to push beyond the boundaries of the 'strict adherence to common life' so prevalent in the mid-eighteenth-century novel by introducing a supernatural agent into his tale (Walpole 1996a: 9). As E. J. Clery argues, Walpole's tale, and the terms of his argument, presented 'an outright challenge to [the orthodoxy] that novelists should remain within the bounds of 'natural horror' (Clery 2002: 23). Walpole was all too aware of the risks of his literary enterprise, however, and chose to 'shelter [his] own daring under the cannon of the brightest genius this country, at least, has produced' (Walpole 1996a: 14). He was, of course, referring to Shakespeare. The military register of his language here – 'shelter' and 'cannon' – are immediately suggestive of a literary battle. This battle was two-fold: earlier, in this same Preface, Walpole had defended Shakespeare from attack by the French critic Voltaire. By carrying out this defence of England's 'brightest genius' first, he placated his readership's anxieties regarding the boldness of his own experimentation. After this patriotically-driven defence of Shakespeare, Walpole was then able to excuse his own literary experiment by arguing that 'I should be more proud of having imitated, however faintly, weakly, and at a distance, so masterly a pattern, than to enjoy the entire merit of invention, unless I could have marked my work with genius as well as originality' (Walpole 1996a: 14). In this invocation of Shakespeare as a national treasure to be defended against foreign criticism, Walpole was then covertly able to import into England, under the 'masterly pattern' of Shakespeare, his own use of the supernatural.[2] Walpole's literary experimentation was quick to establish Shakespeare as a cherished national precedent for Gothic romance. Thus, when Drake grouped together the fictions of Walpole, Reeve and Radcliffe, nominating Radcliffe herself as 'the Shakspeare of Romance writers', he consolidated her reputation as the guardian of a nationally founded literary tradition deemed appropriate for a British readership in the 1790s.[3]

Other critics shared Drake's view. In *The Pursuits of Literature*, for example, the Reverend Thomas J. Mathias had exempted Ann Radcliffe from the charge-sheet of female literary subversives – the three specifically accused were Charlotte Smith, Elizabeth Inchbald and Mary Robinson, all of whom 'turn' 'our girls' heads wild with impossible adventures' – by specifically drawing attention to his belief that 'Mrs Radcliffe' had been 'bred amid the paler shrines of Gothick superstition' (Mathias 1798: 58).

Both Drake and Mathias's approving assessments of Radcliffe's due care for the British nation's moral compass, however, derived from a cursory reading of her use of Shakespeare. As I will argue in the following pages, their assessment was contingent upon several misleading assumptions: first, that the invocation of Shakespeare by any Gothic author in Britain was a gesture of English nationalism during a time of French encroachment, and second, that Ann Radcliffe was fundamentally opposed to the use of the supernatural in her fiction and other writings. Nathan Drake in particular presumed that Radcliffe's engagement with Shakespeare was a comforting constant. Instead, as I will argue, Radcliffe's use of Shakespeare, and the tributes that she paid to him throughout her career, demonstrate a dynamic relationship between romance writer and dramatist. It is a relationship that evolves in response to the reproduction of Shakespeare's work in new editions, the production of his plays on stage, and perhaps more significantly, the changing political stage in England in the 1790s and 1800s.

Samuel Johnson's 1765 edition of Shakespeare contained a Preface where Johnson, like Walpole, defended Shakespeare against the criticism of Voltaire (Johnson 1765: xii). But Johnson's defence of Shakespeare was not as self-interested as Walpole's patriotically defensive endeavours. Johnson's Shakespeare was a more transcendent figure, one who was 'above all writers, at least above all modern writers, the poet of nature' (Johnson 1765: viii). Clearly, Johnson's Preface held enormous importance for Ann Radcliffe: she specifically invokes this Preface in her travel journals, recalling from memory Johnson's insights on Shakespeare.[4] Johnson's transcendent Shakespeare was, however, later challenged in 1790 by another scholar. Almost immediately after Radcliffe began publishing her Gothic romances in 1789, a new edition of Shakespeare was produced. In 1790, Edmond Malone's ten-volume edition, *The Plays and Poems of William Shakspeare*, appeared to great acclaim. In his lengthy 75-page Preface to the first volume, Malone drew attention to the eighteenth century's renewed interest in Shakespeare:

> It is remarkable that in a century after our poet's death, five editions only of his plays were published; which probably consisted of not more than three thousand copies. During the same period three editions of the plays of Fletcher, and four of those of Jonson, had appeared. On the other hand, from the year 1716 to the present time, that is, in seventy-four years, but two editions of the former writer, and one of the latter, have been issued from the press; while above thirty thousand copies of Shakspeare have been dispersed through England.
>
> (Malone 1790: lxxiii)

Renewed interest in the Bard demanded new editions of his works. Although Malone held Johnson's 1765 edition in considerable esteem, he nonetheless believed that 'we are yet without a splendid edition of [Shakespeare's] works' (Malone 1790: lxxiii).[5] Malone's edition aimed to supply this want with a considerable quantity of scholarly notes and criticism.[6]

The date of Malone's edition (1790) places it squarely within the political turbulence that England experienced in the immediate aftermath of the French Revolution. Despite being a work of considerable scholarship that took Malone some years to produce, the edition conveys an impression of its own political stance. Towards the end of his Preface Malone's genuflection before Samuel Johnson is only surpassed by his far more partial (and unscholarly) admiration of Edmund Burke. Where Johnson was 'the brightest ornament of the eighteenth century', Malone had a caveat: Johnson is great only 'if we except a great orator, philosopher, and statesman, now living, whose talents and virtues are an honour to human nature' (Malone 1790: lxviii). The footnote below this caveat informs us that Malone refers to 'The Right Honourable Edmund Burke'. Malone's admiration of Burke was reciprocated. Burke, whose *Reflections on the Revolution in France* was published in the same year, reportedly broke off his denunciation of the French Revolution to praise Malone's edition, equating Malone's 'admiration of Shakespeare' with his own 'perfect abhorrence of the French Revolution' (Boswell 1924: 204). Later, in 1796, Malone would also defend his antiquarian urge 'to keep Shakespeare pure and uncontaminated from modern sophistication and foreign admixtures' (Malone 1796: 2–3). For Malone, the correct editing of Shakespeare thus became associated with the guardianship of a specifically English literary purity.[7] When, therefore, in 1798 Nathan Drake approvingly called Radcliffe 'the Shakspeare of Romance writers', he was inevitably participating in a flourishing tradition of scholarship that grounded Shakespeare politically in a nationalist context.[8] By metaphorizing Radcliffe as '*the* Shakspeare', Drake contributed to her emergent (and questionable) reputation as the Gothic romance's guardian of national literary propriety – a propriety that became linked with an uncontaminated national tradition.

Drake's positive assessment of Ann Radcliffe in 1798 followed the publication of five of her romances and a travel journal. Combined, these provided the substance of her great reputation. With her first two romances, *The Castles of Athlin and Dunbayne* (1789) and *A Sicilian Romance* (1790), Radcliffe did not use epigraphs to direct her readership to the themes and literary heritage which she wished to highlight. Instead, she offered more allusive tributes to Shakespeare. In both works, these tributes come in part from servants debating whether they have seen ghosts, and take their cue from Walpole's own Shakespearean model in *The Castle of Otranto*. In tandem with this comparatively light approach to the supernatural, however, comes a more embedded and considered literary consideration of Shakespeare.

In addition to the formal allusions to Shakespearean plot, Alison Milbank also notes the nascent tribute to Shakespeare offered up by Radcliffe's use of interspersed poetry throughout her narratives (Milbank 1995). In *The Castles of Athlin and Dunbayne*, for example, the three poems offered all pay tribute to fancy. Milbank rightly argues that Radcliffe's chosen theme of fancy is 'a favourite poetic theme from the sixteenth century onwards, and one that is directly associated with Shakespeare in the eighteenth' (Milbank 1995: xiii). Even at this early stage of her writing career, however, Radcliffe's use of this eighteenth-century take on Shakespearean fancy, derived in part from Johnson, is tempered by an awareness of its transience. Early on in *The Castles of Athlin and Dunbayne*, there is a curiously abstract passage added to the initial description of the young, impetuous Osbert who wishes to reclaim his family's honour:

> When first we enter on the theatre of the world, and begin to notice its features, young imagination heightens every scene, and the warm heart expands to all around it. The happy benevolence of our feelings prompts us to believe that every body is good, and excites our wonder why every body is not happy. We are fired with indignation at the recital of an act of injustice, and at the unfeeling vices of which we are told. … As we advance in life, imagination is compelled to relinquish a part of her sweet delirium; we are led reluctantly to truth through the paths of experience; and the objects of our fond attention are viewed with a severer eye.
>
> (Radcliffe 1995: 4)

On the second page of her very first romance Radcliffe concentrates upon the limitations of fancy in 'the theatre of the world'. The transience of youthful fancy will become a major theme to be echoed throughout Radcliffe's works. It is present in this novel in the poem when Osbert listens to the imprisoned Laura reciting her poetry in the castle: 'When first the vernal morn of life/ Beam'd on my infant eye / Fond I survey'd the smiling scene / Nor saw the tempest high' (Radcliffe 1995: 33). Laura touches upon 'Hope's bright illusions' and 'Fancy's vivid tints' and 'fairy prospect', only to draw attention to the dispersion of these imaginative faculties (Radcliffe 1995: 33–34). The 'theatre of the world' is bound to dissipate our imaginations as 'we are led reluctantly to truth through the paths of experience' (Radcliffe 1995: 4). At this early stage of her writing career, then, Radcliffe figures the world as a 'theatre' which is bound to dissipate the imagination. She continues this theme with her second novel, *A Sicilian Romance* (1790), where her heroine Julia composes a poem entitled 'Evening' in which 'To Fancy's eye fantastic forms appear' (Radcliffe 1790, I: 98). Julia's ardent imagination, however, is monitored by her older guardian Madame de Menon, who, it is explicitly stated, has experienced life's disappointments.[9]

However, this presumption – that 'fancy' must inevitably be disappointed by the 'theatre of life' – does not remain constant in Radcliffe's work. During the course of the 1790s, there is an evolution in her fictional practice whereby the very theatricality of the scenes provides and sustains the impetus for 'fancy'. With *The Romance of the Forest* (1791), Radcliffe's novelistic practice transformed her textual allusions to Shakespeare to sustained tribute through the use of epigraph. In the first volume of *The Romance of the Forest* alone, five out of seven epigraphs are taken from Shakespeare, with four from *Macbeth* and one from *As You Like It*.[10] There may be several reasons for this evolution in Radcliffe's novelistic practice. As Rictor Norton rightly observes, the 'revival of interest in Shakespeare during Ann Radcliffe's childhood had a profound impact upon her romances' (Norton 1999: 50). On the basis of the discussions between Mr 'W' and Mr 'S' in Radcliffe's posthumously published 'On the Supernatural in Poetry', Norton conjectures that Radcliffe, during her youth in Bath, may have seen Sarah Siddons performing Hamlet in Bath in 1781, and later her performance of the role of Lady Macbeth.[11] That *Macbeth* remains such a constant throughout Radcliffe's fiction suggests that she was certainly struck by this performance, or at least reports thereof.

And yet, the specific dating of the debut of Radcliffe's epigraph practice in her 1791 novel suggests alternative sources of inspiration. First, as I have already argued, the advent of Malone's edition of Shakespeare in 1790 renewed the study and accessibility of Shakespeare. Second, the opening of the Shakespeare Gallery in London's Pall Mall in 1789, with Henry Fuseli's impressions of key scenes from *Hamlet*, *Macbeth* and *King Lear*, undoubtedly stimulated Radcliffe's very visual and dynamic conceptions of Shakespeare's works.[12] Whilst Malone's authoritative edition provides the impetus for many Shakespearean epigraphs throughout *The Romance of the Forest*, *The Mysteries of Udolpho* and *The Italian*, performances and paintings of Shakespearean scenes provide a more visually dramatic tribute.[13]

With each successive novel, Radcliffe's use of Shakespearean epigraph and allusion becomes increasingly sophisticated. In general, she reserves Shakespearean epigraph for moments of moral quandary and episodes of distress for her heroines. Whilst *A Sicilian Romance* has one Shakespeare epigraph at the very beginning of the novel – 'I could a tale unfold', the lines of the ghost in Act 1, Scene 5 of *Hamlet* – *The Romance of the Forest* is the only novel to begin its first chapter with an epigraph from Shakespeare. This is because it precipitates us almost immediately into visualizing the distress of the heroine Adeline and the moral weakness of Monsieur La Motte. With the later novels *The Mysteries of Udolpho* and *The Italian*, Radcliffe reserves her use of Shakespearean tragedy in particular for the moments when her heroines are thrown into crisis. In *Udolpho*, for example, Chapter Two repeats Radcliffe's second novel's overall epigraph with lines: 'I could a tale unfold, whose lightest word / Would harrow up thy soul' (Radcliffe 1980: 19). This not only hints at the secret at the heart of Emily's father St Aubert's family, but also prepares us for her more visual tribute to *Hamlet* in the second volume, when Emily is taken against her will to Udolpho. The plot of *Hamlet* in particular provides a strong impetus for this section of the novel. The parade of mercenary soldiers on the battlements of Udolpho, and their exchanges of conversation, recall immediately the opening scenes of *Hamlet*. With the incident where the heroine Emily mistakes a waxen figure for a corpse, Emily's immediate reminiscence of her father recalls Hamlet's murder of Polonius behind the arras, as well as Ophelia's consequent insanity:

> With some difficulty, Annette led her to the bed, which Emily exam-ined with an eager, frenzied eye, before she lay down, and then, pointing, turned with shuddering emotion, to Annette, who, now more terrified, went towards the door, that she might bring one of the female servants to pass the night with them; but Emily, observing her going, called her by name, and then in the naturally soft and plaintive tone of her voice, begged, that she, too, would not forsake her. – 'For since my father died,' added she, sighing, 'every body forsakes me.'
>
> (Radcliffe 1980: 351)

Here, Emily suffers a temporary loss of reason that is meticulously chor-eographed. In this particular episode, Radcliffe succeeds in uniting careful movement with one line of speech that carries immediate dramatic, visual impact.

In the later 'On the Supernatural in Poetry' (1826), Radcliffe specifically alludes to Shakespeare's technique of 'accordant circumstances', with Mr W. reflecting that 'No master ever knew how to touch the accordant springs of sympathy by small circumstances like our own Shakespeare' (Radcliffe 1826b: 146). With Radcliffe's *The Italian* (1797), *Macbeth* proves to be the strong narrative influence, with the Marchesa di Vivaldi and Schedoni's concerted attempts to murder the heroine Ellena di Rosalba. Radcliffe employs the technique of accordant circumstances when the

Marchesa di Vivaldi has a momentary reanimation of conscience, whilst consorting with Schedoni to murder the heroine Ellena di Rosalba:

> The organ sounded faintly from the choir, and paused, as before. In the next moment, a slow chaunting of voices was heard, mingling with the rising peal, in a strain particularly melancholy and solemn.
>   'Who is dead?' said the Marchesa, changing countenance; 'it is a requiem!'
>   … The Marchesa was much affected; her complexion varied at every instant; her breathings were short and interrupted, and she even shed a few tears, but they were those of despair, rather than of sorrow.
>
>   (Radcliffe 2000: 206–7)

Whilst in this scene we are only offered by way of the accordant circumstance the aural description of requiem, the effects of it upon the Marchesa's countenance – her changes of complexion, the interrupted breath, as well as the tears – constitute, in the words of the contemporary critic Arthur Aikin, 'a most striking and impressive scene' (Aikin 1797: 283). Again, it is both aurally and visually dramatic, and draws our attention to the careful choreography of Radcliffe's later works.

The Italian's most celebrated scene, in which Schedoni attempts to murder Ellena on the shores of the Adriatic, again combines both the aural and visual to stunning dramatic effect: Ellena is '[a]larmed by his manner, and awed by the encreasing gloom, and swelling surge, that broke in thunder on the beach' (Radcliffe 2000: 257). The anonymous writer for the *Analytical Review* drew particular attention to 'Mrs. Radcliffe's uncommon talent for exhibiting, with the picturesque touches of genius, the vague and horrid shapes which imagination bodies forth' (anon. 1797: 516). As with Aikin's review, the emphasis on the words 'exhibiting' and 'picturesque' here illustrate a particularly strong visual aspect to Radcliffe's scenes. This conjuring of effect can be traced directly to her theorization of Shakespeare's *Macbeth* in 'On the Supernatural in Poetry', in which Mr W. reflects that 'Macbeth shows, by many instances, how much Shakspeare delighted to heighten the effect of his characters and his story by correspondent scenery: the desolate heath, the troubled elements, assist the mischief of his malignant beings' (Radcliffe 1826b: 147).

Taken together, all of the scenes which I have discussed thus far attest to an evolution in Radcliffe's works. Her fiction came to be associated increasingly with a visual and aural dramatic immediacy, which, as her later critical work shows, Radcliffe drew from Shakespeare's own techniques. Where this practice becomes truly striking, however, and to date crucially overlooked, is in the extracts that we have of Radcliffe's own travel observations. A survey of the material indicates that Radcliffe is even further indebted to Shakespeare's technique of 'accordant circumstances' than these examples from her primary fictions would suggest. Her journal and travel memoirs illustrate that 'accordant circumstances' became intrinsic to her own observations on her surroundings. For example, in her published travel memoir *A Journey Made in the Summer of 1794 through Holland and the western frontier of Germany*, Radcliffe, visiting the forest of Carlsruhe with her husband William, makes the following allusion to *As You Like It*:

> The scenery of this forest is very various. Sometimes we found our way through groves of ancient pine and fir, so thickly planted that their lower branches were withered for want of air, and it seemed as if the carriage could not proceed between them; at others we passed under the spreading shade of chestnuts, oak and walnut, and crossed many a cool stream, green with the impending foliage, on whose sequestered bank one almost expected to see the moralizing Jacques; so exactly did the scene accord with Shakespeare's description.
>
> (Radcliffe 1795: 261)

With the 'scenery' 'accord[ing]' with Shakespeare's description, we begin to witness a fascinating development in Radcliffe's writing: landscapes become in themselves backdrops for the recollection of Shakespeare. In *The Mistress of Udolpho*, Norton questionably hints at Radcliffe's own dramatic persona, stating that 'Mrs. Radcliffe herself frequently climbed to the tops of mountains and cliffs, where she imagined herself as Prospero the Magician, and wandered through Windsor Forest fancying herself a druidess' (Norton 1999: 12). As I will proceed to argue, however, the evidence that we garner from her later works suggests a far more profound and potentially political metaphorization of her relationship with Shakespeare's plays.

While the narrator at the beginning of *The Castles of Athlin and Dunbayne* might hint at the disappointments of the 'theatre of the world', her later, more private work appears to argue that it is only through recasting the 'work-a-day' world as a theatre that 'fancy' can be recaptured at all. Her posthumously published works suggest that for Radcliffe, where the reality of the everyday, politically fraught England was doomed to disappoint, the recollection of Shakespeare redeemed it.

By the time of Radcliffe's death in 1823, her first five romances and *A Journey* had secured her the reputation as 'the Shakspeare of Romance writers'. The careful cultivation of such a strong national and financially

successful reputation meant that upon her demise, there were clear bene-
fits to maintaining this intimate connection between Shakespeare and the
Gothic romancer. When, therefore, Thomas Talfourd was asked by her
husband William Radcliffe to compose a *Memoir of the Life and Writings of
Mrs Radcliffe*, the carefully edited excerpts that he offered to the public
from Radcliffe's own journal all testified to the profundity of her engagement with Shakespeare.[14] The fragments that Talfourd cited illustrate how
each English location visited by Radcliffe and her husband recalled for her
a particular Shakespearean association. For example, during a journey
which they undertook along the south coast of England in 1798, Radcliffe
recorded the late-evening impressions that the atmosphere created:

> Near eleven, before we reached Hastings; no moon; starlight; milky-
> way very lucid; seemed to rise out of the sea. Solemn and pleasing
> night-scene. Glow-worms, in great numbers, shone silently and faintly
> on the dewy banks, like something supernatural. Judgment of
> Shakespeare in selecting this image to assist the terrific impression in
> his ghost-scene.
>
> (Radcliffe 1826a: 43)

Her hastily noted observations refer to Shakespeare's atmospheric depic-
tion of the ghost's appearance in *Hamlet*, a scene which clearly haunts her,
judging from the frequent allusions to it in her journals and fiction. On a
visit to Warwick Castle in 1802, for instance, she records that 'Before
those great gates and underneath these towers, Shakespeare's ghost might
have stalked; they are in the very character and spirit of such an apparition, grand and wild and strange' (Radcliffe 1826a: 60). In Radcliffe's
observations, the fabric of the ancient Warwick Castle becomes a catalyst
for recalling Shakespeare's ghost. This is symptomatic of what I have
observed to be an increasing tendency in Radcliffe to recast actual locations through their Shakespearean associations.

Talfourd also presents us with excerpts from the Radcliffes' second
journey to Portsmouth in 1811. Amidst hastily scribbled observations on
the evident Anglo-French military tensions and the surrounding ships of
war in Portsmouth, Radcliffe finds the time to listen with care to the exact
'cadence' of the sea:

> How sweet is the cadence of the distant surge! It seemed, as we sat in
> our inn, as if a faint peal of far-off bells mingled with the sounds on
> shore, sometimes heard, sometimes lost: the first note of the begin-
> ning, and last of the falling peal, seeming always the most distinct.
> This resounding of the distant surge on a rocky shore might have

given Shakespeare his idea when he makes Ferdinand, in the Tempest, hear, amidst the storm, bells ringing his father's dirge; a music which Ariel also commemorates, together with the sea-wave:
> 'Sea-nymphs hourly ring his knell,
> Ding, dong, bell!'

(Radcliffe 1826a: 79)

The accordant acoustics of a sea that visually is despoiled by ships of warfare facilitates Radcliffe's imaginative transport to Shakespeare's act of composition. The peal of bells which she imagines she hears alongside the surge of the sea upon the rocks allows her to meditate upon Shakespeare's own creative inspirations. This not only demonstrates Radcliffe's skill at summoning extracts from almost all of Shakespeare's plays at will; it is also illustrative of the extent to which Radcliffe's own imagination is indebted to the example of Shakespeare. The conditions of creation for Radcliffe's composition were dependent upon this increasingly intimate relationship with Shakespeare's works. It also indicates that, at this time of political turbulence and warfare in England, Radcliffe, during the threat of invasion, can still conjure up Shakespeare's scenes and characters at will. She does not simply do this in order to dispel more pressing concerns; it is also her way of imagining a *better* England where 'fancy' is still a potent force. Taken together, the journal extracts that Talfourd presents to us suggest that Shakespeare and England become almost synonymous in Radcliffe's later writing.

Radcliffe's conflation of England and Shakespeare continues throughout the fragments of her journal that Talfourd edits. Collectively, these extracts seem to suggest that the power of Shakespearean association remained a constant throughout her life and fiction. I would now like to argue, however, that her final, posthumously published work *Gaston de Blondeville*, with its accompanying prefatory dialogue between Willoughton and Simpson, suggests that Radcliffe suffered a crisis of imagination as well as an interruption in her imaginative engagement with Shakespeare. This was possibly grounded in the political disappointment of the early 1800s.

According to Talfourd, *Gaston de Blondeville* was probably composed at some point between 1802 and 1803, but we do not know why it was not published at its time of composition.[15] Many modern critics have judged *Gaston de Blondeville* unfavourably.[16] The Introduction that eventually preceded its publication in 1826 was, according to Norton, written 'sometime between 1811 and 1815' (Norton 1999: 196). Although the published Introduction to *Gaston* and the *New Monthly Magazine*'s 'On the Supernatural in Poetry' of 1826 were published separately, the two essays were clearly originally part of the same essay: in fact, they both contain separate parts of the same argument. The excerpt in the *New Monthly Magazine* summarizes Radcliffe's views on terror and the supernatural, while the remainder of the Introduction which is prefaced to *Gaston* provides us with the imaginative and moral impetus to the tale to follow. The Introduction begins as follows:

> "Well! Now are we in Arden," said an English traveller to his companion, as they passed between Coventry and Warwick, over ground, which his dear Shakspeare had made classic. As he uttered this exclamation of Rosalind, he looked forward with somewhat of the surprise and curiosity, which she may be supposed to have felt, and with an enthusiasm all his own, on beholding the very scene, into which the imagination of the poet had so often transported him with a faint degree of its own rapture. He was not, it appears, one of those critics, who think that the Arden of Shakespeare, lay in France.
>
> (Radcliffe 1826a: 3–4)

Here, at the very beginning, Radcliffe's imaginative traveller Willoughton anticipates with relish his journey through the Forest of Arden precisely because of the renown that Shakespeare has brought it. Willoughton, like his author Radcliffe, is able to summon Shakespeare at will as the source for his knowledge of this part of England. Here, as Frances Chiu has also noted, Willoughton quotes imperfectly from *As You Like It*, conflating two distinct lines uttered by Rosalind and Touchstone.[17] It is important to note, though, that Radcliffe herself also frequently conflated or misquoted lines from Shakespeare, as we see both in Talfourd's extracts from her journal and her use of epigraphs in her later romances. Whilst this may not have been a conscious error on her part, it remains suggestive of her dynamic relationship with Shakespeare. What is important for Radcliffe is the constant *recollection and evocation* of Shakespeare prompted by what she visits, rather than the precise detail from his plays. Willoughton attempts to imagine the 'surprise and curiosity' that Rosalind may have experienced when entering the forest of Arden, but this is accompanied by an attendant 'enthusiasm all his own'.

A potentially nationalist note creeps in here, though, with the observation that Willoughton 'was not, it appears, one of those critics, who think that the Arden of Shakespeare, lay in France'. This qualification undoubtedly came from Malone's 1790 edition, when in his notes for *As You Like It*, he maintains that the location of Shakespeare's Arden comes from the pen of an English author, Thomas Lodge.[18] Radcliffe's use of this corrective note by Malone, however, is at best equivocal with the addition of the caveat 'it appears'. If this first impression of Willoughton leads us to think that he is safe-guarding a national literary treasure against French encroachment, then our belief in the worth of this 'treasure' comes to be sorely tested in what follows immediately after Willoughton's first transport of anticipation:

> But [Willoughton] looked in vain for the thick and gloomy woods, which, in a former age, were the home of the doubtful fugitive, and so much the terror of the traveller, that it had been found necessary, on this very road, to clear the ground, for a breadth of six acres on each side, in order to protect the way-faring part of his Majesty's liege subjects.
>
> Now, albeit the landscape was still wild and woody, he could not any where espy a forest scene of dignity sufficient to call up before his fancy the exiled duke and his court, at their hunter-feast, beneath the twilight of the boughs; nor a single beech, under the grandeur of whose shade the melancholy Jacques, might "lose and neglect the creeping hours of time," while he sadly sympathized with the poor stag, that, escaped from the pursuit of man, came to drop his tears into the running brook, and to die in quiet. Not even a grove appeared, through whose deep vista the traveller might fancy that he caught, in the gayer light, a glimpse of the wandering Rosalind and her companions, the wearied princess and the motley fool, or the figure of Orlando, leaning against an oak, and listening to her song, in a scene so different from the one his fancy had represented to him for the forest of Arden.
>
> (Radcliffe 1826a: 4–5)

This is contemporary rural England, and it disappoints the ardent Willoughton. It is a country where the pragmatics of commercial travel 'to protect the way-faring part of his Majesty's liege subjects' has led to the deforestation of one of its most treasured and dignified cultural icons. Arden does not just stand for a contested English location; it also represents an aspiration that has been lost in what Willoughton later calls 'the plain reality of this work-a-day world' (Radcliffe 1826a: 6). The Romantic critic William Hazlitt would also later write of Shakespeare's Arden that 'Caprice and fancy reign and revel here, and stern necessity is banished to court. The mild sentiments of humanity are strengthened with thought and leisure; the echo of the cares and noise of the world strike upon the ear of those 'who have felt them knowingly,' softened by time and distance (Hazlitt 1818: 305–6). Hazlitt's later rendition of Arden strikes a very similar note to Radcliffe's: Arden is an imaginative space where 'fancy' may reign, whilst 'stern necessity is banished to court'. Radcliffe's Willoughton deplores the intrusion of 'stern necessity' into this imaginative realm. The unwelcome intrusion of state necessities, Radcliffe seems to suggest, disturbs the organic relationship between location and imagination: Willoughton looks in vain for 'a forest scene of sufficient dignity' that may correspond to the picture that his 'fancy' has painted for him.

Yet again, as with the opening to her first work *The Castles of Athlin and Dunbayne*, Radcliffe draws our attention to the destructive curbing of the imagination in this Introduction to *Gaston de Blondeville*. It is a theme which permeates *Gaston*, and one which may be suggestive of why Radcliffe for the first time chose to invoke a ghost in her final work. The disappointment that Willoughton experiences with this mutilated image of Arden leads to a surprising privileging of the artificial:

> "Alas!" said he, "that enchanting vision is no more found, except in the very heart of a populous city, and then neither by the glimmering of dawn, nor by the glow of evening, but by the paltry light of stage lamps. Yet there, surrounded by a noisy multitude, whose cat-calls often piped instead of the black-bird, I have found myself transported into the wildest region of poetry and solitude; while here, on the very spot where Shakspeare drew, I am suddenly let down … "
>
> (Radcliffe 1826a: 5–6)

Here, Willoughton is forced to concede the superiority of 'the paltry light of stage lamps' to the England now before his eyes. Whereas once England itself could inspire 'fancy', now only performance can draw him into 'the wildest region of poetry and solitude'. This sentiment is also emphasized in the excerpt of this Introduction reproduced in 'On the Supernatural in Poetry'. There, more plaintively, 'W' demands:

> "Where is now the undying spirit […] that could so exquisitely perceive and feel? that could inspire itself with the various characters of this world, and create worlds of its own; to which the grand and the beautiful, the gloomy and the sublime of visible Nature, up-called not only corresponding feelings, but passions; which seemed to perceive a soul in everything: and thus, in the secret workings of its own characters, and in the combinations of its incidents, kept the elements and local scenery always in unison with them, heightening their effect."
>
> (Radcliffe 1826b: 145)

This part of the essay forcefully illustrates that 'Visible Nature' is no longer capable of inspiring sublimity in an England where Nature has been disturbed by the intrusions of State demands. In such an altered location, performance is now the only method of conjuring imagination.

The prefatory material to *Gaston de Blondeville* is thus suggestive of Radcliffe's own anxiety about her diminishing 'fancy'. This diminution of imagination is clearly and radically connected to her increasing disillusionment with England's governance. Miles and Norton have both rightly drawn attention to Radcliffe's own radical dissenting heritage (Miles 1995; Norton 1999). More recently, Chiu's 'Introduction' to a new edition of *Gaston* draws attention to the differing contexts of Radcliffe's writing, commenting that 'perhaps [Radcliffe's] frustration with contemporary crises led her consciously to seek the Britain of Henry III as a means of oblique criticism' (Chiu 2006: xxii). I believe that this assessment is entirely right, and that the appearance of Radcliffe's first real ghost is as a direct response to political crisis.

In his *Reflections on the Revolution in France*, Edmund Burke recast France itself as a stage, deploring the French Revolution as 'this monstrous, tragic-comic scene' (Burke 1790: 11). Radcliffe's *Gaston* seems to me to be a direct rebuke of Burke, where she responds by casting England as a stage on which a particular tragedy is played out. The tragedy narrated in *Gaston* is a simple story of injustice, where a humble merchant Woodreeve rightly accuses King Henry III's favourite, the eponymous Provençal Gaston, of murdering his kinsman, a knight who has fought for England's values in the Holy Wars. Whilst it is tempting to read this, as James Watt does, as a 'loyalist romance' with anti-French sentiments, Radcliffe's point appears to be far more nuanced (Watt 1999: 66). *Gaston de Blondeville* is neither a straightforward condemnation of Frenchmen, nor an unambiguous championing of English values. Both its Introduction and the romance itself attest to an increasing disillusionment with the governance of England. King Henry III is portrayed as a vacillating and malleable leader, who is all too prone to persuasion from his closest counsellors. By contrast, his wife, Eleanor of Aquitaine, is portrayed as a kind if somewhat frivolous queen. She may not comprehend the anti-French sentiments that she inspires amongst the nameless English crowd, but she submits to their insults unflinchingly.

The characterizations of King Henry and Queen Eleanor are significant, but they are not the most important element of Radcliffe's final romance. Although E. J. Clery rightly observes the 'distancing devices' which surround this work, she nonetheless figures these as an aesthetic failure on Radcliffe's behalf (Clery 1995: 110). However, it is possible to view them as an integral part of the novel's argument. *Gaston de Blondeville* is a romance that is entirely staged, where the tableaux that serve as epigraphs to each chapter self-consciously establish acts and scenes. This is because *Gaston* is ostensibly a drama. When Willoughton in the 'Introduction' regretfully privileges the imaginative force of dramatic performance over the now 'humbled' present scene, his tangible sadness becomes a lament for a lost England. Radcliffe's romance tells the story of a fallen country, fallen not because of foreign encroachment, but because of a loss of dignity in the role of kingship. Henry III allows himself to be ruled by self-interested advisors, and the court hearing that he stages for the unjustly imprisoned Woodreve is a 'monstrous, tragic-comic scene', to use Burke's turn of phrase.

Exiled justice can only find a location through the means of performance. It is no coincidence that this novel abounds with pageantry and festival. It is up to the travelling minstrels, the performers who serve the court, to narrate this particular tale of injustice. A Provençal minstrel sings the tale of the foul murder to which Woodreve bore witness, and a group of miming actors, clearly inspired by the mimers employed by Hamlet, re-enact the crime. Combined, these re-enactments suggest that performativity and artifice have become more 'authentic' conveyors of truth than justice itself.

And finally, there is Radcliffe's use of a real ghost. In the Introduction, Willoughton responds to Simpson's teasing about his belief in ghosts by protesting 'I am not so fond of ghosts in general, as you seem to think. It is only for a few of particular excellence, that I feel a friendship; for them, indeed, I am willing to own even an affection' (Radcliffe 1826a: 7). We know from Radcliffe's own edited journal extracts, and particularly from her visit to Warwick Castle, that she felt a particular 'friendship' for the ghost in Shakespeare's *Hamlet*. This is the ghost from Shakespeare that she clearly attempts to resurrect in *Gaston de Blondeville*, a ghost of a murdered knight who, due to the failures of justice, is forced to confront his own murderer. Radcliffe's ghost is nowhere near as magisterial as Shakespeare's original; rather, he is a silent, shadowy presence that lurks in the margins of the story. His lack of force is perhaps indicative of Radcliffe's reluctant invocation of him at all. For he is symbolically representative of a crisis of imagination which Radcliffe lamented not only in herself, but also in England at large. Radcliffe argues in this final novel that the lawlessness of the earlier, untamed Arden, where thieves and murderers may lurk, is nonetheless preferable to the suffocating pretence of law and governance from which England suffers.

By way of conclusion, then, I wish to argue for a more dynamic relationship between Ann Radcliffe and Shakespeare than that allowed for by Drake's contemporary assessment of her art. Radcliffe's imaginative engagement with her literary inspiration was not a constant; instead, it was an engagement informed by the performances, editions and exhibitions of Shakespeare that proliferated during her lifetime. Towards the end of her writing career, however, Radcliffe was forced to acknowledge the limitations of her metaphorization of Shakespeare as England. The imaginative recuperation of Shakespeare's Arden was only possible through an increased reliance upon 'the paltry light of stage lamps' in the self-consciously performative *Gaston de Blondeville*. Radcliffe's anxiety regarding her own poetic inspiration, as I have argued, was present from the very beginning of her writing career. Perhaps the change of circumstances which led to her self-perceived diminution of inspiration is best expressed by one of her own heroines. Whilst Emily St Aubert is imprisoned in the castle of Udolpho, she attempts to diminish her anxieties through reading 'the poet' Shakespeare:

> Emily sought to lose the sense of her own cares, in the visionary scenes of the poet; but she had again to lament the irresistible force of circumstances over the taste and powers of the mind; and that it requires a spirit at ease to be sensible even to the abstract pleasures of pure intellect. The enthusiasm of genius, with all its pictured scenes, now appeared cold, and dim. As she mused upon the book before her, she involuntarily exclaimed, 'Are these, indeed, the passages, that have so often given me exquisite delight? Where did the charm exist? – Was it in my mind, or in the imagination of the poet? It lived in each,' said she, pausing. 'But the fire of the poet is vain, if the mind of his reader is not tempered like his own, however it may be inferior to his power.
> (Radcliffe 1980: 384)

We know that 'the poet' that Emily resorts to in vain is Shakespeare, for in the Introduction to *Gaston*, Willoughton too looks forward in vain to beholding the scene of Arden 'into which the imagination of the poet had so often transported him with a faint degree of its own rapture' (Radcliffe 1826a: 4). This is the 'poet of Nature' that Johnson privileged in his 1765 edition of Shakespeare, and which Radcliffe cherished over all subsequent, more scholarly editions. But sadly for Radcliffe, while 'the fire of the poet' may have endured, her own disillusionment with England's changed 'circumstances' disturbed the delicate balance of her imaginative engagement with the Bard himself.

Notes

1 I would like to record my thanks to the editors of this collection, Dale Townshend and John Drakakis, for their encouragement and patience. I am also extremely grateful to Hamish Mathison, of the University of Sheffield, for his helpful and insightful commentary on earlier drafts of this essay.

2 In 'Europhobia: the Catholic Other in Horace Walpole and Charles Maturin', Robert Miles rightly observes that

Walpole's experiment provoked unease, partly because it wilfully inter-fered with the received Whig progress of literary history, from marvellous tales of adventure (fit for children, Catholics and other primitives) to probable representations of everyday life (fit for those living in a Protestant nation); and partly because he was employing the arms of novel-writing innovators in support of a tale whose sole aim appeared to be the under-mining of Protestant rationality of its readers.

(Miles 2002a: 93).

For futher analysis of this, see Clery's edition of *The Castle of Otranto* (Walpole 1996a) and Wright (2007).

3 As I argue elsewhere, however, Radcliffe's reputation as the careful guardian of a national tradition is questionable when we take into account her parallel use of continental inspiration (Wright 2008).

4 See, for example, Radcliffe's *A Journey Made in the Summer of 1794 through Holland and the western frontier of Germany with a return down the Rhine: to which are added observations during a tour to the lakes of Lancashire, Westmoreland and Cumberland.* During her trip through Goodesberg, Radcliffe saw a group of French prison-ers suffering at a roadside, whilst people passed them to attend a local carnival. She comments: 'Misery and festivity could scarcely be brought into closer con-trast. We thought of Johnson's "many coloured life" and of his picture, in the preface to Shakespeare, of contemporary wretchedness and joy, when "the reveller is hastening to his wine, and the mourner is burying his friend"' (Radcliffe 1795: 135).

5 Johnson's 'Preface' to his edition is far more engaging, if less scholarly, than the edition that Malone was to issue later in 1790. Johnson argues for the universal attributes of Shakespeare's characters, and constantly refers to Shakespeare as 'the poet', a practice which, as I will later argue, Radcliffe identifies and enga-ges with herself in her later works.

6 As Margreta de Grazia notes, 'Malone's 1790 edition of Shakespeare was the first to advertise itself as having been 'collated *verbatim* with the most Authentick copies' (de Grazia 1991: 48).

7 The fear of literary and political cross-contamination from the continent was a shared concern amongst many literary commentators of the 1790s, including Mathias in *The Pursuits of Literature* (1798). For further information on this, see Keen (1999).

8 In his 'Preface' to *Literary Hours*, for example, Drake draws specific attention to the contemporary political turbulence. Clearly expecting his readership to share his dismay at the Revolutionary events, Drake situates his scholarship firmly in relation to these politics:

In the present hour of difficulty and danger, when politics and finance appear so entirely to occupy the public mind, it is little to be expected that subjects of fancy and mere elegant literature should greatly excite atten-tion, or meet with adequate support. Long however as our eyes have been now turned on scenes of turbulence and anarchy, long as we have listened with horror to the storm which has swept over Europe with such ungo-vernable fury, it must, I should imagine, prove highly grateful, highly soothing to the wearied mind, to occasionally repose on such topics as lit-erature and imagination are willing to afford.'

(Drake 1798: i–ii)

9 Throughout *A Sicilian Romance*, the term 'fancy' is invoked in total twenty-two times.

10 Volume II of *The Romance of the Forest*, by contrast, only contains three epigraphs from Shakespeare, one from *Julius Caesar*, one from *King Lear* and one from *King John*, and Volume III carries no epigraphs from Shakespeare at all.

11 Norton writes: 'Mrs Radcliffe was among the many novelists and playwrights who had in mind Mrs Siddons's sublime look and utterance when they created their most imperious female characters. She certainly saw her perform the role of Lady Macbeth, whether it was in Bath or London' (Norton 1999: 50–51). He goes on to cite the excerpt from 'On the Supernatural in Poetry' in which the two travellers hold a discussion of Siddons's performance, with one arguing that despite his contempt of the witches, 'the fascination of Mrs Siddons's influence so spread itself over the whole play, as to overcome my disgust, and to make me forget even Shakespeare himself; while all consciousness of fiction was lost, and his thoughts lived and breathed before me in the very form of truth' (Radcliffe 1826b: 147). In relation to this, see also E. J. Clery's excellent analysis of the performance of 'Lady Macbeth in the eighteenth century' in *Women's Gothic: From Clara Reeve to Mary Shelley* (2000).

12 See, for example, John Boydell's *A Catalogue of the pictures in the Shakspeare Gallery, Pall-Mall*. London, 1789. This was reissued in 1790 and 1791, as pictures were added to the collection.

13 With *The Mysteries of Udolpho* (1794), according to my own counts, Radcliffe quotes Shakespeare in 22 chapter epigraphs out of a total of 57 chapters. The most prevalent Shakespeare plays to be quoted are *Hamlet* and *Macbeth*. With *The Italian* (1797), Radcliffe quotes Shakespeare for 12 chapters out of a total of 35. Again, *Hamlet* and *Macbeth* both feature prominently here, although her overall use of Shakespearean quotation is more diverse, with epigraphs also drawn from *Twelfth Night*, *Julius Caesar*, *Romeo and Juliet*, *The Merchant of Venice*, *Othello*, *King John*, *Richard III*, *King Lear* and *As You Like It*.

14 Robert Miles also refers to this posthumous account of Radcliffe as 'rich in ideological nuance, not least because of its managed quality' (Miles 1995: 28). Norton records that

> When Talfourd began editing [Radcliffe's] posthumous works, he was impressed more by these journals than by the unpublished poetry or fiction, according to his friend Mary Russell Mitford: 'Mr Talfourd says that by far the finest things he has seen of hers are her manuscript notes on different journeys in England – simple, graphical, without a single word to spare.'
> (Mitford, Letter to Revd William Harness, 4 March 1826, *The Life of Mary Russell Mitford* (1870), vol. II, 221; cit., Norton 1999: 177).

15 Whilst Talfourd suggests that she wrote it for amusement, Norton suggests that it was *withdrawn* from publication, or possibly rejected (Norton 1999: 193).

16 Miles's otherwise excellent study of Radcliffe (1995) does not analyse the novel at all; E. J. Clery calls it a 'strange contradictory work', and Rictor Norton goes further, even speculating that Radcliffe may not have been the author of *Gaston* by asserting that 'it possesses not a single hallmark of the author's hand' (Clery 1995: 110; Norton 1999: 195).

17 As Frances Chiu notes in her excellent edition of *Gaston de Blondeville*, Willoughton here conflates two lines from Rosalind and Touchstone in *As You Like It* (Act 2, Scene 4, lines 15–16):

> *Ros.*: Well this is the forest of Arden.
> *Touch.*: Ay, now am I in Arden, the more fool I.
>
> (Chiu 2006: 3)

18 Malone's note on the location of Arden reads as follows:

> *Ardenne* is a forest of considerable extent in French Flanders, lying near the Meuse, and between Charlemont and Rocroy. It is mentioned by Spenser, in his *Colin Clout's come home again*, 1595:
>
> "Into a forest wide and waste he came,
> "Where store he heard to be of savage prey;
> "So wide a forest, and so waste as this,
> "Not famous Ardeyn, nor foul Arlo is."

Having quoted Spenser's French location, Malone then carefully distinguishes Shakespeare's differing location: 'But our author was furnished with the scene of his play by Lodge's novel' (Malone 1790, Vol. 4: 123). Here, he is referring to Thomas Lodge's work *Rosalynd* (1590).

7 Gothic Shakespeare on the Romantic stage

Michael Gamer and Robert Miles

Gothic Shakespeare's stage career begins with a single, controversial word: *Vortigern*. This was the allegedly lost and recently discovered play by Shakespeare, mounted by Richard Brinsley Sheridan on 2 April 1796 at Drury Lane, with John Phillip Kemble and Dorothy Jordan in the leading roles. In the aftermath of the debacle that was the play's only performance, the astounded literary world discovered *Vortigern* not to be an early production of Shakespeare, but rather of a twenty-one-year-old law clerk, William Henry Ireland (who gave his age as nineteen to stress his Chattertonian precocity). It was an outrageous literary debut, one that came perilously close to launching Ireland as a second Shakespeare, or at least as a literary genius of staggering proportions. An intense admirer of Chatterton, Ireland had wished to emulate his hero by taking the shortest way to literary fame. Not satisfied with forging the work of a writer whose reputation already was unassailable and sacrosanct, he chose to do it in that writer's most prestigious genre: tragedy (with 'historical' thrown in, for good measure).[1]

Ireland's compositional choices in *Vortigern* were as deliberate as they were governed by fixed assumptions about Shakespeare's prestige and function within British literary history. Of all possible tragic subjects to a country in the grip of bardolatry, those with the greatest cachet, both on London and provincial stages, concerned ancient Britain. Thus, Ireland chose Vortigern, the fifth-century Briton who invited the Saxons, or Goths, to the country they eventually conquered and made their own. Within the hierarchy of cultural status governing tragedy in the final decade of the eighteenth century, Ireland could not have aimed higher. Of all national subjects, none was so resonant as the arrival of the Goths, who with their constitution and manners had made England England. Ireland effectively doubled the national stakes by choosing Vortigern, whose vanquishing, and subsequent retreat westward, made Wales Wales. This logic of national prestige takes us straight into *Vortigern*, Ireland's Gothic Shakespeare.

Gothic counterfeits

First displayed in the house of Samuel Ireland in December of 1794 (Schoenbaum 1991: 139), the so-called Shakespeare Manuscripts took in many of the leading literati of the age. What had begun as a deed bearing Shakespeare's signature grew, over the course of 1795, to include promissory notes, correspondence, testaments of faith, library catalogues, love poems to 'Anna Hatherrewaye', and, finally, a lost five-act tragedy on the subject of Vortigern and Rowena. The person fabricating these documents, in the sixteen months that separated the December 1794 discovery of the deed and the April 1796 premiere of *Vortigern*, was Samuel Ireland's son William Henry. The story does not lack pathos: long considered an embarrassment and dolt by his bardolatrous father, William Henry Ireland produced his first forgery when Samuel declared he would give half his library for a document bearing Shakespeare's signature. After some research and experimentation with papers and inks, William produced a signed deed, and was showered with affection by Samuel. With each document he produced, he received this same fatherly approval – so much so that he moved, in little more than a fortnight, from forging simple documents to claiming the existence of a full play in manuscript. The next months must have proven heady indeed for Ireland, as learned gentleman after learned gentleman testified to the authenticity of the documents. Among these were Poet Laureate Henry James Pye, biographer James Boswell (who after a stiff glass of brandy prostrated himself before the holy relics, expressing thanks for having lived long enough to see them), and 'Doctors Wharton and Parr', who, as William Cobbett indelicately reminded them, though 'deemed the two most learned men in the Kingdom … declared and certified that it was their conviction that no human being could write those manuscripts but Shakespeare'.[2]

Given such encomiums, Ireland expected to be treated at the very least as a second coming of the 'marvellous boy' Thomas Chatterton when he confessed the truth. Instead, as a sympathetic Cobbett put it, although 'there was nothing illegal and nothing immoral' in Ireland's actions, as soon as 'Mr. Ireland was discovered to be the real author, the whole band of literary ruffians fell upon him, and would have destroyed him, if they had been able, with as little remorse as men destroy a mad dog'. The ire of those duped, moreover, did not dissipate with time. His father Samuel at once disbelieved his confession (declaring him too stupid to perpetrate such an ingenious hoax) and disowned him. Years later when Ireland encountered one of his persecutors, James Boaden, a successful playwright and one of the manuscript's early dupes, Boaden provided a telling explanation:

You must be aware, sir, of the enormous crime you committed against the divinity of Shakespeare. Why, the act, sir, was nothing short of sacrilege; it was precisely the same thing as taking the holy chalice from the altar; and ******* therein!

(Ireland 1832: xiii)

Under his own name and various pseudonyms over the next four decades, Ireland wrote some twenty more books; in most cases, his authorship was discovered and the books did not sell well. As a result, he spent most of those years in debt, at times forced into re-forging multiple copies of the Shakespearean manuscripts to sell to book collectors as the 'original' forgeries. It's an interesting concept in itself, and one suggestive not just of Ireland's career and psyche, as Jack Lynch has argued compellingly (Lynch 2004; 2007b: 150), but also of the oxymoronic position Shakespeare played within the drama of the Romantic period, of being the period's most reproduced original.

German bards and scotching reviewers

As the most rapid survey of late-eighteenth- and early-nineteenth-century drama will testify, Romantic writers from Joanna Baillie and Lord Byron to Walter Scott and Percy Shelley regularly wrote plays drawing simultaneously from Shakespeare's *oeuvre* and from the Gothic. These two traditions can be said to constitute popular taste in the period, and to have almost single-handedly revived tragedy as a viable form during these years (see Cox and Gamer 2003). Throughout this same Romantic period, however, to bring Shakespearean tragedy and the Gothic together on stage was to risk censure for having committed aesthetic sacrilege. Such hyperbole belongs entirely to the period. We experience it not just in Boaden's outrage but also in the iconic mudslinging, in the years immediately following *Vortigern*, of Romantic writers against the theatre itself, their dismissals coming even as they desperately tried to get their own Gothic tragedies in blank verse staged at Drury Lane or Covent Garden. Thus, the same years that see Samuel Coleridge writing *Osorio* and William Wordsworth *The Borderers* also see Coleridge dismissing *The Castle Spectre* (1797) as 'Schiller Lewis-ized', while Wordsworth in the Preface to *Lyrical Ballads* (1800) would condemn successful adaptations from Auguste von Kotzebue like *Lovers' Vows* (1798) and *Pizarro* (1798) as 'sickly and stupid German Tragedies' bent on driving the 'invaluable works of our elder writers, I had almost said the works of Shakespeare … into neglect' (Wordsworth 1974: 129).

Wordsworth was hardly alone in condemning tastes informing his own earlier works. One of the great refrains of critical writing in the 1790s is its perpetual grieving over the decay of British theatre. The sudden popularity of Kotzebue and other German dramatists in London, coming, as it did, in the wake of *Vortigern* and its accompanying scandal, merely increased the frequency and intensity of the collective lament. And the effect that this lament had on the audience for British drama was at once ambivalent and contradictory. On the one hand, war with France raised bardolatry to new patriotic heights, inviting theatre manager John Philip Kemble in 1794 to revive *Macbeth* without the ghost of Banquo (in the name of aesthetic and intellectual purity) but *with* a scene in the witches' cave featuring fifty supernatural dancers and a full orchestra (Bartholomeusz 1969: 133–34). On the other hand, it became a critical commonplace to associate such Gothic excesses with corrupt 'foreign' dramas while staunchly maintaining the unequalled excellence of Shakespeare as a dramatic model.

Thus it was that Walter Scott, having translated five German plays and written his own Gothic tragedy, *The House of Aspen* (composed in 1799), found himself persuaded by various *Anti-Jacobin* friends in the Tory establishment to abandon, in the name of prudence and patriotism, what he called his 'German mad' and 'drum and trumpet' productions: 'should I ever again attempt dramatic composition, I would endeavour after the genuine old English model' (Scott 1932, Vol. I: 124; Sutherland 1995: 73–74). And thus it was that Joanna Baillie, writing in the aftermath of *Vortigern*'s failure at Drury Lane, would publish *A Series of Plays ... on the Passions* (1798), which included a sizable 'Introductory Discourse' painstakingly linking her own dramatic experiments with the practice of Shakespeare and other Renaissance English playwrights. In her 1804 *Miscellaneous Plays*, Baillie would be even more explicit in her national politics, positively denying her play *Rayner*'s affiliation to contemporary German drama:

> A Play, with the scene laid in Germany, and opening with a noisy meeting of midnight robbers over their wine, will, I believe, suggest to my reader certain sources from which he will suppose my ideas must certainly have been taken. Will he give me perfect credit when I assure him, at the time this play was written, I had not only never read any German plays, but was even ignorant that such things as German plays of any reputation existed?
>
> (Baillie 1804: xii–xiii)

The uneasiness of Scott and Baillie was not without reason. Beginning with the 1797–98 season, German plays, and especially the plays of August von Kotzebue, became fixtures on the London stage, accounting over the next three years for over a quarter of all mainpiece representations at the two Theatre Royals, with Kotzebue outperforming Shakespeare by a four-to-one margin.[3] Writing as the century closed and in the same year that Wordsworth penned the Preface to *Lyrical Ballads*, Thomas Dutton of *The Dramatic Censor* could thus argue that modern theatre's fondness for Gothic spectacle amounted to an invasion by a foreign dramaturgy. Kotzebue's popularity, he argued, represented nothing less than an 'usurpation on that throne, which SHAKESPEARE, and his compatriot race of drama-tists, once filled with equal honour to themselves and to the national character (Dutton 1800: 98). As Ireland learned only too well, such cul-tural xenophobia, once aroused, did not dissipate for decades, at least when raised in defence of the most sacred figure in British dramaturgy.

Nowhere, for example, do we find this familiar compound of vitriol as unleavened by irony as with Samuel Coleridge's attack on *Bertram* (1816), the wildly successful play written by the Irish writer Charles Robert Maturin, best known to us as the author of the late Gothic masterpiece *Melmoth the Wanderer* (1820). Coleridge's review is especially pertinent because it makes clear the web of literary influence that ties *Vortigern* toge-ther with that collection of novels, plays and poems belatedly dubbed 'Gothic' by the Victorians. But the review is also central to this essay because it places in such a stark light the issues faced by Ireland in com-posing a Shakespearean tragedy about modern Britain's national origins. In this sense, what this essay dubs 'Gothic Shakespeare' is not just a pro-blem of genre or ancient history. It also constituted a problem of con-temporary literary history at the end of the eighteenth century. In the same decades that saw English theatres regularly running bowdlerized or otherwise 'improved' versions of *Hamlet* and *King Lear* – and that saw Samuel Johnson preferring Shakespeare's comedies to his tragedies in his own edition of the *Plays* heading his long list of Shakespeare's deficiencies with the declaration that '[i]n his tragick scenes there is always something wanting' (Johnson 1765: xvii) – German dramatists and critics were cele-brating him, and especially his tragedies, with unreserved abandon. And the contrast between English moderation and German exuberance became only starker after Johnson's death, in the decades separating Henry Mackenzie's 'Account of the German Theatre', which introduced *The Robbers* to Great Britain in 1788, and the translation of August Wilhelm von Schlegel's *Course of Lectures on Dramatic Art and Literature* into English in 1815 (Mackenzie 1790: 154–92; Schlegel 1815: iv).[4] For Mackenzie, Shakespeare's true heir had landed, phoenix- and Saxon-like, in England in the form of Schiller. And for English readers of Schlegel, here was a true critic whose Goth credentials came not just from his country of origin, but from his ability to understand Shakespeare's genius better than even native-born Britons: 'It will hardly fail to astonish us … that admiration of the English for Shakespeare should first obtain a truly enlightened interpreter in a critic of Germany' (Schlegel 1815: 4). Coleridge's review comes, then, at the end of nearly three decades of English ambivalence over German and Gothic drama, in which audiences, reviewers, and literati first embraced this new literature as a true likeness of Shakespeare, and then (as the 1790s and the war with France progressed) rejected it for its perceived immorality and revolutionary principles. This accumulated tension explodes in the review of *Bertram*.

Running an astounding forty nights in its first season, *Bertram; or, The Castle of St. Aldobrand* broke all existing nineteenth-century attendance records for tragedy, partly because its high, hectic, Shakespearean blank verse fitted perfectly with the acting style of the great Shakespearean actor Edmund Kean, who played the title role. Steeped in adultery and murder, Bertram at once recalled and exceeded recent literary hero-villains, from Walter Scott's guilty Marmion and Lord Byron's gloomy Giaour to the fatalistic *stürm und drang* heroes of Goethe and Schiller. The irony is that the play thrilled audiences in spite of being only a diluted form of Maturin's original composition. In the original version of the play sent to Scott (whose influence, with Byron's, did much to secure its staging), Maturin had tried to outdo Matthew Lewis's infamous German-influenced novel *The Monk* (1796), by placing not just the Devil's minions on stage but the Devil himself. Though such scenes accorded with his own dramatic predilections, Scott did fear London audiences might balk at *Bertram's* potent combination of 'diabolical agency' and 'unnecessary horror'.[5] In advising Maturin to revise, Scott was especially prescriptive about *Bertram's* violent and protracted ending, which in its various aspects resembled the catastrophes of Shakespeare's *Lear*, Joanna Baillie's *De Monfort* and Friedrich Schiller's *The Robbers*. 'We especially object to the death of the child', he advised Maturin, 'in a piece where there are three deaths beside … try to assemble your persons toward the conclusion & precipitate the whole' (Scott 1932, Vol. 12: 353). Six days later, Maturin wrote agreeing to adapt most of Scott's proposed changes; a year and a half later, *Bertram* became the most popular tragedy of the young century.

Still, for Coleridge, the stage version of *Bertram* was toxic enough to embody everything radical and wrong with modern theatre. Here was yet another example of the pernicious influence of German drama on English theatre; and here were unpleasant reminders for Coleridge of the signal failure of his own translation of post-*stürm* Schiller, *Wallenstein* (1800), through which he had intended to correct this same debauched public taste sixteen years earlier.[6] Coleridge's attack, moreover, did not begin simply by labelling this Gothic school 'German'; his critical predecessors had engaged in precisely this practice for two decades.[7] Initially welcomed by critics and literati in the years following Mackenzie's 1788 'Account of the German Theatre', German drama's cultural status had plummeted in the mid-1790s because of the scandal surrounding German-inspired productions like Lewis's *The Monk* and *The Castle Spectre* (Drury Lane, 1797), the success of free adaptations from the German like Elizabeth Inchbald's *Lovers' Vows* (1798), and the host of translations of the poetry of Gottfried August Bürger and the plays of Auguste von Kotzebue.

Rather than arguing for that school's unwholesome foreignness, Coleridge instead adopted the counterintuitive tactic of proclaiming the school's essential Englishness, albeit tainted by foreign influences. Put succinctly, his review argues that English tragedy had been corrupted by 'German drama', but that the 'German' dramas so popular on the London stage were not really German at all. Instead, they were originally adapted (and perverted) from English sources, particularly the plays of Shakespeare. Schiller's *Robbers* may have originated the so-called craze for German drama that closed the eighteenth century, he concedes; but Schiller himself had fashioned his dramas by grafting Renaissance tragedy and English Graveyard poetry onto the minutely self-reflexive introspections of Richardson's *Clarissa* (1748). To this, he then added the 'horrific incidents and mysterious villains … the ruined castles, the dungeons, the trap-doors, the skeletons, the flesh-and-blood ghosts, and the perpetual moonshine of a modern author' (presumably Ann Radcliffe), themselves recycled from 'the literary brood of the *Castle of Otranto*' (Coleridge 1983: 211). Schiller might thus have founded 'the German drama'; but his plays were really conceived from English materials subsequently corrupted by Kotzebue and embraced by London audiences. In short, Coleridge concludes, we are at once innocent and guilty of this corruption of taste and principles: innocent in being instinctively drawn to anything derived from Shakespeare, guilty for embracing Shakespeare in such perverted and debased forms.

Maturin's *Bertram* thus stands accused of being, in effect, a copy of a copy of a copy:[8] of Kotzebue; of Schiller; and of English Shakespearean originals, which, as any student of Shakespeare knows, were themselves derivative:

> The so called *German* drama, therefore, is *English* in its *origin*, *English* in its *materials*, and *English* by re-adoption; and till we can prove that Kotzebue, or any of the whole breed of Kotzebues, whether dramatists, or romantic writers, or writers of romantic dramas, were ever admitted to any other shelf in the libraries of well-educated Germans than were occupied by their originals, and apes' apes in their mother country, we should submit to carry our own brat on our own shoulders.
>
> (Coleridge 1983: 212)

In Coleridge's formulation, the characteristic that ties this new and corrupt band of writers together is their lack of education (signalled by their presence on the low shelves of the circulating library), their Classical deficit (shown through their status as the debased progeny of Walpole and Richardson) and their generic illegitimacy (proclaimed by their status as unacknowledged 'brat[s]'). Under Coleridge's handling, the problem of 'German drama' (and, hence, of the British Gothic plays inspired by it) is the problem posed by low or popular writing more generally – that is, the problem of a literature produced for mindless consumption. German drama thus occupies, by the end of Coleridge's review, part of the broader and more omnivorous literary space we now call the Gothic, that aesthetic comprising popular novels, poems and plays.

Politics play a conspicuous part in Coleridge's review as well, since the ostentatious target of his critical fury is *Bertram*'s supposed sympathy with French revolutionary principles – what Coleridge calls the play's 'Jacobinism'. Ironically, this same quality had entirely escaped the play's earlier conservative readers, from its sponsor Walter Scott to its reviewers at *Blackwood's Edinburgh Magazine*.[9] With such accomplished Tories missing *Bertram*'s corrosive radicalism, it is tempting to regard it as a phantom of Coleridge's imagination. Still, his reasoning is worth pursuing, in part because of the way he relentlessly reduces cultural practice to ideological essence. Thus, in Coleridge's review of *Bertram*, Jacobinism's 'whole secret … consists in the confusion and subversion of the natural order of things in their causes and effects', so that we discover 'liberality, refined feeling, and a nice sense of honour' in scoundrels, such as banditti, while virtuous sympathy is directed towards those 'criminals whom law, reason, and religion have excommunicated from our esteem' (Coleridge 1983: 21). Schiller's mysterious villains are 'geniuses of supernatural intellect, if you will take the author's word for it, but on a level with the meanest ruffians of the condemned cells, if we are to judge by their actions and contrivances' (Coleridge 1983: 11).

What Coleridge identifies and condemns, then, is less a problem of Maturin's dramaturgical politics than one inherent in Shakespeare's tragedies. All tragedy may turn on a recognition of the unyielding reality of 'law', as Northrop Frye argues;[10] but in Shakespeare's version of it such inexorability is most often parsed, not as a vaguely symbolic fate, but as the law itself. Accordingly, Shakespeare's plays create a tension between his charismatic tragic heroes and the laws they flout. To use Coleridge's formulation, virtuous sympathy is directed towards, say, Othello, Macbeth or Hamlet, even though their actions indict them as 'criminals whom law, reason, and religion have excommunicated from our esteem' (Coleridge 1983: 21). The moral conundrums of Shakespearean tragedy might pass in a pre-Revolutionary era, but in a revolutionary one the exceptional nature of the tragic hero inevitably calls into question the laws they would over-leap, whether as 'supernatural intellects' or as figures of extraordinary martial prowess. In a period of heightened political alarm, such question-ing of 'things as they are' was not sustainable. Shakespeare's 'Jacobinism' was beyond reproach, but translated to Maturin, it was a wide-open target.

Prophetic hindsight

As Coleridge helps us realize, what this essay dubs 'Gothic Shakespeare' is anything but an isolated special case. Rather, the term points to cruxes central to Romantic writing. If Shakespearean tragedy represented the zenith of aesthetic achievement in English, then how was one to bring Shakespeare's example into the modern age, into a new nineteenth cen-tury, without repeating – via his exportation to Germany and subsequent reimportation – this Gothic 'Jacobinism'? Associated with this conundrum is one of Shakespeare's key legacies: his historical practice and use of var-ious pasts to inform a sense of the present, where history remains (as it frequently does in Scott's novels) half-explanation and half-national gen-ealogy. If there exists a single crux constitutive of *Vortigern* and its vision of Shakespearean tragedy, it is this juggling of historicities. Here, we find Shakespeare's legacy vibrantly alive in the Gothic of his self-conscious imitator, Horace Walpole, whose *Castle of Otranto*, we recall, is a five-act prose romance based on Shakespearean tragedy. And here we find the central problem facing Ireland in composing *Vortigern*: how to bring Shakespeare's historical practice into the modern age when that modern age is a decade (the 1790s) that saw Britain arguably more politically divided than at any point since the English Civil War?

To read *Vortigern* closely is to find it playing both sides of this con-temporary cultural divide at once, most notably in its handling both of ancient and of recent history. In an age when performed dramas were assiduously censored by the Licenser of Plays John Larpent, who, employed by the Lord Chamberlain, routinely excised from all new plays their contemporary political and religious references, *Vortigern* invoked subjects usually barred from theatrical representation.[11] Part of its strange political licentiousness stemmed from its dual position as both new play and historical document, a status recalling Ireland's later phrase 'authentic forgery' but also buttressed by its unique cultural status. This was, after all, a Shakespeare play about how the Goths, or Saxons, came to England,[12] a play about Britain's national origins supposedly written by Britain's national author. One can only imagine Larpent's quandary as he read the manuscript in late March, 1796. Here is a play replete with scriptural quotations – which Larpent routinely excised in the texts of new plays as blasphemous during his career – whose opening act represents the murder of a king in a decade where the act of imagining the killing of a king was treasonous.[13] Even more provocatively, here is a play whose hero (Aurelius) is not just a young pretender to the throne of Britain, but one who sails from Rome to assert his rightful claim to it, landing in Scotland in open rebellion against an existing monarch (Vortigern) constitutionally appointed by the Lords of Britain. Such scenes recall nothing so strongly as the second Jacobite rebellion of 1745, and make *Vortigern* read as both Jacobite allegory and fantasy. There, the young pretender Aurelius avenges the earlier removal of his father, King Constantine, by the tyrant Vortigern, who is willing to exploit anti-Scottish sentiment to shore up his hold on power. With such narrative trajectory, the dilemma for Larpent must have been severe: how to censor such a play, one that he would likely have rejected for representation if presented to him as new?

Now housed in the Huntington Library, the Larpent manuscript of *Vortigern* shows signs of this strain. Submitted to Larpent on 2 February 1796, the manuscript's excisions appear to be pre-emptive, written not by Kemble but by either Samuel Ireland or some Drury Lane representative.[14] For the most part they are formulaic, consisting either of biblical lines or phrases like 'murdered king': but also gone are all lines referring to the divine right of kings, no longer suitable in a country boasting a constitutional monarchy since 1688:

> Oh! Sleep thou god of calm and soft repose
> Sweet nourisher of man and babe alike
> Soother of sorrow that alone can'st bury
> The care-worn mind in sweet oblivion,
> To thee o' gentle sleep I pawn my soul!
> Here then upon my bended knee, great God
> Let me implore thy grace and look for mercy:
> ~~Tho' thou has plac'd me Sovereign over men~~
> ~~And on my brow hath plac'd a Diadem~~
> ~~Yet am I subject still to human frailty,~~
> ~~And nought can boast more than my meanest Vassal.~~[15]

Along similar lines, the manuscript entirely deletes the scene in which King Constantius is murdered, anticipating Larpent's customary objections to any scene representing the murder of a king and demoting that event to the status of off-stage occurrence. As 135 years of successful rewritings and adaptations make abundantly clear, London audiences were long used to Shakespeare revised and excised; such pre-emptive practices are designed to invite a bureaucratic response in line with existing precedents. With all 'objectionable' passages either deleted or flagged, Larpent is invited to ignore the play's broader, more troubling representations of historical figures and events. Larpent's minimal response – he appears merely to have agreed with the offered changes[16] – suggests that he was grateful to have the work done for him, especially in the face of such a daunting question: how to prune a play whose authenticity and cultural status depended on its being performed whole before an impartial audience?

This same issue of authenticity worked to inoculate the play from accusations of partisanship, since *Vortigern*'s status as a play written two centuries prior to its stage premiere transformed all contemporary political references into the stuff of prophecy. Outside of its startling Jacobite allegory, other moments of the drama point not to 1745 but to later decades, such as the association of Vortigern with opposition leader Charles James Fox, self-styled 'Man of the People' and lifelong opponent of George III:

> *Vort.* Oh! you ha' struck me where I am indeed
> Most vulnerable – "*The voice o'th' people!*"
> For them I will surrender liberty.[17]

As political allusions go, Ireland's is stunningly economical, invoking not just Fox's populist title but also his 17 December 1783 speech on the defeat of the East India Bill, in which, out-manoeuvred by George III, he warned the House of Commons that under such royal overreaching 'We shall certainly lose our liberty' (Wright 1815: 275). At once invoking Fox and associating him with a violent usurper, the passage presents democratic feeling as a mere rhetorical fiction, a blind to disguise one man's will to power. Such a reading is confirmed by the play's next scene, in which Vortigern is appointed Lord Protector by his fellow barons but finds the position not enough:

> Their niggard shew of liberality
> Suits ill my lofty aim, and but the semblance wears
> Of that my soul is thirsting for – Dominion!
> (1.7.15)

Here, the association is not limited to Fox but arguably reaches back in time (through the play's prophetic logic) to fellow Protector, regicide, and scourge of Scotland and Ireland, Oliver Cromwell. And again the position is staunchly royalist, though this time in a way more in line with Hanoverian orthodoxy.

When we argue that *Vortigern* plays both sides of the partisan divide that was the mid-1790s, we do not mean to suggest that the play is ideologically divided or duplicitous. Like the rest of the Shakespeare forgeries, which presented Shakespeare as a devout Protestant, loving husband, steady businessman, hearty reveller, popular courtier and avid boater, *Vortigern* speaks from a coherent position, but one historically in and out of synchronization with the contentious politics of 1796. As such, the play is at once recognizably Jacobite and exuberantly nationalistic: the former still anathema at the end of the eighteenth century, the latter welcome in an age of war. Thus, even as it presents a recognizable allegory of Stuart deposition and reaccession – one that laments the oppression of Scotland and associates the Saxons with Vortigern's desire to subjugate and divide the people of Britain – the play also prophesies a future British empire whose greatness will depend on the national unity of its people, a unity based in each tribe having an equal stake in governance.

This strange historical practice of producing a timely play yet indulging in out-of-date forms of nostalgia is mirrored by *Vortigern*'s prevailing aesthetics, which alternate between displays of authenticity and flights of literary-historical fantasy. As one might expect of an attempted forgery, *Vortigern*'s first scene reads like an accelerated version of Shakespeare's *Complete Works*, in which King Constantine presents Vortigern with half of Britain to rule, and Vortigern instantly resolves to murder Constantine and rule the entire kingdom himself. Resembling *King Lear*, *Macbeth* and *Richard III* in its plot devices, the scene displays little of those plays' penchant for dramatizing psychological processes or developing character.[18] Instead, it provides pure plot through recognizably Shakespearean situations and motifs – and produces surprisingly shrewd results, particularly for a young man manufacturing a tragedy by a supposedly young Shakespeare.

To read *Vortigern*, then, is to be always on a trial run for the mature article, always on the lookout for the truly authentic dramatic gesture or flight of fancy, always on the edge of identifying a quotation that dissolves, on closer inspection, into mere allusion. It is an experience reinforced, moreover, by the play's composition and production history and by its status as a stage representation.[19] Tried on the stage rather than on the page, transmitted to John Philip Kemble in instalments as quickly as Ireland could compose it, the play existed only as a transient, single performance until its publication in 1799, by which point its cultural status had irrevocably altered. For an audience with no text to consult and dependent on the aural evidence of a single night's representation, *Vortigern*'s opening scene must have been bewildering indeed. Was this rapid barrage of quasi-quotations plagiarism or forgery? Or was it the predictable apprentice work of England's Bard warming to his themes and language? Equally baffling must have been the play's unsettling historical allegories. Had Shakespeare anticipated the ascension of the Stuarts to the English throne? Had he feared a violent transition of power? Or was this something more, something closer to inspired prophecy? Coming from the genius of young Shakespeare, and in a play dramatizing a turning point in English history, such premonitions no doubt were to be expected. But they understandably rankled the enemies of the Irelands.

Led by the great Shakespearean scholar Edmond Malone, opponents of the Irelands responded by mocking the Shakespeare Manuscripts' hopeless anachronisms as proofs of their inauthenticity. Their complaints were not without reason. This anachronistic tendency in the earlier manuscripts, moreover, carried on into *Vortigern*, where it is easy to cite examples, such as Ireland's dutiful attempt to establish Shakespeare's Protestantism once and for all by having the saintly Constantius appeal directly to God for grace:

> *King.* O sleep, thou nourisher of man and babe,
> Soother of every sorrow, that can'st bury
> The care-distracted mind in sweet oblivion,
> To thee, O gentle pow'r! I pawn my soul!
> Here then, on my bended knee, great God,
> Let me implore thy grace, and look for mercy;
> Though thou hast plac'd me sovereign over men
> (1.4.8)

Or we could look to Pascentius's speech to his sister Flavia on their father's disturbed state of mind, which combines references to eighteenth-century theories of sensibility with nods to the acting style of Garrick informed by them:

> *Pas.* My Flavia say!
> What is't hath ruffled thus thy gentle bosom?
> I fear our father hath occasion'd this,
> For late as passing through the hall I saw him,
> He paced to and fro in great disorder,
> Sometimes in deep thought lost, he'd stop and pause,
> Then o'er his troubled breast crossing his arms,
> Would utter words, but in a voice so low,

> That they distill'd themselves I'th' gentle air.
> Tho' I did thrice address him, yet he brake
> Abruptly from me, and no answer made.
> I never saw the conflict of his soul
> So plainly in his countenance pourtray'd.
>
> (1.8.15–16)

Or, finally, we could look to Edmunda's laudanum-taking (2.3.24) or to Aurelius's confrontation with the Romantic sublime, sounding almost Wordsworthian were it not for the deflating effect of an unfortunate ending verb:

> *Aurelius.* Here prostate then I fall before thy face,
> And, tho' unworthy of thy mercy, pray; –
> If giant form doth more enlarge the mind,
> Would that my front did with the mountains vie;
> That so my heat amazed brain might work
> Thoughts suiting more this vast immensity!
> O most expanded, O most fertile mind!
> When thou would'st copulate with thoughts like this,
> Thou art mere nothingness.
>
> (3.2.83)

Similar anachronisms comprise much of Edmond Malone's analysis in his exhaustive *Inquiry into the Authenticity of Certain Miscellaneous Papers and Legal Instruments … Attributed to Shakspeare* (1796), published on the eve of *Vortigern*'s 2 April 1796 performance. However, Malone's chief charge was that Ireland's anachronism displayed sympathy towards Jacobinism, as evinced in the periphrasis 'gyldedde bauble', for crown, from the letter to 'Anna Hatherrewaye'. In the *Inquiry*, Malone reasons that 'from the present contemptuous mention of Kings, it is no very wild conjecture to suppose that the unknown writer' is one of those 'modern republican zealots' who has endeavoured to 'diminish that love and veneration which every true Briton feels … for Royalty, so happily and beneficially interwoven in our inestimable constitution' (Malone 1796: 148). For many, Malone's conjectures were indeed 'wild' – sufficiently so to bring his sanity into question – but they did have the merit of becoming notorious, a notoriety that has subsequently obscured the complexity of Ireland's way with history. 'Gyldedde bauble' was Malone clutching at a straw, with which he hoped to break the camel's back.[20] As for most of the opposers of the Shakespeare manuscripts, for Malone the stakes were nothing less than national culture and national pride:

Every individual of this country, whose mind has been at all cultivated, feels a pride in being able to boast of our great dramatick poet,
Shakespeare, as his countryman: and proportionate to our respect and
veneration for that extraordinary man ought to be our care of his
fame, and of those valuable writings that he has left us; and our soli-
citude to preserve them pure and unpolluted by any modern sophistication or foreign admixture whatsoever.

(Malone 1796: 2–3)

Published in the same month that Matthew Lewis published his own piece
of gothic 'admixture', *The Monk*, Malone's treatise is nothing short of a
declaration of war, a call to a self-consciously British aristocratic and
scholarly militia to 'preserve … pure and unpolluted' their national culture. Supplying, as the *Inquiry*'s subtitle advertised, 'fac-similes of the genuine hand-writing of that Nobleman [the Earl of Southampton], and of
her Majesty [Elizabeth I]; a new fac-simile of the hand-writing of
Shakspeare, never before exhibited; and other authentick documents',
Malone sought to bring the entire force of Shakespearean scholarship to
bear on *Vortigern*'s public hearing at Drury Lane. And with the assistance of
John Philip Kemble in the lead role, the play was not just condemned, but
remained unrepresented for over two centuries, until it enjoyed a successful bicentenary run of four weeks at London's Bridewell Theatre.[21] The
charge of Jacobinism helped focus the attack, but it also simplified
Ireland's play, not least in obscuring the curious circumstance that *Vortigern*
is as much Jacobite as Jacobin.

The crux of anachronism

As we hope we have demonstrated thus far, the term 'anachronistic'
cannot adequately represent Ireland's historical practice in forging a
Shakespearean tragedy about the Goths. One of the most interesting
aspects of William Henry Ireland's many confessions – first published in
December 1796 as *An Authentic Account of the Shakespeare Manuscripts*, then
reworked in 1805 as *Confessions of William Henry Ireland*, and finally retold in
1832 in a new Preface to *Vortigern*[22] – is the elusive nature of his descriptions of sources. The idea for *Vortigern*, Ireland explained, was suggested by
'a large drawing by Mr. S. Ireland (being a copy from a design of
Mortimer's) representing Rowena in the act of presenting wine to
Vortigern, and which hung over the chimneypiece in Mr. Ireland's study'
(Ireland 1969: 133–34). Inspired by the painting, Ireland immediately
ransacked Holinshed's Chronicle for his story. And, like a true latter-day
Shakespeare, Ireland altered much of what he found there. Thus, in

Holinshed, Constantius' murder by a Pict happens ten years before Vortigern's ambitions take shape, whereas Ireland renders it the inevitable result of those ambitions. Holinshed's account, in fact, smacks more of the *Henry VI* triad than *Macbeth, Lear* or *Richard III*. In Holinshed Vortigern does not have his ambition piqued by an incautious king offering him half his kingdom; instead, he plots against Constans, Constantius' son, a devoted monk who exposes himself to Vortigern's depredations through his lack of ambition and unworldliness.

Ireland's version of this same story recasts Holinshed's account to markedly different effect. His two most fundamental revisions are geographical: first, he relocates Constantius' other sons, Aurelius and Uter, from what Holinshed calls 'lesser Britain' to Rome; second, he conflates Pict and Scot into a single northern race, thus allowing Aurelius to invade from the same northern kingdom (and with the help of the same northern people) that Vortigern has spent most of the play opportunistically oppressing as an excuse for seizing power. Combined, these two changes effectively transform the tale of Vortigern and Rowena into the stuff of political prophecy. Arriving from Rome, Aurelius joins his own cause to that of the Scots against Vortigern, mirroring the 1745 actions of Charles Edward Stuart by invading Britain from the North to recover his kingly rights from the usurper. Ireland, in fact, improves upon this Jacobite allegory in several ways – not just by having Aurelius achieve victory, but also by making him a true native Briton (rather than a Scottish Stuart) triumphing over a usurper whose only resemblance to the Hanoverians derives from his having invited the Saxons to what would become their native soil. Of all *Vortigern*'s interested parties, in fact, the invited Saxons come to occupy a position most similar to the transplanted Hanoverians of the eighteenth century.

What emerges in Ireland's version of Holinshed's chronicle is a Jacobite allegory as eye-catching as it is incomplete, remaking both ancient and recent history even as it transposes key players and events. Yet, as *Vortigern*'s burlesques of Fox already have suggested, the play's acts of historical allegory are hardly limited to the 1745 rebellion. For, in stirring up hatred against northern Britons, Vortigern resembles no one so much as John Wilkes, who in the decades following the second Jacobite rebellion founded the periodical *The North Briton*, specifically to attack governmental minister John Stuart, 3rd Earl of Bute, and more generally to foment anti-Scottish feeling in England. Even here, however, Ireland inverts the order of key events, allowing him to invoke Wilkes and vilify him as an unprovoked oppressor. Thus, unlike the historical events of 1745, the Scottish rebellion in *Vortigern* does not precede but rather follows Vortigern's unwarranted and opportunistic oppression of the Scots. Such a reversal, at the very least, exonerates the North's rebellion by giving it just cause for grievance. But, like Ireland's decision to transform Aurelius into a Briton and to align the Saxons with the Hanoverian dynasty, the reversal here again renders *Vortigern*'s Jacobite allegory at once less problematic and less legible. And where historical figures are altered and historical events transposed, allegories face the danger of losing their transparency.

If it did not confuse the Drury Lane audience of 2 April 1796, this restructuring of the play's dominant allegory must at least have opened up other possibilities for interpretation for them. Among their many choices, audience members must have associated the character of Vortigern with contemporary figures like the Prince of Wales, who in the late eighteenth century aligned himself with the Foxite Whigs so strongly favoured by William Henry Ireland's father, Samuel. Here, indeed, the son might be found to be mocking the father, by aligning his favourite political party with one of history's great losers, Vortigern, whose unprincipled man-oeuvres not only cost him his kingdom but also brought about the per-manent exile of the ancient Britons to the inhospitable mountains of Wales. One thing is certain: in Ireland's treatment, Vortigern is at once a proto-Macbeth swathed in tragic grandeur and a bumbling embarrass-ment, appearing at times as Fox, the people's tribune, and at other times as Fox's political master, the Prince of Wales, whose disappointment with the outcome of the Regency crisis of 1788 nicely mirrors Vortigern's own disappointment at being offered only half a kingdom.

Part of the play's strange layering of allegory may stem, in fact, from the painting and source story that inspired it. Commenting on the picture that hung over the chimneypiece in Samuel Ireland's study, Juliet Feibel notes that Mortimer's painting of Vortigern and Rowena would have comme-morated not one but two contending histories of the Saxon invasion. The first, an older Welsh one, presents Rowena as the willing lure by which Vortigern was ensnared (and Britain lost) to the Saxon-Goths. The second, a more modern, English version, paints Rowena as the chaste inspiration for the marriage of ancient Briton and Saxon that produced modern England:

> In representations of Vortigern and Rowena, a London-based artistic culture subverted a mournful Welsh tale of betrayal and loss, turning it into a celebration of the Saxon descent and the assimilation of the original Britons into the Saxon, or English, line. In less than a cen-tury, a legend whose purpose was to remind audiences of the primacy of the Welsh people and the loss of their birthright in the Saxon des-cent was thoroughly revised, losing its original meaning entirely.
> (Feibel 2000: 3)

These English representations of Rowena increasingly stressed her role as the type of the wild English girl, a Gothic stem to a transcendent English rose. For Feibel, what was originally a 'Welsh legend became an English mythology of origins, reinterpreted to represent the glorious foundation of England, Wales' ancient enemy' (Feibel 2000: 3). As this handling of historical sources and contemporary personages demonstrates, *Vortigern* exists in a confusing space somewhere in between these two traditions. Ireland's Rowena is at once a willing and a seductive trap for Vortigern; yet, she brings with her all the premonitions of the future marriage of Briton and Goth that distinguished the English reinvention of Rowena as a type of English futurity. In Ireland's version, this ambiguity is never settled. Instead of producing a mythic British-Gothic futurity, Rowena perishes, as do Hengist and Horsa, without producing a single miscegenated issue. Vortigern, to be sure, is spared, but only to sponsor a sullen Welsh race nursing grudges in the distant, mountainous west.

Writing at a time when the French Revolution had polarized British politics, Ireland plays both sides of the 1790s divide less out of opportunism than necessity. Such divided loyalties, moreover, produce similar divisions even of literary genre. As the subtitle of *Vortigern: An Historical Tragedy* reminds us, Ireland's play is an uneasy amalgam of two distinct Shakepearean modes. And unlike Shakespeare, whose histories appear untroubled by his own propagandist practice – forging Tudor myths whereby regicide, civil war and usurpation are reduced to a few local difficulties and duly expiated in the course of the emergence of a divinely endorsed order – Ireland, writing in the aftermath of the French Revolution, could not help finding such matters newly problematic. Shakespeare's Tudor histories are first about king-making; and when it appears at all, the place of nation-building takes a distant second. Put another way, *Vortigern* is also about king-making; but it faces the added difficulty of finding ways to represent British history as at once inevitable, tragic and providential. Small wonder that the play's allegories sometimes sound discordant notes. If a political unconscious is present in any aspect of Ireland's play, it manifests itself not through anachronistic references to Fox and the Jacobite Rebellion of 1745, but rather through a plot in which a monarch foolishly divides his kingdom not once, but twice: Constantius in 1.1 when he makes the offer to Vortigern that sets the plot in motion; and Vortigern in 4.6 when he purchases Rowena by selling Kent to the Saxons against the wishes of his Barons. Both acts end in ruin. And while one certainly could read Vortigern's historic act of betrayal through standard Whig ideology – as an offence against Magna Carta – the fundamental argument governing the play is that dividing the country is impossible, and that any man who attempts to do so engages in tragic hubris.

Where unspoken supreme value is placed on the indivisibility of the nation, to ransack the past for evidence of England's heterogeneity is to threaten the belief that England is an immemorial, homogeneous unity. It is a belief that, as the eighteenth century closed, united Shakespeare as the national Bard with 'Gothic' as a code for Englishness. In *Vortigern*, this same belief defeats all attempts to narrate history as a single cohesive fable. Two of the most aesthetically successful Shakespearean tragedies of the Romantic period, Wordsworth's *The Borderers* and Shelley's *The Cenci*, failed, not because they were unstageable closet dramas, but because they confronted the same historical and aesthetic cruxes that condition *Vortigern*. Both are highly sophisticated meditations on modern English history, with Wordsworth's text exploring the destructive power of the unhinged charismatic figure (Rivers) in an age defined by its breaking of customary restraints and by its revolutionary lurch to modernity, and Shelley's systematically condemning patriarchal power in domestic, religious and political spheres. Both plays defy resolution, leaving viewers with an irremediable sense of modern life's inexorable contradictions; neither play charts a way forward toward any kind of recuperative, organic synthesis. If Ireland's *Vortigern* is a literal attempt to write Gothic Shakespeare, *The Borderers* and *The Cenci* represent the same impulse, figuratively understood, of mixing tragedy's aporias with a sense of history and the present. Writing on the difference between history and romance in 1798, William Godwin had condemned history's narratives as at once less instructive and less 'true' than the fables of romance, as sorry tales of greed, murder and illegitimacy whose internal contradictions could not sustain their moral and didactic charge. Speaking from three historical perspectives (ancient, renaissance and romantic) at once, *Vortigern* threatens to dissolve into a similar Godwinian incoherence, unable to transform historical conflict into a providential principle of national synthesis.

Such a principle eventually emerged in the shape of a new genre of fiction: the 'historical romance' of Sir Walter Scott. E. J. Hobsbawm describes the principle:

> Merely by dint of becoming a 'people', the citizens of a country became a sort of community, though an imagined one, and its members therefore found themselves seeking for, and consequently finding, things in common, places, practices, personages, memories, signs and symbols. Alternatively, the heritage of sections, regions and localities of what had become the 'nation' could be combined into an all-national heritage, so that even ancient conflicts came to symbolize their reconciliation on a higher, more comprehensive plane. Walter Scott thus built a single Scotland on the territory soaked in the blood

of warring Highlanders and Lowlanders, kings and Covenanters, and he did so by emphasizing ancient divisions.

(Hobsbawm 1990: 90)

In *Ivanhoe* Scott applies the same principle to England. As Feibel points out, Scott's Rowena loses all traces of her origins as the Saxon temptress, becoming, instead, an idealized fusion, on a higher, symbolic plane, of Saxon and Norman. In Scott's reformulation, such a providential evolution naturally excludes tragic elements from the chief protagonist, including all traces of Shakespeare's charismatic heroes. Instead we find, as we do in Scott's prototype, a vacillating non-entity – a Waverley – who bears a closer relationship to the protagonists of object narratives (such as *Chrysal; or, the Adventures of a Guinea*) than he does to Shakespeare's 'Jacobinical' over reachers. For Ireland, the romance solution to 'tragical history' lay very much in the future. If Ireland mediates, and juggles, the decade's irreconcilable historicities, as we have argued, he also serves as a crux in the other sense of the phrase, meaning a parting of the ways. As the period wore on, 'high tragedy' retreated further into the closet, where Romantic cruxes could be turned without incurring charges of Jacobinism, while the storm and stress that habitually accompanied tragedy weltered unconfined in the genre we retrospectively know as 'Gothic'.

Notes

1 For Ireland's career in forgery see John Mair (1938); Bernard Grebanier (1966); Ian Haywood (1986); S. Schoenbaum (1991); Peter Martin (1995); Jeffrey Kahan (1998); Paul Baines (1999); Nick Groom (2002); and Jack Lynch (2004).
2 The article is W. H. Ireland's obituary from Cobbet's *Register*, but is pasted in, with neither date nor page numbers, in British Library Manuscript BL 37, 831.
3 These figures are compiled from volume three of Charles Beecher Hogan, *The London Stage 1660–1800; Part V: 1776–1800* (Hogan 1968).
4 Henry Mackenzie's address was given on 21 April 1788.
5 The first sketches of Scott's own Gothic drama, *The Doom of Devorgoil* (composed in 1817), would project an elaborate spectre feast replete with supernatural disasters. See *The Letters of Sir Walter Scott*, 4:402–6, 4:437–38, 5:77, 5:88–89, 5:150 (Scott 1932). Further references are cited parenthetically in the text.
6 Coleridge also was likely angered by the fact that *Bertram* had been chosen by the Drury Lane Committee over his own play, *Zapolya*, submitted that same year.
7 For a detailed account of the reception of German drama and poetry in England at the end of the eighteenth century, see Michael Gamer's essay, 'National Supernaturalism: Joanna Baillie, Germany, and the Legitimation of Gothic Drama' (Gamer 1997).
8 For an excellent reading of the function of forgery and counterfeiting in Gothic writing, see Jerrold E. Hogle, 'The Ghost of the Counterfeit and the Genesis of the Gothic' (Hogle 1994).

9 Scott helped bring *Bertram* to the stage during a period in which he was establishing himself as a quiet, yet spectacularly efficient, scourge of radicalism. In these same years, *Blackwood's* succeeded in establishing themselves as the true heirs to the tradition of raucous Tory satire established by the *Anti-Jacobin* (1797–98) two decades earlier. After Coleridge's review appeared, both acted in character: Scott counselled Maturin to ignore Coleridge's attack, while *Blackwood's* took Coleridge to task for his poltroonish behaviour towards an Irish cleric.

10 '[W]hether the context is Greek, Christian or undefined, tragedy seems to lead to an epiphany of law, of that which is and must be' (Frye 1957: 79).

11 The performance manuscript of *Vortigern* read by John Larpent is housed in the Huntington Library, Larpent MS 1110. On the 1737 Licensing Act and Larpent's practices as Licenser, see Richard Findlater (1967) and L. W. Connolly (1971–72; 1976).

12 For a lucid account of the cultural function of this myth in Britain, see Samuel Kliger (1952).

13 On 6 November 1795, six months prior to *Vortigern*'s debut, the Treasonable Practices Bill was introduced, which, among other things, made 'a second offence of speaking or writing any words inciting the people "to hatred or dis- like of the person of his Majesty"' punishable by transportation for seven years. See John Barrell (2006: 140–41) and more generally Barrell (2000).

14 See Huntington Library Larpent MS 1110. The manuscript itself is written in three hands: Act 1 in one hand; Acts 2 and 3 in a second; and Acts 4 and 5 in a third. Our reasoning stems from the fact that two of the play's deletions are accompanied by notes that could not be written by Larpent, and that do not appear to be in Kemble's handwriting. In Act 5, Scene 1, for the phrase 'Death thou King of Kings', the hand-written note reads, 'King of Kings is a scriptural phrase and Mr. I. conceives here unexceptional but shou'd this line be objected to Mr. I. will substitute the following. "And to whom? 'To thee O Sovereign Death"' (5.5). In this same speech a second note is added to the lines 'And when thou wou'dst be merry thou dost chuse / The gaudy chamber of a dying King': 'These two Lines it is presumed can only be considered as a figure in Poetry and as their ejection wou'd materially hurt the sense of the speech which is one of the best in the piece Mr. Ireland wou'd be glad to preserve them' (5.5). Our thanks to Terry F. Robinson of the University of Colorado at Boulder for sharing her work on this manuscript with us.

15 Larpent MS, pages I.8–9. The 1799 published text of *Vortigern* also notes this excision; see 1.4.8.

16 While there are some small differences between the Larpent MS and the pub- lished version of the play, it is difficult to determine whether these were at Larpent's behest or simply made during the process of rehearsal.

17 [William Henry Ireland], *Vortigern, An Historical Tragedy, in Five Acts, Represented at the Theatre-Royal, Drury Lane. And Henry the Second, an Historical Drama*, Act I, Scene 6, page 13. Subsequent references to this text will be cited by act, scene and page number.

18 The play's comic scenes, particularly those with Flavia and Clown, assiduously invoke *Twelfth Night, As You Like It* and *Pericles*.

19 Samuel Ireland's diary (British Library Add MS 30346) and the Richard Brinsley Sheridan–Samuel Ireland correspondence (housed in the British Library and at Princeton University) show that negotiations were protracted and at times

rancorous. Promised new scenery and dresses for the production, Ireland became increasingly frustrated by the many delays that attended *Vortigern*'s production, at one point finally writing to Sheridan, 'y^r conduct & that of some persons ab^t ye theatre has done an irreparable injury to the interests of the My Son as well as to ye publication of ye papers in general'. See BL Add. MS 30348, fol. 59v; quoted from Jack Lynch (Lynch 2007a: 215).

20 For the contemporary critique of Malone's accusations of Jacobinism, see Robert Miles (2005).

21 Tour de Force Production Company, Bridewell Theatre, 22 October–19 November, 1997. Patrons: Alan Ayckbourn and Kenneth Branagh.

22 This list does not include the opening to Ireland's Gothic novel *The Abbess* (1798), or his *Full and Explanatory Account of the Shakespearean Forgery by Myself the Writer William Henry Ireland*, composed in 1802 or 1803, which exists only in manuscript and predates the *Confessions*, from which it markedly differs. For particulars of this final text, see S. Schoenbaum (1991: 578–79, note 71). Jack Lynch describes Ireland's *Full and Explanatory Account* in 'The Truth, the Whole Truth, and Anything but the Truth: What Can You Say about William Henry Ireland?', delivered as the first annual David Hosford Lecture, Rutgers University, Newark, 11 April 2005 (Lynch 2005).

8 Theatres of blood

Shakespeare and the horror film

Peter Hutchings

Dracula meets *Hamlet*

There comes a moment in Universal's 1931 production of *Dracula*, a film which is now seen as a founding text in horror cinema, when Renfield, an insane acolyte of Dracula, quotes from *Hamlet*. The scene takes place in a sanatorium to which Renfield has been confined since his return from Transylvania (a journey made by Jonathan Harker in Bram Stoker's original novel). Van Helsing is explaining to Doctor Seward, the head of the sanatorium, and Jonathan Harker his method for destroying Dracula – a method which, unsurprisingly, involves driving a stake through the vampire's heart. Enter Renfield, commenting, for once not unreasonably, 'Isn't this a strange conversation for men who aren't crazy.' When challenged by Van Helsing, he answers dismissively, 'Words, words, words'.

Why Renfield feels the need to quote one of Hamlet's retorts to Polonius in Act 2, Scene 2 is not entirely clear. Hamlet might pretend to be mad, but Renfield really is insane and generally seems aware of this. The scene's relativization of sanity – with apparently sane men subscribing to irrational and supernatural beliefs while in the company of a certified madman – is striking enough but does not seem to relate, in any obvious way at least, to the situation in which Hamlet finds himself, and Van Helsing, while capable of a certain amount of pomposity, is no Polonius. Renfield's earlier Hamletesque reference to 'bad dreams', when he worries that his nocturnal howling might disturb Mina's sleep, is not as obtrusive as 'Words, words, words' but arguably makes more sense, if only as a statement of literal fact.

If not a remark arising from a particular dramatic context, then, 'Words, words, words' might well be a gesture to a world outside the drama. It could be seen as part of the film's own bid for a kind of cultural reputability, for a horror genre characterized by its low cultural status might in certain circumstances seek a higher standing through attaching itself to a more prestigious area of culture: Shakespearean drama. If this were the case, however, a better-known quotation than the one deployed by Renfield might have been more suitable and effective. After all, 'words, words, words' is hardly the most memorable or resonant line to be found in Shakespeare's work.

In any event, *Dracula* was far from being a low-budget project of insignificant status. On the contrary, it was an ambitious undertaking that represented a significant investment for Universal Pictures. Moreover, at the time of its production it was not thought of nor marketed as a horror film, for this generic category or label would not begin to circulate widely until later in the 1930s. Instead, *Dracula* was presented by its makers to the prospective audience as a macabre thriller. Its retrospective designation as a horror film, and all the assumptions about cultural value that go with that designation, has sometimes distorted or obscured its position within the American entertainment market of the early 1930s.[1]

From such a historical perspective, the fact that *Dracula* was a theatrical adaptation – taken from the 1927 Broadway hit that itself had been adapted from a 1925 English stage drama – becomes more significant. Universal's film has often been criticized over the years for what are perceived to be its 'theatrical' elements, with 'theatrical' here denoting a failure by the filmmakers to exploit fully the resources offered them by the cinematic medium. In particular, critics have commented on the staginess of *Dracula*'s *mise-en-scène*, with numerous lengthy shots and a limited use of camera movement bestowing a visually static quality upon the proceedings. The one partial exception to this is the film's opening Transylvanian sequence – a sequence absent from the stage versions – although even here the camerawork tends to be stately and reserved. It is easy to understand why *Dracula* has been compared unfavourably by critics with the more stylish Universal production of *Frankenstein* (1931), which was also based on a stage play but which more successfully transcended those origins, or even the Spanish-language version of *Dracula* that was shot on the same sets as the English-language version but which offered a considerably more mobile use of the camera and more dynamic visualizations of such key scenes as the vampire's famous appearance at the top of his castle's staircase (see Skal 1990).

However, *Dracula*'s theatrical qualities can also be viewed in terms of its marketability, for its status as a valuable property in the entertainment market of the early 1930s resided almost entirely in its earlier success in the theatre. One can speculate as to whether the flat staging of the drama was consciously intended to direct the film's audience back to that original theatrical experience or whether this was instead the accidental side-effect of some unadventurous filmmaking. Whatever its cause – and there continues to be debate as to why the film, directed by the talented Tod Browning, turned out to be so disappointing in visual terms – there is potentially another context here for Renfield's 'Words, words, words'. They might be functioning here as a gesture to the theatre, one that connects with the film's more general aura of theatricality and which therefore operates less as an appeal to cultural value or esteem and more as a straightforward reference to the stage uttered within a film's sense of its own commercial existence.

Ultimately, Renfield's Shakespearean reference remains opaque, just as the film in which it features remains a decidedly ambiguous production. The *Hamlet* quotation is sufficiently odd to be noticeable but insufficiently elaborated to be fully meaningful. Yet its opacity is itself revealing inasmuch as it troubles some of our 'common-sense' assumptions about the shape of our culture: that horror cinema is overwhelmingly of low cultural status while anything Shakespearean invariably rests higher in a cultural hierarchy of value, and that any relationship between them is necessarily corrupting or parasitic, with either Shakespeare-themed horror seeking to rise above its 'natural' state of abasement or Shakespearean films drawing upon horror in order to secure a commercial popularity that they might otherwise lack. As it turns out, there is something to be said for the latter point in relation to particular films. But the case of the 1931 *Dracula* suggests that there might be a more complicated and context-specific set of intermedial and commercially driven relationships at work here between apparently disparate areas of culture, cutting across cultural hierarchies in unpredictable ways.

What follows is a discussion of some of those moments since the 1931 release of *Dracula* when horror cinema and Shakespearean drama have briefly engaged with each other, either in the form of Shakespearean cinematic adaptations deploying imagery associated with horror, or in the form of horror films that have drawn upon Shakespearean material. In particular, the focus will be on films produced in two periods offering small clusters of relevant activity: the mid-1990s to the present day, and the early 1970s. It follows that this chapter will not provide an exhaustive account of the interaction between Shakespeare and the horror film, although it does seem that the films caught up in this are small in number and often isolated or marginal in both Shakespearean and horror cinema. Neither will the chapter rely on any sense that these two areas of our culture are in themselves cohesive or in possession of distinctive and commonly agreed identities. Indeed, the value in looking at the films discussed below, aside from their intrinsically interesting features, resides in the way that the business of locating them within their cultural contexts underlines how mutable those contexts actually are.

Shakespeare into horror

In their own ways, Roman Polanski's *Macbeth* (1971), Kenneth Branagh's *Hamlet* (1996) and Julie Taymor's *Titus* (1999) align themselves (or can be aligned with) the horror genre. The nature of that alignment might vary from one film to another – ranging from partial or temporary in *Hamlet* and *Titus* to something more substantial in *Macbeth* – but all of them contain scenes that would not be out of place in a contemporaneously produced horror film. In part, this has to do with the way in which horror cinema since the 1930s has appropriated particular themes and ideas, to the extent that any pre-existing works containing these themes can be, and sometimes are, retrospectively classified as part of the horror genre. The witches in *Macbeth*, the ghost in *Hamlet* and the mutilations, torture and cannibalism in *Titus Andronicus* are all now conventional horror elements, and *Macbeth* and *Titus Andronicus* in particular are consequently often thought of as Shakespeare's most horror-like plays, even to an embarrassing extent with the critically unloved *Titus Andronicus*. It follows that film versions of such plays will have to engage with this in some way, if only to disavow it.

Alongside such thematic elements, some of the key creative personnel involved in the production of the films cited above just happen to have significant connections with horror; critics and audiences might well have been predisposed by this fact alone to view their subsequent work in the light of that genre. Prior to making *Macbeth*, for example, Roman Polanski had been responsible for the disturbing psychological thriller *Repulsion* (1965), the spoof vampire film *Dance of the Vampires* (1967) and the groundbreaking and highly successful Satanic horror film *Rosemary's Baby* (1968); he would go on to direct the similarly disturbing *The Tenant* (1976) and *The Ninth Gate* (1999). The most notable earlier screen credits for Jon Finch, who played Macbeth, were two Hammer horror films, *The Vampire Lovers* in 1970 and *The Horror of Frankenstein* in 1971. Critics writing about *Macbeth*, both at the time of its original release and since, have often used Polanski's authorship as a way of approaching it, with the real-life horror of the murder of Sharon Tate, Polanski's pregnant wife, by followers of Charles Manson in 1969 enhancing the film's horror-centred qualities. Kenneth Branagh lacked that sustained association with horror, but his biggest and most expensive film as director prior to *Hamlet* had been the horror film *Frankenstein* (1994), and Samuel Crowl, for one, has found echoes of the snowy opening scenes of that earlier film in *Hamlet* itself, especially in the 'My thoughts be bloody or be nothing worth' soliloquy that leads up to the film's intermission (Crowl 2000: 232). As for *Titus*, the film's star Anthony Hopkins might have had a distinguished career in the theatre, but he had experienced only intermittent success in the cinema until his Academy Award-winning performance as master serial killer Hannibal Lecter in *The Silence of the Lambs* (1991), a part he would reprise in *Hannibal* in 2001 and *Red Dragon* in 2002. Although he has only played occasionally in horror since – most notably a grandstanding turn as Van Helsing in Francis Coppola's 1992 version of *Dracula* – it is Lecter that has in large part defined his post-1991 screen persona, irrespective of his acting abilities or his versatility. It follows that his presence amidst the atrocities evident in *Titus* functions as yet another element pulling the film into the gravitational vortex of the horror genre.

One strategy adopted by filmmakers – and sometimes by critics – in relation to finding themselves in the presence of something that might be interpreted as filmic horror is to seek to suppress that 'horror' in favour of a more decorous or intellectual treatment of the material. For the appearance of the ghost in *Hamlet*, for example, Laurence Olivier in his 1948 screen version, Grigori Kozintsev in his highly regarded 1964 Russian version and Franco Zeffirelli in a 1990 adaptation all opt to distance us from the ghost and avoid any 'scare' or 'shock' tactics through adopting a slow, artful and meditative pacing. Underlining this, Neil Taylor has noted of the Kozintsev film that 'Each frame is an aesthetic composition worthy of exhibition in its own right, and the average length of shot is long enough (just under twenty seconds) to allow the spectator time to appreciate the beauty of the image' (Taylor 1994: 185).

Critics, too, can respond to films in ways that marginalize or explain away horrifying elements. Note, for instance, Martha Nochinson's review of *Titus*: 'The result is a film that realizes the subtlety and breadth of Shakespeare's treatment of a story that in its narrowest interpretation is a Roger Corman dream scenario of non-stop atrocity' (Nochinson 2001: 48). The respect paid here to Shakespeare's *Titus Andronicus* is surprising given that it is generally thought of as the author's most unsatisfying play. Equally significant, however, is the invoking of American film producer and director Roger Corman, best known for a series of horror films he directed that were based on Edgar Allan Poe stories and which often starred Vincent Price, among them *House of Usher* (1960), *Pit and the Pendulum* (1961), *Masque of the Red Death* (1964) and *The Tomb of Ligeia* (1964). Nochinson's hyperbolic characterization of this work in terms of 'nonstop atrocity' is thus placed against *Titus*'s 'subtlety' in a manner clearly designed to inoculate the film against being viewed as belonging in any way to the horror genre. This juxtaposition reproduces in a fairly straightforward manner a dichotomy between high-cultural Shakespeare and low-cultural horror, although, as was the case with the 1931 *Dracula*, a schematic division of this kind is hard to sustain in the face of both textual nuances and contextual specificities. As already noted, *Titus Andronicus* is usually interpreted as a crude rather than a subtle work, and, on the side of horror, Roger Corman's considerable reputation as a horror director most certainly does not reside in the provision of 'non-stop atrocity'. Indeed, his Poe films in particular have come to be viewed as a prime example of an ambitious, intelligent and cultured tendency in horror production.

So what of those Shakespearean adaptations that seem less restrained and less subtle, adaptations of which *Titus*, despite Nochinson, might be one? What in particular of those elements in such films that might reasonably be described as horror-like? Let us take, for example, Hamlet's encounter with the ghost in Branagh's *Hamlet*. While obviously aware of, and to some extent influenced by, other screen versions, Branagh's film engages far more enthusiastically with the possibilities for a horrifying and excessive experience in relation to the ghost. In his account of the supernatural in Shakespearean cinema, Neil Forsyth is unimpressed by the results, claiming that Branagh's rendition of the scene 'has little sureness of touch'. As Forsyth continues, 'The film then whisks us suddenly outside into the surrounding woods and blue-grey coloured night, to a place insistently and facilely Avernian, where the ground cracks mysteriously to release smoke (updated dry ice) and noise. In a sudden silence the ghost speaks in close-up, always in a stage whisper that becomes increasingly tedious as the long speech about the murder unfolds' (Forsyth 2000: 278).

One of the things that Forsyth seems to be objecting to is the way in which this particular scene sits uneasily within the film as a whole, with its 'facile' nature deriving from the obvious artifice of the setting – this was clearly filmed in a studio – and the rapid, excitable editing, with shots cut together in a manner that gives little sense of the overall topography of the location. The wood, in all of its dry-ice artificiality, is actually reminiscent of rural settings in Italian and American Gothic horror films of the 1960s (among which could be numbered the Poe adaptations of Roger Corman). While there is no evidence that this is in any way a direct homage to that particular school of filmmaking, it is arguably more reasonable to view this kind of setting in terms of the horror genre than through the 'Avernian' reference offered by Forsyth. To this can be added a slasher film-like use of offscreen space, with the ghost's hand suddenly emerging from beneath the frame line and grasping at Hamlet in a manner designed to produce a startling effect. The milky contact lenses worn by the ghost are also a common device in horror cinema, used for signifying the presence of evil or the monstrous. Other than the clear intent to provide a scary, thrilling experience, the deployment of horror conventions here also connects *Hamlet* with a set of popular generic practices. This, in turn, can be related to a broader impulse exhibited by the film of seeking to appeal to as broad an audience as possible, an impulse evidenced in the film's starry cast (which includes cameos for Charlton Heston, Billy Crystal, Jack Lemmon and Gerard Depardieu) and its lavish production values.

Something similar could be said for the apparently very different *Titus*. Its stars Anthony Hopkins and Jessica Lange, its array of state-of-the-art special effects and, in places, its MTV-like editing all contribute to an updating of the cinematic presentation of Shakespeare's work. In the midst of what is a decidedly busy production, horror elements also make an impression. In part, this affiliation with the horror genre derives from the gory nature of the story, but it also has to do with details in Hopkins's performance. The scene in which Chiron and Demetrius are suspended upside down and naked before Titus as he cuts their throats prior to baking them in a pie brings together in a spectacular fashion both of these elements. With its emphasis on an epicurean violence, it is the most Hannibal Lecter-like situation in the film. Accordingly, Hopkins is at his most Lecter-like, both in terms of some of his gestures and in the sardonic coolness he exhibits in the face of extreme body-centred horror. In fact, one wonders whether it actually provided inspiration for a scene in the later *Hannibal*, in which Hopkins cooks part of someone's brain while the brain's unfortunate owner looks on. One might also detect echoes of Hopkins's manic performance as Van Helsing in the later scene where Titus reveals to Tamora that she has just unwittingly consumed her sons' flesh.

It seems from this that both Branagh's *Hamlet* and Taymor's *Titus* are picking up elements, both visual and thematic, associated with the horror genre and deploying them both for their considerable affective power and as a way of connecting, if only momentarily, with a popular film genre. This takes place in the wider context of a stylistic eclecticism, with references made by both films to a range of fictional genres and historical periods. This is obvious in *Titus* from the opening sequence, with its combination of period and contemporary detail, onwards; the film could readily be placed within what has been termed 'post-modern' Shakespearean cinema, defined by Neil Sinyard as 'an approach characterized by irony, explicit allusions to modes of production, a mixture of "reality" and fantasy' (Sinyard 2000: 70). Sinyard excludes Branagh's *Hamlet* from this post-modern grouping on the grounds that 'it is basically conservative and traditional. ... The emphasis is on reverence for the text, not relevance: it preaches to the converted, not to a new audience' (Sinyard 2000: 69). However, while it is certainly the case that *Hamlet* avoids the multi-media games played by *Titus* (or by that prime example of post-modern Shakespeare, Baz Luhrmann's *Romeo + Juliet*), it is an allusive project nevertheless, containing, as it does, some fairly explicit references to a range of epics – notably the quality historical epic associated most of all with David Lean (with some critics picking up on the resonances of Lean's *Doctor Zhivago* in the snowbound setting); Errol Flynn swashbucklers (note Hamlet swinging on a chandelier in the climactic swordfight); contemporary action thrillers (most evident in the spectacular storming of Elsinore by Fortinbras's shock troops); and, of course, horror cinema itself. Horror figures, then, in both *Hamlet* and *Titus* as part of a broader strategy of framing Shakespearean drama within popular forms in a manner designed to render it relevant to contemporary audiences not necessarily accustomed to such a mode.

By contrast, Polanski's 1971 *Macbeth* offers a very diffrent version of a Shakespeare/horror conjunction. As a Playboy Production, with Hugh Hefner as one of its producers, its pop-cultural credentials are immaculate, but at the same time there is little of the breathless, crowd-pleasing eclecticism found in more recent Shakespeare films. Instead, the film turns out to be even grimmer than Shakespeare's original, entirely lacking in the faith in the essential integrity and necessity of royal authority that is evident in the play. So while Shakespeare's *Macbeth* concludes with a clear sense that a just rule has been restored, Polanski's *Macbeth* ends with an equally clear sense that the social disorder inaugurated by Macbeth's murder of Duncan will continue after Macbeth's own death.

Critics writing about the film have tended to assign this nihilistic quality both to Polanski's biography (which encompassed traumatic experiences as a Jewish child in Nazi-occupied Poland and the later murder of his wife) and to the social unrest evident in the late 1960s and 1970s, much of which was driven by a newly politicized youth culture (see Pearlman 1987; Williams, 2004). *Macbeth* emerges from this as potentially a *zeitgeist* work, a filtering of Shakespeare through the troubled spirit of the times. In this context, it is unsurprising that the film has been appropriated for the horror genre, not just for some of its intrinsic disturbing features, but because it was made by a director whose most successful previous film had been *Rosemary's Baby* and also because it can be aligned with a nihilistic form of horror popular at the time. Harvey Fenton and David Flint's *Ten Years of Terror: British Horror Films of the 1970s*, an exhaustive survey of 1970s British horror production, includes it as a matter of course.

However, the question remains of the legitimacy and value of such an appropriation. Recent theoretical work on film genres has suggested that appropriation is in fact a key element in their formation, that genres do not exist in fixed states but instead that films have moved in and out of them according to commercial pressures and audience tastes, and that this process is ongoing and in some instances contentious, with different groups arguing about where certain films belong (see Altman 1999). *Ten Years of*

Terror's inclusion of *Macbeth* therefore involves making a claim for it as horror, a claim that might not be acceptable to everyone but which nevertheless offers a strategy for contextualizing the film. It is certainly true that a number of the changes made by Polanski and his collaborators to the theatrical original fit neatly with what was going on in American and British horror cinema during the late 1960s and early 1970s, most notably in the American work of George Romero (*Night of the Living Dead* in 1968; *The Crazies* in 1973); Polanski himself with *Rosemary's Baby*; and in the British work of Michael Reeves (*The Sorcerers* in 1967; *Witchfinder General* in 1968); Gordon Hessler (*Scream and Scream Again* in 1969); and Pete Walker (*House of Whipcord* in 1974; *Frightmare* in 1974). The features shared by these and other films include:

- a cynicism about the efficacy of social institutions and the powers of good, often resulting in open endings where evil remains undefeated;
- a focus on young people, who are often destroyed in the course of the film;
- a realist approach that refuses the more stylized Gothic approach that had dominated horror production earlier in the 1960s;
- more explicit violence and gore than had been evident earlier in the history of the genre.

All of these clearly connect with elements in Polanski's *Macbeth*. The film's open ending – with Donalbain meeting the witches prior to what presumably will be his own rebellion against his brother, the new king – and the youth of Macbeth and Lady Macbeth are combined with a grubbily realistic *mise-en-scène* only occasionally interrupted by moments of stylization, sparing no detail in the various executions and murders that litter the narrative.

Attempts to establish *Macbeth* as 'really' or exclusively a horror film are almost certainly doomed to failure, given the considerable cultural pull exerted by the film's Shakespearean source. However, that is not the real point of the exercise. Instead, the important question is 'Does thinking about Polanski's *Macbeth* as a horror film develop our understanding of it as a film?' It can be argued in this respect that locating the film within the specific generic context in which it seems to fit can help to clarify its nature as a work emerging from a precise moment in social and cultural history. In particular, it can give a more nuanced and grounded account of that film than simply viewing it as a *zeitgeist* expression of the times. Such an approach can potentially also offer a more revealing and meaningful historical engagement with the film than an approach that places it in a long line of *Macbeth* adaptations, thus necessarily prioritizing the idea of the film as a version of an original theatrical source rather than as a distinctive text in its own right. Similarly, *Titus* and *Hamlet*'s forays into the representational territory claimed by horror direct our attention away from Shakespeare as a point of origin and instead encourage us to focus on a more immediate context, one that is characterized by specific genre formations and cultural relations.

Horror into Shakespeare

Tony Howard has described the British horror film *Theatre of Blood* (1973) as 'the highpoint of bad taste Shakespeare' (Howard 2000: 312). One can see what he means. The film's narrative involves the actor Edward Lionheart taking revenge on the critics who have wronged him through killing them via methods inventively drawn from Shakespeare's plays. *Theatre of Blood* sits somewhat oddly within British horror history, however. On the one hand, it is a decidedly old-fashioned for a film released in 1973, exhibiting few of the socially critical qualities found elsewhere in the genre at the time and which, as we have seen, are also manifested in Roman Polanski's *Macbeth*. It has an old-time horror star in Vincent Price – whose association with the genre went back to *Tower of London* (1939) and *The Invisible Man Returns* (1940) – and also contains performances from ageing, well-known character actors, among them Michael Hordern, Jack Hawkins, Arthur Lowe and Harry Andrews. The idea of youth in revolt so evident in other 1970s horror films is also absent; Lionheart's daughter (played by Diana Rigg) turns out to be a model of filial devotion, to the extent that at the end of the film she is compared with Lear's Cordelia. Stylistically, too, the film is defiantly old-school, eschewing the subjective camerawork and fragmented narrative structures popular in the genre in this period. At the same time, however, *Theatre of Blood* clearly looks forward to the serial killer dramas that would become popular from the 1990s onwards. The idea of the serial killer as a kind of artist whose killings have an overall pattern and which exhibit a distinctive 'signature' – for example, killing according to the seven deadly sins in *Se7en* (1995) or re-enacting earlier classic serial killings in *Copycat* (1995) – works well for Edward Lionheart, who emerges as a Shakespearean serial killer *par excellence*.

The 'bad taste' here would seem to derive from the bringing together of venerable Shakespearean drama and the vulgar activity of serial killing, and indeed, the series of murders presented by the film involves not just doing violence to the victims but to Shakespeare's plays too, as Lionheart cheerfully reinterprets the classics in order that they might fit his own agenda. In some cases the transposition of Shakespearean material into the film's contemporary settings is relatively straightforward – for example, one victim is stabbed to death by a group of assassins in the manner of *Julius Caesar* – but elsewhere the distinction between the original and Lionheart's version can be striking and, indeed, positively grotesque. For example, the scene from *Titus Andronicus* in which a mother consumes the flesh of her sons baked in a pie becomes a scene in which a critic, played by Robert Morley as the gayest of gay stereotypes, is fed his beloved poodles, while the execution of Joan of Arc in *Henry VI* becomes a scene in which a female critic is electrocuted by a malfunctioning hairdryer, thus achieving the 'flame with ash highlights' look promised her by Lionheart. Most outrageous of all is the re-enactment of *The Merchant of Venice*, where yet another unfortunate victim actually does lose a pound of flesh, with fatal consequences. 'It's Lionheart alright,' comments one of the surviving critics when he realizes what has happened, 'Only he would have the temerity to rewrite Shakespeare.'

Of course, it could be argued that 'rewriting Shakespeare' is what most of the adaptations cited in the first part of this essay have achieved, and this in the interests of rendering the plays relevant to contemporary audiences. Yet there is something particularly egregious about Lionheart's versions, and *Theatre of Blood* connects this with the performance tradition from which his activities derive. Much like the film in which he features, Lionheart is presented as an old-fashioned figure whose declamatory renditions of Shakespearean verse have been derided by critics for being hopelessly out-of-date. However, *Theatre of Blood* itself is more ambivalent than are the critics in the film about Lionheart and the type of Shakespearean drama he represents. It does this partly through showing the critics as a smug, pompous lot (with the possible exception of the youngest of them, played by Ian Hendry) but mainly through revelling in Lionheart's performances, for this is indeed a witty revisionary interpreter of Shakespeare who is also given a few moments of pathos as he laments his situation. In fact, the film generally seems to be offering an elegy for a lost style of Shakespearean drama, a style that involves approaching the plays as barnstorming melodramas and one which is characterized by a reliance on non-naturalistic forms of acting within extreme situations, on scenes that emphasize pathos, cruelty and suffering, and on the presentation of wrongs done and of wrongs righted. This is apparent from the film's beginning, with the credit sequence consisting of excerpts from silent film adaptations of Shakespeare's work – adaptations that even in their complete versions presented highly truncated renditions of the plays – and coupling this with sad, mournful music. Although Lionheart himself is clearly not old enough to be in these films, he deploys a comparable adaptive method in his murders, selecting individual scenes from a variety of plays – including, in addition to the titles already mentioned, *Cymbeline*, *Othello*, *Richard III*, *Romeo and Juliet* and *Troilus and Cressida* – and reworking these in order to achieve maximum dramatic impact, with little respect shown for the integrity of the original text.

It would be hard to deny that this is a version of Shakespeare that lacks the nuances evident in more critically valorized adaptations, but *Theatre of Blood* permits its own moments of grandiosity and emotive power – for example, in the scene where Lionheart confronts the Critics' Circle and then delivers Hamlet's 'To be or not to be' soliloquy before apparently committing suicide, or in the final scene when he carries his dead daughter through a burning building while speaking some of Lear's lines. Implicitly, this is a form of Shakespearean drama intended as popular entertainment for the mass audience; Lionheart himself states that 'For thirty years the public has acknowledged that I was the master.' However, the film never clarifies the extent to which Lionheart's performances were popular in this way. On no occasion do we see Lionheart performing for an actual theatrical audience; instead, he performs only for his victims and for the band of drunken indigents who aid him in his murders and who sporadically function as a degraded image of the audience. Interestingly, neither does *Theatre of Blood* offer a sense that there is any alternative way of presenting Shakespeare in this contemporary world. At one point, Ian Hendry goes so far as to encourage Lionheart to abandon Shakespeare and work in modern drama, the implication being that to be modern in the theatre necessarily entails leaving Shakespeare behind. This makes for an intriguing contrast with films such as Taymor's *Titus* or Branagh's *Hamlet* that have sought to update Shakespeare for contemporary audiences but which, as verse dramas, had, perhaps inevitably, a limited box-office appeal. Located much more comfortably within the commercial mainstream, *Theatre of Blood* presents Shakespearean drama instead as hopelessly antiquated and irrelevant. Lionheart emerges from this not as someone who besmirches the integrity of the Bard but rather as someone who, for all his crudity and egoism, works hard to keep Shakespearean drama alive in a world that is apparently indifferent to it.

It is worth considering here, if only briefly, another 1970s British horror film that 'dabbles' in Shakespeare, admittedly to lesser effect than *Theatre of Blood* but in a thematically comparable manner. *The Flesh and Blood Show* (1972) was directed by Pete Walker, the later films of whom – notably *House of Whipcord* (1974), *Frightmare* (1974) and *House of Mortal Sin* (1976) – have since earned him a significant reputation as a director of low-budget cult horror.[2] *The Flesh and Blood Show* is less accomplished than these and is considerably more downmarket than *Theatre of Blood*, both in its rather seedy production values and in its extensive, gratuitous and exploitative use of nudity. Its narrative is similarly theatrical, however, centring, as it does, on a group of young actors rehearsing a play, each of whom is stalked and killed by a mysterious assailant. The killer turns out to be an old Shakespearean actor by the name of Sir Arnold Gates, who many years before murdered his unfaithful wife and her lover in the theatre after a performance of *Othello*, a performance in which he played the Moor and his wife Desdemona. In this, the film seems to be referring back to George Cukor's 1947 film *A Double Life*, which also presented the part of Othello as one capable of driving insane the actor who plays it. This has left him with an insane hatred of actors, whom he considers promiscuous 'scum', hence his anonymously arranging for the actors to be hired and then murdering them.

What is interesting about this scenario is the way in which, like *Theatre of Blood*, *The Flesh and Blood Show* registers Shakespearean drama as a cultural practice associated firmly and irredeemably with the past, as something of little relevance to the present. In an otherwise colour film, the Shakespearean scenes are filmed in black and white as if to underline the point. At the same time, this type of drama is shown to possess a residual power and to exert a curious fascination. Edward Lionheart's final performance of Lear before his death in *Theatre of Blood* might be old-fashioned and overblown but it is also intensely heartfelt, and Ian Hendry's comment on it – 'He was madly overacting as usual' – seems a distinctly sour and churlish response. By contrast, *The Flesh and Blood Show* does not afford its old actor much by way of pathos, but neither does it have much faith in the alternative to his Shakespearean performance provided by the young actors. Lionheart in *Theatre of Blood* describes one of his young theatrical competitors as 'a twitching, mumbling boy', and *The Flesh and Blood Show*'s theatrical troupe might also be seen to fall into that category. They are not preparing a Shakespearean drama so much as working on what one of them describes as 'a happening', this involving, from the little we are shown of it, a largely improvised mixture of dance, mime and inarticulate dialogue that gives every impression of being of no immediate or lasting value whatsoever. Even in this debased and perverse context, it seems, Shakespearean drama lives on.

Words, words, words

This chapter began with a madman quoting from *Hamlet* and the observation that Shakespeare was present at the very beginning of horror cinema, if only in the form of that one cryptic line. Since that moment, Shakespeare and horror have tended to go their separate ways, with examples of interaction still few in number. But what is striking about the interactions discussed in this chapter is the confidence with which they negotiate their way across what some would consider an uncrossable cultural divide. There is no awkwardness or embarrassment here, no snobbishness or cap-doffing to high culture, and no sense either of Shakespeare slumming it with the horror proles. It is undeniably the case that powerful cultural distinctions, and an accompanying sense of what is proper and improper in the adaptation of Shakespeare to the screen, have limited opportunities for such interactions, albeit without preventing them entirely. The apparent transformation or at least reconfiguration of such distinctions in recent times – arguably reflected in the likes of Branagh's version of *Hamlet* and Julie Taymor's *Titus* – suggests that more could be done to explore the possibilities in this area, and that such enterprises could potentially cast a new light both on Shakespeare and on the horror genre. In particular, they could further develop a cultural relationship based not on simplistic high/low distinctions but instead on productive differences and some rather surprising similarities.

Notes

1 For more on this, see Hutchings (2004: 1–33).
2 For a discussion of Walker's films, including *The Flesh and Blood Show*, see Chibnall (1998).

9 'As one dead'

Romeo and Juliet in the 'Twilight' zone

Glennis Byron

At this very moment precisely, according to my personal *Eclipse* web counter, one hour, ten minutes, and thirteen seconds remain until publication … and I have just learned that the book will not appear in the UK until 4 October. OMG!!!!!

Confused? If so, you are clearly not one of the hordes of teenage girls (and a significant number of their mothers) participating in the hysteria surrounding the publication on 7 August 2007 of the third book in Stephenie Meyer's hugely successful vampire romance saga, the 'Twilight' series. As I write this, only two books have been published, *Twilight* (2005) and *New Moon* (2006). Combined, they have sold well over a million copies and have both been on the *New York Times* bestseller list for young adult fiction for over thirty weeks. With an initial print run of one million copies in the USA, the publishers are clearly expecting, and ensuring through their marketing strategies, even more of a demand for *Eclipse*. An *Eclipse* quotation of the day is displayed on Meyer's official website, and the first chapter of the novel is available for reading on Meyer's official website, working fans into a frenzy of anticipation. Discussion forums on the numerous 'Twilight' websites are full of anxious speculation about the future of Bella Swan, the vampire she loves, Edward Cullen, and her best friend, Jacob Black, a werewolf and consequently ancient enemy of the 'cold ones'. Two other books are well underway: *Breaking Dawn*, to be published in the autumn of 2008, and *Midnight Sun*, the story of *Twilight* from Edward's perspective.

As J. K. Rowling's *Harry Potter* series comes to its end, Meyer's 'Twilight' books seem set to slide into place as the most popular fiction among adolescents. Unlike Rowling, however, Meyer appeals specifically to a female fan base, young girls from about age thirteen up, and she is promoted as a kind of combination of Anne Rice and prom queen (*Twilight* concludes with Edward taking Bella to the prom). The personal web counter available for download, counting off the moments until the publication of

Eclipse, is just one of the many strokes of genius in the marketing of Meyer's series, marketing directed very specifically at this young female audience. To celebrate a special edition of her second book, *New Moon*, and promote the coming *Eclipse*, for example, Meyer held a 'prom' in Arizona in July 2007, attended by hundreds of teenage girls, all dressed in prom outfits, and Meyer herself, looking notably vampiric in the photographs, in a huge red dress (Irwin 2007).[1] With the publication of *Eclipse* imminent, various websites, including those of a number of bookshops and Amazon.com, carry video interviews with Meyer, some with just Meyer speaking, others with her responding to questions from groups of fans.

While young girls often identify with Bella, it is Edward that is of primary interest. 'I love Edward Cullen' T-shirts, thongs and barbeque aprons are available for sale through various websites. A selection of comments from one of many discussion forums suggests that what Bella desires is precisely what they desire:

> 'omg omg omg i loooooooooooove edward'; 'so sad how guys arent realy like that ... i love edward!!!!!!! i cant wait for eclipse or midnight sun'; 'Edward Cullen aww if only all guys were like that..'; omg startrekkin said it was her favorite book and an obbsessiopn MINEE TOO omg I THOUGHT I WAS THE ONLY ONE ... now i m obsses with having the perfect fairytale ... just like the book'; 'OMG i absloutly LOVE edward cullen! Im OBBSESSED w/that book & new moon!' 'holy crap lve that book i wanna marry edward!!! lol he is my love..'[2]

'If only all guys were like that': the fantasy lover, living out one's own 'perfect fairytale'; these are desires that the series may on some level interrogate, but also desires that it perpetuates and exploits.

Each book in the series appropriates a classic love story in which there is some kind of barrier between hero and heroine. *Twilight* vaguely gestures towards Jane Austen's *Pride and Prejudice*, and *Eclipse*, the information on Meyer's website suggests, will be in some ways indebted to Emily Brontë's *Wuthering Heights*. But Shakespeare's *Romeo and Juliet*, the iconic story of romantic young love that overtly structures the narrative of the second book, *New Moon*, underlies them all. And one of the most telling of Meyer's comments in the video on the Amazon.com webpage for *Eclipse* deals specifically with the issue of love: '*Twilight* is about finding true love; *New Moon* is about losing true love; and *Eclipse* is about choosing true love' (Stephenie Meyer talks about *Eclipse*). True love, Meyer suggests, is not as straightforward a concept as it might initially appear, and the 'Twilight' series appropriates *Romeo and Juliet* in order to negotiate, primarily through the body of the vampire, competing ideologies of love for the teenager of the modern world. At the same time, it also somewhat disturbingly promotes a suspension of development, with the adolescent reader encouraged to desire a prolonged fantasy 'twilight' of her own, a twilight that is, as Edward tells Bella, 'the safest time of day … But also the saddest, in a way', as it leads to 'the end of another day, the return of the night' (Meyer 2005: 204). If J. K. Rowling wrote for a readership that she assumed would grow up with her, Meyer keeps her readers in a state of delayed development. Progression, endings, these are things that Meyer's 'Twilight' zone is, as far as possible, anxious to avoid.

Before moving on to discuss the fantasy of the 'Twilight' series in some detail, however, I want to begin by providing some background to the transformations that have enabled what may initially appear to be the incongruous coupling of Shakespeare's play with the vampire. In particular I want to consider the ways in which the quintessential Gothic monster and the iconic 'star-crossed lovers' have been simplified and commodified, emptied of threat and tragedy, welcomed into the collective iconography of popular culture, and now, merged together in the 'Twilight' series, reappear in the form of a sanitized teen clean fantasy.

Star-crossed lovers

> From forth the fatal loins of these two foes
> A pair of star-cross'd lovers take their life,
> Whose misadventur'd piteous overthrows
> Doth with their death bury their parents' strife.
> (*Romeo and Juliet*, Prologue: 5–8)

While *Hamlet* is generally considered to be the most frequently appropriated, quoted and recontextualized of Shakespeare's plays within popular culture, *Romeo and Juliet* certainly runs a close second. 'Each generation rewrites Shakespeare for its own purposes', R. S. White notes, and the effectiveness of *Romeo and Juliet* 'must largely derive from its capacity for recontextualisation' (White 2001: 3). 'The phrase "Romeo and Juliet"', White adds,

> has become proverbial, two names fused into a single concept signifying a certain kind of love and a certain kind of tragic destiny. How often do we see newspaper headlines like 'Romeo and Juliet in Belfast', 'Romeo and Juliet in Bosnia', Romeo and Juliet double teenage suicide'? They refer to young lovers from 'different sides of

the tracks', divided by the families who represent warring religious or ethnic groups or who disapprove for other reasons of their children's choices in love. They die for their love, either as a result of social persecution or in acts of self-destruction.

(White 2001: 2)

The ways in which the phrase 'Romeo and Juliet', or alternatively 'star-crossed lovers', is appropriated by the media suggest a further possible refinement to White's assessment. The *San Francisco Chronicle* for 15 May 2005, for example, contained the following news report:

> Bethlehem's star-crossed lovers
>   Christian girl runs off with young Muslim – Vatican, U.S., Palestinian president intervene after street violence erupts.
>   A love feud straight out of 'Romeo and Juliet' has erupted in the West Bank over the clandestine romance of a 16-year-old Christian schoolgirl and a wealthy Muslim eight years her senior.
>
> (Kalman 2005)

Similarly, a BBC news report from 28 February 2007 announces:

> Star-crossed lovers quit West Bank
>   She is a 26-year-old Jewish Israeli. Her name is Jasmine Avissar. He is a 27-year-old Palestinian Muslim, Osama Zaatar. …
>   'Our marriage was a human thing. We just fell in love,' says Jasmine. 'The society around us is making it political.'
>
> (Price 2007)

In Shakespeare's play, 'A pair of star-crossed lovers take their life' (Prologue: 6). To be a contemporary Romeo and Juliet, these news stories suggest, such drastic measures are quite unnecessary. The focus is instead on conflict, on the 'ancient grudge' (Prologue: 3) and, as the second example most clearly suggests, on the autonomy of desire, on a love that, like the love ultimately valorized by the play, is seen as intensely personal, something that transcends the public and the political: 'We just fell in love … The society around us is making it political.'

The feud is also, of course, central to Shakespeare's play, and its importance stressed by the way the play begins with the fight between servants of the two opposing families and concludes with the scene in which peace is made between the families. But while the feud in Shakespeare's play seems motiveless, the reason for the 'ancient grudge' unknown, modern rewritings often politicize the play far more overtly and focus on what seems particularly threatening in the modern world – most frequently the clash between different ethnic groups or religions.

Even in adaptations that remain relatively true to source and include tragic death, the feud's the thing. In the 1960s, the best-known film adaptations of *Romeo and Juliet* began to appropriate the story in order to explore social problems: *West Side Story* (1961) replaced the Montagues and Capulets with feuding gangs; Franco Zeffirelli's *Romeo and Juliet* (1968) targeted a generation unwillingly caught up in a war initiated by their parents; and, more recently, Baz Luhrmann's *Romeo + Juliet* (1997) updated the conflict and rescripted Shakespeare's feud to offer an attack on corrupt multinational corporations. For all these political rewritings of the play, however, there has also been an equal impulse to simplify, sentimentalize and commodify the story of the star-crossed lovers, an impulse particularly evident in the ways in which writers of popular romance fiction have appropriated *Romeo and Juliet*.

Romance and the vampire

> 'Taste me,' she gasped, looking deep into his startled eyes. 'I want to know what it feels like.'
>
> (Marjorie M. Liu, *A Taste of Crimson*)

The 'Romance Writers of America' association sets out the two basic elements necessary in the romance genre as follows:

> A Central Love Story: In a romance novel, the main plot centers around two individuals falling in love and struggling to make the relationship work. A writer can include as many subplots as he/she wants as long as the relationship conflict is the main focus story.
>
> An Emotionally Satisfying and Optimistic Ending: Romance novels are based on the idea of an innate emotional justice—the notion that good people in the world are rewarded and evil people are punished. In a romance, the lovers who risk and struggle for each other and their relationship are rewarded with emotional justice and unconditional love.
>
> (Romance Writers of America 2007)

Given the second of these guidelines, *Romeo and Juliet* would at first glance appear an unlikely narrative to interest writers of romance. However, as the story has been transformed in the popular imagination, with the downplaying of death and the foregrounding of conflict, *Romeo and Juliet* has in fact proven eminently amenable to appropriation by popular romance fiction. 'The barrier drives the romance novel', Pamela Regis argues, and 'more than the marriage' is at stake (Regis 2003: 32). Romance novelists find the feud of Shakespeare's play usefully fulfils the function of this barrier although their appropriations do not usually extend far beyond a simple borrowing of this basic plot element and the use of either the names of the characters, or the shorthand term 'star-crossed lovers'. Jeanne Ray's *Julie and Romeo* (2000) exemplifies such an approach, with Julie Roseman and Romeo Cacciamani as florists who find love in their sixties despite an ancient feud between their families. The twist to the storyline reclaims the ideology of romantic love epitomized by *Romeo and Juliet* for a somewhat less youthful generation. Rosemary Poole-Carter's more recent *Juliette Ascending* (2007) rewrites Shakespeare in the context of the civil war, although despite the setting, as in most popular romances that appropriate *Romeo and Juliet*, the feud loses much of its political flavour. It functions primarily as a barrier, and in both these books, and others like them, true love prevails, the families are reconciled, and the lovers have, in romance fiction terminology, their HEA (Happily Ever After).

If, as White suggests, the effectiveness of *Romeo and Juliet* stems largely from its capacity for recontexualization, much the same argument is offered to account for the enduring popularity of the vampire. In Nina Auerbach's oft-quoted words, 'every age embraces the vampire it needs' (Auerbach 1995: 145). Recent years have seen the vampire quite literally embraced with the growth of a massive vampire romance industry, now generally considered to be the most popular subgenre of paranormal romance. A quick glance at any paranormal website reveals just how prolific writers of this subgenre have been. Interestingly, these websites also show how frequently vampire romances are written in series, possibly an indication of the need to delay the narrative thrust towards death, or rather undeath, but also, of course, to delay bringing to an end a lucrative commodity.

'Romance by You', which markets personalized romances, has capitalized on the enthusiasm for vampire romance by adding *Vampire Kisses* to the list of books on offer. For just under US $40, you can be the heroine of the story and have your personal details inserted (name, hair colour, eye colour, best friend's name, pet's name, hero's name, and so on). Since *Vampire Kisses* takes place on a modern college campus, where 'our heroine is a brilliant researcher and our hero spends his time in reclusive research of his own', I found it hard to resist taking advantage of the personalized preview on offer, and filled in the required questionnaire. Unable to decide on my hero's name, I took their advice and settled for Brad Pitt. A summary of my story appeared as follows. The information from the questionnaire rather disconcertingly appeared in bold but, I was assured, it would not appear this way when I ordered the book:

> A college campus is the setting for *Vampire Kisses* and where **Glennis Byron** and **Brad Pitt** first cross paths. It's love at first sight, but as they become closer, **Glennis** discovers that **Brad** has a horrifying secret – he's a vampire doomed to a bloodthirsty immortality! Although **Glennis** senses danger beneath his soft-spoken manner, and even after **Brad** himself warns her away, **Glennis** is drawn to this creature of the night and loves him as she has loved no other.

The summary is followed by four excerpts, detailing the first meeting '**Glennis** and **Brad** meet at the library'; part of the heroine's conversation with her best friend, '**Glennis** and **Judy**: a little intellectual repartee'; a romantic interlude, '**Brad** has vampire lust'; and a steamy encounter, '**Brad** – the first bite', with all the necessary throbs and fangs. The whole thing is artificial to an extreme: 'The dim light fell gently on his **dark brown** hair and shoulders. Impossibly wide shoulders … '; 'dripping the essence of his need onto **Glennis**, her perfect skin glistening in the dim light.' There is something of a touch of irony in the way that romantic love – something intensely personal, according to the dominant ideology – has here been commodified and reduced to an exercise in filling in the blanks: love by numbers. The vampire is indistinguishable from Jared Ryder, Rafe Cassidy, Raoul Valmy, Brig McCord or any other of the dangerous men, just waiting to be tamed, that are found in popular romance.

Shakespeare's Romeo may not fit easily into the category of dangerous man, but *Romeo and Juliet* has nevertheless been so frequently appropriated in vampire romance as to have become a convention, part of the genre competence demanded of the readers. The conflict provided by the feud provides a perfect template for the problems encountered in romances between vampire and werewolf or vampire and human, the two most common couplings. Vampires are usually male, but in the case of vampire–werewolf relationships, since the werewolf is the epitome of the Alpha male, women assume the vampiric role, often metaphorically somewhat defanged and transformed to what can only be described as the feisty cuteness so often associated with heroines of romance fiction. Shiloh Walker, an extremely prolific author of paranormal romances, provides just such a story in 'The Blood Kiss', where wolf king Roman Montgomery and Julianna Capiet, daughter of the vampire king, find their HEA despite the problems produced by their warring clans. There is no trace of anything the least bit Gothic in such works as these. The monstrous functions purely as a figure of, supposedly, erotic frisson, and is ultimately little more threatening than Count Chocula.

Vampires and *Romeo and Juliet*

> JULIET: O God, I have an ill-divining soul!
> Methinks I see thee, now thou art below,
> As one dead in the bottom of a tomb:
> Either my eyesight fails, or thou look'st pale.
> ROMEO: And trust me, love, in my eye so do you:
> Dry sorrow drinks our blood. Adieu, adieu!
>
> (*Romeo and Juliet*, 3.5: 54–59)

In 1997, an excerpt from *Romeo and Juliet* appeared in John Richard Stephens's *Vampires, Wine and Roses*, an anthology of vampire literature. While the play may seem to have enough in the way of apparently vampiric language and imagery to claim a place in such an anthology, there is nevertheless something anachronistic about its inclusion. In looking to explain a Romeo who 'locks fair daylight out, / And makes himself an artificial night' (1.2: 136–37) or a Juliet who describes him 'as one dead' (3.4: 56), it would probably be more useful to consult Robert Burton's *Anatomy of Melancholy* (1621) than vampire mythology. Lawrence Schimel's brief story of a vampire Romeo and his human Juliet, 'Swear Not By The Moon', makes the point clear. This Juliet plans to kill herself, unable to contemplate life as a vampire with her lover, and taking his dagger from the table she clutches it to her body:

> Romeo murmured as she left his side, and half-opened his eyes to watch her pale form walk to the window and stand before the curtains. She opened them.
> Romeo jerked upright. 'What light through yonder window breaks?' he cried. 'Art thou mad?'
>
> (Schimel 1994: 193)

As Schimel's ludicrous rewriting of the play as vampire story demonstrates, the language and imagery of *Romeo and Juliet* may occasionally duplicate those later found in vampire fictions, but they belong to entirely different systems of representation. To apply the term 'Gothic' to Shakespeare's play would be to drain an already threatened term of any meaning whatsoever. Nevertheless, as the vampire infected popular romances during the late twentieth century, so vampire fictions were by no means immune to the contagion of romance, and the number of vampire stories that have appropriated *Romeo and Juliet* suggests some transformation has occurred in the traditional vampire that now allows this figure and the equally iconic star-crossed lovers to merge together with apparent ease.

In the late twentieth century, Fred Botting notes, the monstrous, once 'terrifying objects of animosity expelled in the return to social and symbolic equilibrium', became 'sites of identification, sympathy, desire, and self-recognition. Excluded figures once represented as malevolent, disturbed, or deviant monsters are rendered more humane while the systems that exclude them assume terrifying, persecutory, and inhuman shapes' (Botting 2002: 286). Once the vampire had been demystified, humanized, and all too often sentimentalized, rewritten to embody some aspect of our contemporary condition, it was only a small step towards producing him as a tragic romantic hero. This was a move that first came to the attention of a wide popular audience with the release of Francis Ford Coppola's *Bram Stoker's Dracula* (1992), with its ubiquitous trailer: 'Love Never Dies'. Coppola's story is in fact far from being Stoker's, and as Ken Gelder has noted, with its opening narrative sequence, the film actually 'drew attention to just how far it had *departed* from the novel' (Gelder 1994: 90). In Coppola's reimagining of *Dracula*, the count does not become a vampire because he makes a pact with the devil in order to defeat the Turks; instead, it is the result of love. The film begins not with establishing its faithfulness to Stoker, but rather by connecting, through the idea of a false death leading to a double suicide, with *Romeo and Juliet*. This Romeo, of course, does not really die, but becomes undead, with his Juliet reincarnated as Mina in Victorian London.

The growing centrality of the play to the 'new' vampire was confirmed when Anne Rice, frequently credited with initiating the domestication of the vampire, loudly heralded the publication of *Vittorio the Vampire* (1998) as her vampire *Romeo and Juliet*. The majority of these vampire fictions, however, much like the popular romances, tend to appropriate the play in a rather superficial manner, primarily as shorthand for a forbidden love, forbidden because of some conflict between human and vampire, vampire and werewolf, or vampires from opposing clans. *As One Dead* (1996), a spin-off from the popular White Wolf role-playing game *Vampire the Masquerade*, provides a typical example. Focusing upon the feud between two vampire sects, the Sabbats that rule Toronto and revel in their own inhumanity, and the Camarilla, vampires who deny the beast within, the novel is also a tale of the forbidden love of Bianka and Lot. In addition to appropriating the idea of the feud, as the title immediately reveals, *As One Dead* recontextualizes the lines from Shakespeare's play to emphasize the tragedy not just of vampire love, but of vampire existence. And to offer an example familiar to a wider public than the cult audience for White Wolf, human Buffy's romance with good vampire Angel in *Buffy the Vampire Slayer* was repeatedly presented in terms of *Romeo and Juliet*. The connection was perhaps too frequently hammered home, as suggested by the decision of the creator of the series, Joss Whedon, to break the couple up: 'You can only play variations on "Romeo and Juliet didn't die" for so long before you get bored. You know, a "Romeo's Working Out to Get Rid of His Spare Tire" episode is not going to be that exciting' (Vineyard 2007).

Stephenie Meyer's 'Twilight' series

Be Safe.

(Stephenie Meyer, *New Moon*)

Romeo and Juliet has always had a particular appeal for adolescents, partly because it epitomizes *young* love in Western society, partly because it is so widely taught in schools, and perhaps also because of the frequent sentimentalization and modernization of the play by those who teach it. Teenagers are encouraged to identify with the love story and the challenge to parental authority that it stages, considering these and other aspects of the play from varying modern perspectives. Vampires are equally popular with the teen audience. Indeed, the majority of Western vampire films and books, from the late 1970s onwards, are specifically directed at middle-class youth culture, tending, as Ken Gelder notes, to focus on 'anxieties centred around the adolescent's relations to the family and to sexuality, and which have to do with questions of law and lawlessness' (Gelder 1994: 103). In bringing the vampire together with the star-crossed lovers of Shakespeare's play, Meyer's 'Twilight' series continues both the simplification and the commodification of these iconic figures. Teetering on the boundary of law and lawlessness, these books exploit their appeal to the teenage audience with a combination of titillation and denial long familiar to those in the consumer society of the big tease.

In exploring romantic young love in this modern world, Meyer begins by setting the idea of love as a cultural construction, a kind of 'false consciousness', against the idea of love as instinctual, spontaneous, and experienced on the body in a manner vaguely reminiscent of Shakespeare's play. Throughout Act 1, Romeo assumes the role of the Petrarchan lover, and the lack of authenticity in his love for Rosaline is suggested by the clichéd language and images upon which he draws. Here, love is a cultural construction, something that is performed. Romeo himself seems to recognize the lack of authenticity, seemingly aware, as he is, of the fact that his true identity is not expressed through the role that he assumes: 'I have lost myself, I am not here: / This is not Romeo, he's some other where' (1.1.197–98). On the other hand, what Shakespeare ultimately valorizes as true love, or what Romeo feels for Juliet, is seen as unscripted, as the expression of authentic identity: it is spontaneous and private, and validated not through conventionalized language so much as through the body.

If Romeo initially bows to the authority of Petrarchan conventions, then the 'Twilight' series demonstrates that *Romeo and Juliet*, through its repeated appropriations and re-narrations, has assumed much the same authority for the contemporary world. *New Moon* begins on the night of Bella's eighteenth birthday, something she is not eager to celebrate as it moves her further away from the eternally seventeen-year-old Edward. Excusing herself from coming to the home of his 'family', the Cullens, Bella insists that she is too busy: 'I haven't watched *Romeo and Juliet* yet for English.' Edward's 'sister', Alice, dismisses the excuse:

> Alice snorted. 'You have *Romeo and Juliet* memorized.'
> 'But Mr Berty said we needed to see it performed to fully appreciate it – that's how Shakespeare intended it to be presented.'
> Edward rolled his eyes.
> 'You've already seen the movie,' Alice accused.
> 'But not the nineteen-sixties version. Mr Berty said it was the best.'
> (Meyer 2006: 11)

Edward agrees to watch the film with Bella, but is completely scathing about Romeo:

> first of all, he's in love with this Rosaline – don't you think it makes him seem a little fickle? And then, a few minutes after their wedding, he kills Juliet's cousin. That's not very brilliant. Mistake after mistake. Could he have destroyed his own happiness any more thoroughly?
> (Meyer 2006: 17)

Bella is slightly offended: 'Romeo was one of my favorite fictional characters. Until I'd met Edward, I'd sort of had a thing for him' (Meyer 2006: 17). Replacing Romeo with Edward, however, is not such a big step.

The series is told from Bella's somewhat unreliable perspective, and in Chapter 1 of *Twilight*, entitled 'First Sight' – with the unspoken 'love at' only implied – Bella first sees the Cullens on her first day at her new school in the cafeteria. She does not know at this point that they, supposedly the adopted children of Dr Carlisle Cullen and his wife Esme, are actually all vampires that have been made by Carlisle, but immediately notices their difference. In one sense, she observes, 'they were all exactly alike. Every one of them was chalky pale, the palest of all the students living in this sunless town' (Meyer 2005: 16). But what makes her stare is that their faces are all 'devastatingly, inhumanly beautiful. They were faces you never expected to see except perhaps on the airbrushed pages of a fashion magazine. Or painted by an old master as the face of an angel' (Meyer 2005: 17). What Bella notes here, and what is emphasized throughout *Twilight* and *New Moon*, is that the vampires look, not human, but like idealized reproductions of the human form. Even totally wet and dishevelled, Edward looks 'like he'd just finished shooting a commercial for hair gel' (Meyer 2005: 37).

As Jerrold E. Hogle argues, the 'ghost of the counterfeit' has been integral to the Gothic from its inception, and the 'Twilight' series appears to place itself within this tradition through the representation of the vampire. Here the human is emptied out to create a space into which is poured a consumer fantasy, a celebrity, a teen icon, a hero of popular romance. Edward is not just a simulation of the human; he is a simulation of what is already a simulation, a reproduction of something found only on 'the airbrushed pages of a fashion magazine'. The vampires even feel like reproductions; they are hard like stone, and just as cold. But it is precisely what makes Edward inhuman that attracts Bella. Leaning against him she claims that 'It wasn't exactly as comfortable as a sofa cushion would be, what with his chest being hard and cold – and perfect – as an ice sculpture, but it was infinitely preferable' (Meyer 2006: 17). The characteristics of the hero of popular romance are here literalized in the vampire's form.

When his true appearance is revealed, Edward, rather than becoming a figure of horror, becomes even more an object of commodified beauty. As the cloudiest place in the USA, Forks is a most useful residence for vampires trying to pass, since in Meyer's reworking of vampire mythology, they avoid the sun not through any fear of being burned up, but because it is in sunlight that their true natures are revealed. Edward first demonstrates when he takes Bella to an isolated sunlit meadow:

> Edward in the sunlight was shocking … His skin, white despite the faint flush from yesterday's hunting trip, literally sparkled, like thousands of tiny diamonds were embedded in the surface. He lay perfectly still in the grass, his shirt open over his sculpted, incandescent chest, his scintillating arms bare. … A perfect statue, carved in some unknown stone, smooth like marble, glittering like crystal.
>
> (Meyer 2005: 228)

Marble, crystal, and diamonds: Edward is a spectacle that glitters and thrills: 'I'd never seen him so completely freed of that carefully cultivated façade. He'd never been less human … or more beautiful' (Meyer 2005: 232).

Bella's desire to be turned into a vampire is a desire to be forever young, beautiful and united with Edward in a fantasy world where nothing changes. In exchange for her self-centred mother and somewhat indifferent father, she wants the Cullens – not a real family, of course, but a gorgeous simulation of one with that enviable celebrity lifestyle so often affected by vampires today. As the first book in the series ends, Edward, aware of the problems involved in vampire life, refuses to turn her. But Edward's sister Alice, who has special talents, has seen Bella becoming a vampire in the future. Alice has occasionally been wrong, but Bella remains optimistic: 'I'm betting on Alice' (Meyer 2005: 418). It is a phrase that will echo throughout the series.

The second book begins by suggesting her wish will be granted. As *Romeo and Juliet* begins with a Prologue that reveals the eventual fate of the lovers, 'a pair of star-crossed lovers take their life' (Prologue 6), so *New Moon* begins with an apparently similarly ominous epigraph from the play, the warning of Friar Laurence:

These violent delights have violent ends
And in their triumph die, like fire and powder,
Which, as they kiss, consume.

(2.6.9–11)

Recontextualized within a vampire story, however, these initial portents of death assume new meaning. If in Shakespeare's play, as Lloyd Davis observes, the love of Romeo and Juliet 'ends in reciprocal death, with the Petrarchan images fatally embodied and materialised' (Davis 2001: 29), then in *New Moon*, the narrative thrust, it is suggested, is towards a meta-phorical enactment of the ending of *Romeo and Juliet*, with Bella joining Edward in a 'death' that, in the context of vampire fiction, may well be, in another sense, life – what Bella sees as her HEA. Will Bella, the reader is encouraged to ask, get her desire at the end of *New Moon*? Will Edward finally agree to turn her into a vampire?

To a certain extent, the 'Twilight' series clearly questions Bella's desire, contesting the obsession with youth and beauty and challenging the preference for fantasy over the 'real'. Not only does Bella fall in love with an image, a simulation of an idealized human form, but she also refuses to contemplate what Edward tries to make her understand about the dangers of vampire life. Even when confronted with evidence of what a 'real' vampire does, she remains determined to maintain her fantasy world. In the vaults of the Volturi, the most menacing and powerful of the vampires, groups of tourists are lured to their deaths. When told that the human who works as their receptionist hopes to be made into a vampire herself someday, Bella is horrified:

'How can she want that', I whispered, more to myself than really looking for an answer. 'How can she watch those people file through to that hideous room and want to be a part of *that?*'

Edward didn't answer. His expression twisted in response to something I'd said.

(Meyer 2006: 488)

Edward understands the irony of Bella's response, her refusal to make the obvious connection between her desire and that of the receptionist. But Bella, who as she notes in *Twilight* has 'always been very good at repressing unpleasant things' (Meyer 2005: 146), only retreats back into fantasy, concentrating on her happiness in being with Edward once more, in 'a fairy tale again' (Meyer 2005: 488).

The 'Twilight' series may interrogate Bella's desires, and suggest her love for Edward is the product of a consumer culture obsessed with empty images, with youth and beauty, but this by no means undercuts Edward's appeal. As the fans' reactions to Edward well demonstrate, they are as seduced as Bella is by this glittering fantasy world. And the series relies upon this for its success. Bella may (or may not) eventually become a vampire, but the moment is endlessly delayed. With each book, Meyer introduces a new reason to defer the moment of satisfaction, keeping her readers, like Bella herself, in a prolonged state of thrilling anticipation, as they hope with the purchase of each new book that this time there will be closure. While this is clearly part of the marketing strategy, it is also closely connected to the ways in which Meyer deals with adolescent sexuality.

If through Bella's response to Edward, Meyer simultaneously interrogates and perpetuates the fantasy of romantic love, then through Edward's response to Bella Meyer examines the idea of love as something spontaneous, instinctive and focused on the body. What initially attracts Edward to Bella is nothing more than her scent. She is his singer, as the Volturi recognize, 'la tua cantante' (Meyer 2006: 471): her blood sings to him, making her irresistible; his first impulse on catching her scent in the classroom is to drain her to the death (Meyer 2005: 236).

But as Edward explains, vampires also 'have human instincts – they may be buried deep, but they're there' (Meyer 2005: 244). And so while her irresistible scent means that he hungers for her blood, he also grows to love her in a more human way. She 'resurrects the human' in him' (Meyer 2005: 265). He also begins to feel 'other hungers. Hungers that I don't even understand, that are foreign to me … I'm not used to feeling so human' he tells Bella (Meyer 2005: 243). One of these other hungers, the text suggests, is love, and it is love that allows him to control his senses and restrain his desire for her blood. But the threat to Bella is constant. 'When we hunt', Edward tells her, 'we give ourselves over to our senses ... govern less with our minds. Especially our sense of smell. If you were anywhere near me when I lost control that way ... ' (Meyer 2005: 197). And Alice expresses her reservations about turning Bella herself in similar terms: 'We're also like sharks in a way. Once we taste the blood, or even smell it for that matter, it becomes very hard to keep from feeding' (Meyer 2005: 362).

As Robert Mighall, in the face of the critical insistence on reading vampirism in sexual terms, has rightly argued, 'a vampire is sometimes only a vampire, and not a sexual menace' (Mighall 1998: 74). Not in the 'Twilight' series: this vampire is most definitely both a sexual menace and a sexual enticement. The hunger for love is not the only human hunger that Bella resurrects within Edward, and he produces a similar hunger in her. The love scenes between Edward and Bella are always suggestive, the vampiric desire to drink blood quite overtly conflated with sexual desire. When Edward first kisses Bella, the passage suggests the problems he experiences have little to do with his desire to drink her blood:

> Edward hesitated to test himself, to see if this was safe, to make sure he was still in control of his need.
> And then his cold, marble lips pressed very softly against mine.
> What neither of us was prepared for was my response.
> Blood boiled under my skin, burned in my lips. My breath came in a wild gasp. My fingers knotted in his hair, clutching him to me. My lips parted as I breathed in his heady scent.
>   ...
> 'Oops,' I breathed ...
> 'Should I. ... ?' I tried to disengage myself, to give him some room. ...
> 'No, it's tolerable. Wait for a moment, please.' ... I kept my eyes on his, watched as the excitement in them faded and gentled.
> (Meyer 2005: 247)

Edward here functions much like Stoker's Dracula: his threat and his allure lie in the way he works as a catalyst for desire. Even as he tests himself to ensure he is 'safe', Edward releases something in Bella that is even more threatening: her own desire for him. 'Be safe', the words Edward constantly repeats to the accident-prone Bella, and which have been taken up as a kind of mantra by numerous fans, take on new meaning. Meyer, a thirty-three year old Mormon mother of three who claims she has never read a horror novel nor seen a horror film, is quite clear about her position: 'I grew up in a community where it was not the exception to be a good girl. It was sort of expected. And all of my friends were good girls too, and my boyfriends were good boys' (Kirschling 2007). In 'Twilight', there is the continual incitement of excess, the thrilling suggestion that boundaries will be overstepped, followed by the emphatic reassertion of prohibition. The vampire may assume the traditional function of the monstrous, to serve as warning and as demonstration. But as the prolonged eroticism of such encounters between Edward and Bella shows, he disturbs, as well as defines, moral boundaries.

The importance of the need for control is further connected to the disruptions caused by adolescent hormones through the reworking of the feud. Rather than overtly focusing on social or political conflict, the feud is represented in Gothic terms, and enacts the conventional construction of the human through the abjection of the monstrous. Sites of horror, this feud well demonstrates, are essential to the construction of subjectivity and otherness, even in the odd dynamic of werewolf and vampire. The werewolves call themselves the 'Protectors'; as Jacob explains to Bella, 'we only protect people from one thing – our one enemy. It's the reason we exist – because they do' (Meyer 2006: 309). The good vampires, those who abstain from human blood, name themselves the 'stregoni benefici'. Each group aligns itself with the civilized and rational through the construction of the other as what is bestial and irrational. Edward dismisses the werewolves as 'immature, volatile' and 'dogs' (Meyer 2006: 506), while Jacob, in turn, despises the 'filthy, *reeking* bloodsuckers' or 'leeches' (Meyer 2006: 267). What each man identifies in the other, however, is what he fears most in himself.

Above all, both fear the resurgence of the body, the senses. 'The hardest part' of becoming a werewolf, according to Jacob, is feeling 'out of control … Feeling like I can't be sure of myself – like maybe you shouldn't be around me, like maybe nobody should. Like I'm a monster who might hurt somebody' (Meyer 2006: 345), and he particularly worries about 'the way it comes so easily to me … does that make me even less human … Sometimes I'm afraid that I'm losing myself' (Meyer 2006: 346). Edward uses much the same language when telling Bella the story of Carlisle, the 'father' of his family, who, when first made into a vampire, realizes there is 'an alternative to being the vile monster he feared'. Through drinking from animals, rather than humans, he finds he 'could exist without being a demon. He found himself again' (Meyer 2006: 295). Carlisle, in Gothic terms a representation of the paternal law that redraws the boundaries of the human, has founded his vampire family on the principle of abstaining from human blood, speculating that 'abstaining makes it easier for us to be civilized, to form bonds based on love rather than survival or convenience' (Meyer 2006: 428). To avoid 'losing' oneself, then, is above all to be able to control what is instinctual, to be able to control the demands of the body, the senses, the monster within. Carlisle, after hundreds of years, finds this easy; the younger vampires do not. In this way both vampire and werewolf become less the monstrous other than the expression of the adolescent condition, and, given that the resurgence of the monstrous body is linked to the bestial, and the control of it with the human, they offer a slightly disturbing site of identification.

If *Romeo and Juliet* validates a spontaneous and instinctual love as the expression of authentic identity, the 'Twilight' series represents such love as both thrilling and dangerous, a threat to authentic identity, and a new Paris is introduced to suggest the possibility of a more mature and socially responsible companionate love. When Edward has left, Bella at one point considers the possibility of actively deviating from the script she sees as dominating her life. She dreams a series of pictures, only one of which stays in her head:

> It was meaningless – just a set on a stage. A balcony at night, a painted moon hanging in the sky. I watched the girl in her nightdress lean on the railing and talk to herself. Meaningless … but when I slowly struggled back to consciousness, Juliet was on my mind.
>
> (Meyer 2006: 369)

Meaningless it is not. As the striking emphasis on the artificial, to be Juliet is to exist in a world of performance, to live on 'a set on a stage'. Resisting the thrust of the play, she begins to wonder 'what if': what if Romeo had lost interest in Juliet? What if Paris had been Juliet's best friend? What if 'she loved Paris? Not like Romeo. Nothing like that, of course. But enough that she wanted him to be happy too' (Meyer 2006: 371). However, the script, she recognizes, is resistant to such drastic change: 'Romeo wouldn't change his mind. That's why people still remembered his name, always twined with hers: Romeo and Juliet. That's why it was a good story. "Juliet gets dumped and ends up with Paris" would have never been a hit' (Meyer 2006: 371).

Bella here comes close to seeing romantic love as nothing more than a 'good story', socially scripted, believing that another kind of love, one based on companionship and comfort, may be both more preferable and more authentic. Rejecting the 'stupid play', she thinks about 'reality' instead, about the effects of her actions on others, including her father, and begins to consider another perspective: 'it would be downright miserable to give up my hallucinations and try to be a grown-up. But maybe I should do it. And maybe I could. If I had Jacob' (Meyer 2006: 372). Bella's feelings for Jacob are not just 'brotherly' (Meyer 2006: 375). 'I couldn't imagine my life without Jacob now', she realizes. 'Somehow he'd become essential to my survival' (Meyer 2006: 374).

As Bella moves towards a valuation of a companionate, adult love that is less dictated by fantasy, the kind of ending associated with classic Gothic texts momentarily seems imminent. In the fairy-tale endings of such works as Ann Radcliffe's *The Mysteries of Udolpho* (1794), passions and superstitious fears are ultimately rejected. Transgression gives way to the reinstatement of the heroine's position and property, excess is controlled, and desire is regulated; with the heroine's marriage to the acceptable hero, moral systems are restored. While it may appear somewhat ironic that this could be seen as being achieved through an alliance with a teenage werewolf, context is all, and in contrast with the transgressive sexuality of Edward, Jacob is, as Bella puts it, what is 'warm and comforting and familiar. Safe' (Meyer 2006: 375).

But as Meyer is clearly aware, this kind of fairy-tale ending holds little interest for her modern readers, and so, just as Bella begins to accept that the 'prince was never coming back to kiss me awake from my enchanted sleep' (Meyer 2006: 411), the phone rings, setting in progress a series of events that leads her to discover that Edward, believing she has committed suicide, has gone to Italy to provoke the Volturi into destroying him; he is about to push the script towards its doomed conclusion and only she can save him. The call of romantic love is far stronger than that of comfortable companionship; being a modern Juliet, with all its accompanying dangers, is preferable to being an Emily settled down into domesticity. Even Edward, initially scathing of Romeo, recognizes that he has made much the same kind of errors. 'Mistake after mistake', he says, appearing to validate the authority of the play. 'I'll never criticize Romeo again' (Meyer 2006: 508).

The time for Bella to be turned seems ripe, and she puts the decision about whether she should become a vampire to the vote with the Cullen family, and, reluctantly, Edward agrees to change her, even if she must wait until graduation; betting on Alice, having faith in Alice's vision of her becoming a vampire, seems justified. However, instead of ending here, in 'Epilogue – Treaty', another barrier is introduced as Jacob reappears, seeking Edward. Bella, typically, begins scripting her fears in accordance with *Romeo and Juliet*, recalling with anxiety the lines '*They fight; Paris falls*' (Meyer 2006: 555; emphasis in text). But Jacob comes to warn Edward, not to fight. According to the treaty agreed upon many years ago, as Jacob reminds them, the werewolves leave the vampires to themselves with one condition:

> 'The treaty is quite specific. If any of them bite a human, the truce is over. *Bite*, not kill,' he emphasized. Finally, he looked at me. His eyes were cold.
>
> It only took me a second to grasp the distinction, and then my face was as cold as his.
>
> (Meyer 2006: 558–59)

If *Romeo and Juliet* ends with the death of the lovers and the reconciliation of the two families, *New Moon* ends by, once again, delaying Bella's 'undeath' and introducing the possibility for intensified conflict.

But hope remains. As the preview to the third book, *Eclipse*, reveals, Bella is going to be forced to choose between Edward and Jacob, 'knowing that her decision has the potential to ignite the ageless struggle between vampire and werewolf. With her graduation quickly approaching, Bella has one more decision to make: life or death. But which is which?'[3] The tension between Bella's 'romantic' love for Edward and her feelings for Jacob, this suggests, is likely to take on a more dominant role, but also once more the tantalizing possibility is dangled before us that, finally, Bella will be turned. And yes, we have certainly been here before. Still …

We're betting on Alice.

Notes

1 See the report in the *Phoenix New Times* for 12 July 2007. Online at http://www.phoenixnewtimes.com/2007-07-12/news/charmed/ (accessed 16 July).

2 Comments taken from 'Iconator'. Online at http://www.iconator.com/icon.php?IconID=591317 (accessed 6 August).

3 Stephenie Meyer's official website, *Eclipse* home page. Online at http://www.stepheniemeyer.com/eclipse.html (accessed 18 July).

10 Gothspeare and the origins of cultural studies

Fred Botting and Scott Wilson

28 January 1581

The wind was howling like the plague. Thunder and lightning barracked and briefly illuminated the distress of a ship against black storm clouds as, rudderless and with topsail gone, it yawed towards the treacherous coast of Northern Lancashire. Abandoning the dire spectacle of the wreck, Sheikh Zoubeir struggled to the shore where he hoped to die at least a dry death.

The ship had been in flight non-stop since it left Tunis only a few days before, pursued by Barbary pirates up the coast of Portugal until it was caught in a vicious storm blowing from the West across the Atlantic. There was no turning back, just a line of flight born on icy winds towards the Gothic wastes of Northern Europe.

In Tunis, Sheikh Zoubeir had been usurped by his brother as the head of the Arab resistance against the Ottomans who had finally seized control of the city in 1575. Zoubeir was renowned for his erudition and his passion for poetry. His Arab heritage went way beyond the austerities of Islam, being steeped in the poetry of the nomadic Arab tribes that 'maintained a tradition of chivalrous valour in which violence was combined with prodigality, and love with poetry' (Bataille 1988: 90–91). Such sublime poetry, as it headed North, provided the basis for the Troubadour tradition in Spain and Southern France, and ultimately the development of courtly love in Europe, which until about the twelfth century had little or no recognizable modern poetry outside of religious liturgy and bardic narrative. Zoubeir's depth of Arab and Islamic learning was nourished and enhanced by his passion for the classics of the Roman era, for Ovid, Virgil and Plutarch in particular. Frustrated by the amount of time Zoubeir spent on the 'liberal arts' in place of pursuing his *jihad* against the Turks, Zoubeir's brother staged an uprising in their camp in Sidi Bou Said, a few miles outside the city of Tunis. Defeated and bloodied, Zoubeir was allowed a ship and a small crew, and sent into exile. Now his ship, his crew and his books were gone, drowned in the Irish Sea.

Washed up on the freezing, muddy sands of Morecambe Bay, Sheikh Zoubeir would often reflect on this, the lowest point of his life. As Stephen Greenblatt writes:

> Again and again in his plays, an unforeseen catastrophe – one of his favourite manifestations of it is a shipwreck – suddenly turns … smooth sailing into disaster, terror, and loss. The loss is obviously and immediately material, but it is also and more crushingly a loss of identity. To wind up on an unknown shore, without one's friends, habitual associates, familiar network – this catastrophe is often epitomized by the deliberate alteration or disappearance of the name and, with it, the alteration or disappearance of social status … all of its conventional signs having been swept away by the wild waves.
>
> (Greenblatt 2004: 85)

This is how Sheikh Zoubeir, when he became Shakespeare for political, racial and commercial reasons, would romantically recall it. But as he began to recover on the desolate beach and head South, Zoubeir was not without hope. He had at least a contact, a fellow poet, indeed a poet celebrated by Edmund Spenser: Fernandino, Lord Strange, son of Henry Stanley, the fourth Earl of Derby. Fernandino had corresponded with Zoubeir and even visited him in Tunis. Fortunately, Zoubeir was recognized and welcomed by Fernandino, and given shelter. But penniless, Zoubeir's Arab pride would not allow him to live indefinitely on Lord Strange's hospitality. Nor would he allow a message of his survival to be sent to his brother in Tunis. On the run from both the Turks and his brother, Sheikh Zoubeir resolved to make his fortune using his natural talent under an assumed name.

As fortune would have it, Lord Strange employed 'a talented, professionally ambitious group of players who were licensed by the Privy Council as Lord Strange's Men' (Greenblatt 2004: 104). Fernandino introduced his Tunisian poet to the principal players – Will Kempe, Thomas Pope, John Heminges, Augustine Philips and George Bryan.[1] At the back of the company was a gangling, spotty young fellow who looked about 17 or 18. Shakeshafte or Shagspeare was his name, he couldn't seem to make up his mind, or remember. Shakeshafte had been lodged with the Earl of Derby at the request of the will of Alexandre Hoghton in whose household he had been an ineffectual tutor (Greenblatt 2004; Wilson 2004).[2] 'Sheikspeare!' exclaimed the Arab in delight. 'I like that.'[3]

To London, Bankside, and the world's first commercial theatre. A fortune made and the assemblage of a war machine whose nomadism and chivalric martial virtue bore such a kinship to the ancient tribes of Araby. In disguise … a Gothic invention.

Gothspeare

Shakespeare is a Gothic invention, a fiction. 'He' emerges as an effect of the modernity for which Gothic becomes fiction's purest modality, a language to infinity (Foucault 1977). While he invented nothing – or very little – apart from himself, Shakespeare has become the fictive name for the limitless horizon of an infinity of fictions that endlessly sustains both the modern myth of culture and its postmodern generalization in and as an aestheticized, 'objectivized and autonomized medium of exchange' that has 'created its own order' (Goux 1998: 48).

The eighteenth-century 'Gothic revivalists', Edward Young, Horace Walpole and Richard Hurd, are among those for whom the playwright served, against prevailing neoclassical taste, to distinguish natural, indigenous genius and imagination, thereby paving the way for a modern aesthetic. The new critical vocabulary in which Shakespeare became a paragon did not embrace Gothic forms for very long: Romanticism, in canonizing the Bard and elevating Nature and the Imagination to the pinnacle of aesthetic value, established itself on the basis of a fundamental exclusion of Gothic productions. The latter came to connote all that was low and base, all that could be associated with an unruly, undiscriminating mob, everything, indeed, that took the form of what would later be identified as popular culture. Significantly, in becoming the basis, the necessary antithesis, for the formation of modern Culture, the negative against which Romantic values could be asserted, Gothic forms delineated the conditions for aesthetic evaluation and remained in the shadow of high Romanticism.

Gothic forms, however, associated with the 'machinery' of non-organic, formulaic cultural productions from the start, do not simply remain as the inert opposition sustaining aesthetic categories, but manifest a popular machine of production which escapes the frame of both Culture and cultural studies. Raymond Williams and Stuart Hall, for instance, while contesting the bourgeois exclusions to which post-Romantic Culture gave rise, nonetheless endorse (with a socially inclusive, democratic materialism) modern cultural categories. The transformations of postmodernity render those categories redundant, trashing distinctions between high and low and diffusing any unifying imperative other than economic performance. Now, of course, Shakespeare serves as a leading brand in the heritage industry while Gothic, with its dark frisson of sex and death, serves as one locus of the 'belief market' where spectrality can be readily flipped into (lifestyle) spirituality: 'Gothspeare', in this context, signifies the com/modifications of a culture thoroughly homogenized by the new economy.

Walpole capitalized on the dramatic and sensational machinery of Shakespearean drama. But he was unable to control the effects – and affects – of his monstrous new species. Among the origins, fabricated though they may be, of Gothspeare, there remain assemblages, machinic rather than mechanical, that hint at a culture less easily assimilated or territorialized than the one supposedly imbued with the imaginative, spiritual and creative ideals so precious in contemporary capitalizations. Gothic, in the fictions of the nomadic Northern tribes or in Worringer's 'northern line' (Deleuze 1986: 51), traverses cultural and aesthetic borders with a deterritorializing force: its nomadism represents an anti-classical and anti-Roman war machine. It discloses anorganic and inhuman shapes and affects, that, while they appear to serve the abstract machine of an accelerated bourgeois culture and capital, turn the war machine of modern progress and Enlightenment inward, making culture, too, a machine of war in class, (trans)national and psychological terms. Such total war – as is evident in the totalizations of contemporary terror – threatens, and constitutes, the borders of all contemporary pseudo-innovations: of new technology, of new media, of New Labour, of the new universities, of the new economy and the new world order.

Prolific swarm

Nomadic, fierce, warlike, free, Gothic tribes roamed the cold climates of the Northern plains and forests, existing beyond the control of Roman imperial power. These tribes lived outside classical order, unbound by Roman codes, a 'free people' and a 'law unto themselves' (Kliger 1952: 20), their very identity multiple and in flux: Goths, Scythians, Scalds, Vandals, Huns, Saxons. Sir William Temple, contributing in 1695 to the Whig political and aesthetic history of the English, described these Gothic nations as 'swarming from the Northern Hive' (Kliger 1952: 7). The image was developed poetically in James Thomson's *The Seasons*:

> Wide o'er the spacious Regions of the North,
> That see *Boötes* urge his tardy Wain,
> A boisterous race, by frosty *Caucus* pierc'd,
> Who little Pleasure know and fear no Pain,
> Prolific Swarm. They once relum'd the Frame
> Of lost Mankind in polish'd Slavery sunk,
> Drove martial Horde on Horde, with dreadful Sweep

Resistless rushing o'er th' enfeedbled South,
And gave the vanquish'd World another Form.
(Thomson 1981: 'Winter', 834–42)

The 'prolific swarm', free, fearless and formless, descended upon soft Southern empires reduced to civilized subservience and excessive refinement. It becomes a potent notion in an eighteenth century whose Enlightenment is presented in neoclassical terms: it rekindles, out of the formlessness of 'swarm' and 'sweep', a glimpse of a stronger and prouder human form, attached to native traditions and liberties, unbowed by and unbound to any order imposed from without. It purveys a persistent counterpoint in narratives of modern cultural development: civilization, if too refined, weakens and corrupts itself, losing touch with the very natural, and savage, strengths, that, albeit in an ill-formed manner, enabled its emergence (while music may soothe the savage breast, the savage – both threat and potentiality – is never far away).

Other forms, too, are given to the world by the 'prolific swarm': political (Gothic liberty and parliament), legal (Gothic law) and romantic (chivalry and martial prowess) institutions. The swarm, nomadic and unbound, however, is a war machine that empires of powerful regimes would find it difficult to direct or control. 'Gothic government' appears oxymoronic: how can a fierce and warlike swarm give form to the world? For P.-H. Mallet, in his *Northern Antiquities*, the model derives from a mythologized idea of a bellicose spirit of freedom: characterized as prizing liberty above all else, and preserving it, to the death if need be, with force of arms, Gothic government emerges out of a warrior code. The marauding tribes upheld a (very English) notion of government 'dictated by good sense and liberty' and underpinned by 'a restless unconquered spirit, apt to take fire at the very mention of subjection and constraint, and a ferocious courage, nourished by a savage and vagabond life' (Mallet 1847: 56). The Goths' love of liberty and martial free spiritedness, their tradition of parliaments and chivalric codes, is translated by Whig historians of the eighteenth century into a myth of native Englishness upheld by the democratic freedoms of parliament and constitutional monarchy (Kliger 1952; Keane 1995).

While a prolific swarm is made to serve (against its own free character) a model of government and nation favoured by Whig political history, its re-emergence in the Enlightened and neoclassical eighteenth century is less easily – in aesthetic terms – contained: the appeal of the Goths, in terms of their chivalric and romantic characteristics, gave rise to an antiquarian movement. Mallet's English translator, Bishop Percy, collecting and publishing old English poetry and ballads, was among those not only recovering a native literary tradition: he was also establishing a different aesthetic line, one associated with the 'Gothic Revival' in architecture (Percy 1966). New poetry also took inspiration from the myth of the Goths: William Collins's 'The Bard' celebrated the tribal mediator and warrior of the Druids, proud singer of heroic songs and fierce defender of indigenous independence. Against the order, uniformity and harmony of imported classical geometric lines and regulated heroic couplets a native tradition was formed, to be associated with a wilder nature, with imagination and genius in which originality and emotion became prized over artful imitations of classical models (Young 1966: 10). Another 'bard' creeps upon the stage. Richard Hurd's re-evaluation of native culture, writing and customs moves away from neoclassical aesthetic judgements to celebrate the imagination, genius and originality of pre-classical writers: Shakespeare, of course, is high on Hurd's list of writers able to draw on the power and mystery of a less cultivated nature in the production of imaginative works (Hurd 1963: 93). From chivalry and romance – and their Arabic and Gothic forebears, the bards of old – to the power of the rediscovered 'bard of Avon', the line sketched by Hurd came to be emphasized in modern and high Cultural terms as a major contribution to Romantic Nature, Genius and Imagination.

On the way, however, there is another juncture, a convergence and divergence in the threads of political, cultural and aesthetic history in which Goth, romance and Romanticism head in high, low – and other – directions. Horace Walpole, son of a Whig Prime Minister and undistinguished MP himself, displayed a love of all things antiquarian, from old poetry and chivalric history to the ornate refinements of interior design and architecture. He also wrote the first 'Gothic story', combining the strands of historical setting (significantly, it is set in the period of the Crusades), chivalric custom (tales of honour, knights and patrilineal order) and architectural style (the castle is as much a protagonist as any character). *The Castle of Otranto* (1764) is notable, also, for its deference to the then still-to-be-rediscovered Shakespeare: ghost and phantom scenes from *Hamlet* and *Macbeth*, lovers' trysts in caves or on balconies (*Cymbeline* and *Romeo and Juliet*) add to a rapid dramatic repertoire of trap-doors, dungeons, duels and supernatural incident (Walpole 1982: xiii–xiv). In his discussions of the story, Walpole makes some very modern claims about the creative process, commenting that a dream served as the visionary inspiration for the tale and stating that the writing was driven by imagination and passion rather than critically approved rules of imitation. Shakespeare presides over the process: in the second Preface, in which Walpole, buoyed by the reception of his anonymously published tale admits authorship, the method of composition is outlined and the Bard's genius is celebrated as being of greater magnitude than that of Voltaire. It is the former from whom Walpole takes his bearings, England's 'brightest genius', who, in appropriate metaphorical strain, becomes a guiding star enabling Walpole's invention and originality, and giving him freedom to lay down new rules of composition and create a 'new species of romance' (Walpole 1982: 11–12).

Walpole's admission of authorship clearly imagines a high aesthetic flight for his new species. More than other antiquarians, who in recovering and re-evaluating the work of indigenous poets, chivalric customs and Northern bards promoted a new taste for a reconstructed feudal past, Walpole's antiquarian and bardic aesthetic accidentally stimulated an appetite that allowed another swarm to emerge: the 'new species of romance' creates the disturbing and monstrous hybrid that became known – and vilified – as the Gothic romance, that is, as Walpole's 'spawn' (Matthias 1805: 422). Emerging as a popular form in the mid-eighteenth century, Gothic fictions, defined against the morality of the novel, were attacked from neoclassical critical positions as signs of a 'flood' or 'torrent' of vicious aesthetic tastes, 'monsters' of undiscriminating fancy: they were seen to loose inappropriate imaginative and libidinal energies amongst young – and particularly female – readers and threaten the bonds of paternal authority maintaining familial and social structures (Williams 1970: 151–62). Romance and adventure, love and war set readerly fancies in flight, taking them beyond filial duty, propriety and subservience. As the century drew to a climactic close in continental revolution, sex and politics entwined literary judgements to the extent that the genre became part of literature's 'great engine' of subversion or conservation (Matthias 1805: 244). Walpole's new species – in its effects imagined more as monster than autochthonous product of native imaginative genius – was more mechanical than organic in form from the start: its narrative machinery and borrowed rude mechanicals, its supernatural devices and its engines of terror and excitement cranked up an array of formulas and sensation-inducing techniques that directly generated a sub-species of fiction for another fifty years. *The Castle of Otranto* loosed a war machine in which fascinations with feudal, martial and aristocratic class codes were seen to generate and use up excess energies in irrational, unproductive and immoral ways. Contained in part as the antithesis of a high Romantic trajectory – as 'frantic novels' (Wordsworth 1920: 936); or a delusional mechanism (Coleridge 1975: 28) – that would reach its apex in organic, spiritual and imaginative claims, the Gothic war machine – part monster, part swarm – continued to rumble among the shadowy realms of low culture.

Monster

Cultural Studies is a creature of Romanticism. The second chapter of *Culture and Society*, one in which Young's *Conjectures* are described as an 'early document' of Romanticism, outline the significance of the Romantic artist. Raymond Williams undoes the later nineteenth-century dissociation (itself 'in part a product' of Romantic aesthetics) in which the poet 'is by nature indifferent to the crude worldliness and materialism of politics and social affairs' and questions the assumption of the apparently 'disparate' activities of attending to either 'natural beauty' and 'personal feeling' or government and 'the nature of man in society' (Williams 1961). For Williams, Romanticism, as it engages an emerging middle-class reading public, makes no choice between 'poet or sociologist' but sees their fields as 'interlocking interests' with Wordsworth writing political pamphlets, Blake and Paine being tried for sedition, Coleridge writing political journalism and Percy Shelley distributing his own political diatribes. These activities were neither 'marginal nor incidental'; rather, they were integral to a Romantic idea of culture: 'a conclusion about personal feeling became a conclusion about society, and an observation on natural beauty carried a necessary moral reference to the whole, unified life of man' (Williams 1961: 48–49). Identified with a unified early Romanticism and occupying both its major fields of interest, Cultural Studies emerges as its effect and quietly absorbs Romantic oppositions in taking its bearings from a high line of critical and aesthetic judgement.

Another founding text of Cultural Studies, and one that sets out to investigate the distinctive features of working-class culture, replays the very judgements through which Romantic writers defined their own aesthetic project. Writing of the sex and violence of popular imported crime novels and of the popular US music played on jukeboxes in milkbars, Richard Hoggart describes the desultory audience: 'they form a depressing group and one by no means typical of working-class people; perhaps most of them are rather less intelligent than the average, and are therefore even more exposed than others to the debilitating mass-trends of the day' (Hoggart 1958: 248). While this audience typifies one version of the post-war mass of culture, its features – lower intelligence and a lack of aesthetic and moral discrimination that leave it unprotected against a deluge of formulaic and sensational texts – replay Romantic individualism's higher aspirations and its horror of the undiscriminating swarm of readers with their excitable appetites for delusional fictions. Hoggart's critical judgement presents his dismal representative working-class audience as the mirror and effect of the low and mass cultural productions they consume, defined by the modern entertainment machine around which they huddle. This ill-formed crowd, visually unappealing and intellectually dulled, an illustration of a mass that is little more than a side-effect of the homogenizing and demeaning machinery of 'mass-trends', also has its precursor in the judgements and oppositions arising from constructions of Gothic readerships and romances in the late eighteenth and early nineteenth centuries.

Walpole's 'new species', in becoming a monstrous spawn that loosed a variety of vicious, libidinal and anti-social energies among an emergent reading public, found itself consolidated as a threatening figure against which familial, social and political order reconstituted itself: the slow, lumbering monster, ill-formed and morally repugnant, took various shapes from revolutionary mob or 'swinish multitude' unleashed by radical ideas (Burke 1969: 173), to the wretched and disenfranchised mass excluded from the realm of rights, freedom and human dignity (Wollstonecraft 1989: 17). Though apparently stabilized in the Romantic oppositions of high and popular culture informing modern critical judgement, the misshapen energies underlying the opposition and the incoherence of what was informed as 'mass' or 'monster' disclosed a fundamental instability: the very formation of modern culture rested upon some Thing formless.

Telespeare

If Shakespeare were alive today he'd be hosting the 'Late Review' and chairing a heated debate about who was better, Keats or Dylan. In this debate, Shakespeare would smugly remind his guests that Shakespeare provides the standard by which all cultural evaluation is measured.

If Shakespeare were alive today he'd be what he is: an impassable horizon protecting the Anglo-American world from anything resembling culture. He's the buffer-zone protecting the Anglo-American world from the claims of any form of writing that struggles to generate a new mode of perception or a new image of thought (everything is always already in Shakespeare), just as he provides the point of demarcation that delegitimizes any form of popular cultural expression (nothing is more popular both in sales and in the affections of the groundlings than Shakespeare).

Shakespeare thus sustains the oppositional couplet, high–low culture, by being both and neither at the same time. Critical and cultural appropriations of Shakespeare, his name, work and myth, articulate multiple contradictory and conflicting positions within a given horizon. As such his fiction sustains a border that remains unstable, but also flexible within his large compass, site of the formation, reversal and dissolution of cultural values. 'Popular culture', as Stuart Hall's deconstruction elucidates, exemplifies this mode of disturbance as it is played out upon the 'Shakespearean' screen. In Hall's terms, set out in a similar historical period to that of Williams, 'popular culture' remains a shifting, contested and dynamic site: it does not lie outside the dominant formation of bourgeois modernity as an authentic set of traditional aesthetic and cultural practices specific to ethnic, regional or class groupings, practices either pushed aside by or resistant to the modern imposition of new forms. Instead it designates a 'locus of transformations', of containments and resistances rather than authentic working-class cultural forms (Hall 1992: 284–85). The subject of popular culture emerges in the eighteenth century in the Whig differentiation of polite civic society from a 'turbulent and ungovernable people', the latter threatening to erupt, 'yet never quite overturning the delicate strands of paternalism, deference and terror within which they were constantly, if insecurely constrained' (Hall 1992: 285). Locus of 'struggle', 'dialectic', 'battle', popular culture is shadowed by something monstrous, and Culture, for all its bourgeois, homogenizing intent, remains rife with the tensions and class antagonisms of its historical formation. As Hall develops Williams's dominant-emergent schema, 'emergent forces reappear in ancient historical disguise; emergent forces in pointing to the future, lose their anticipatory power, and become *merely backward looking*; today's cultural breaks can be recuperated as a support to tomorrow's dominant system of values and meanings' (Hall 1992: 289). The monstrosities associated with Gothic, for all their fabrications of an aristocratic, barbaric – yet romantic – past, press forwards to solidify as the necessary antithesis of bourgeois forms and judgements.

If Shakespeare were alive today he'd be writing a biography of Shakespeare entitled *How Shakespeare Became Shakespeare.*

Beneath or outside the confines of post-romantic opposition, something else rumbles, combining and unravelling in a process that exceeds attributions of the locus of opposition, of subversion or containment. Beneath these pressures, monstrous energies continually threaten, or shed their 'anticipatory power' to be commodified and assimilated. At the same time, the dynamic interplay of dominant and emergent forces allows the (albeit obscure) formless locus for other forces to appear. The question of excess (one of the threats monstrous metaphors are designed to fill) remains as an interior yet externalized disturbance. More than just class forces and oppositional movements are disclosed in the monstrous emergence of Gothic forms: mechanical metaphors and narrative machinery take on their own momentum in the technical emergence and disturbances of Gothic innovation in which the pulses and repulsions of terror and horror oscillate in relation to styles, cultural forms and media as much as content. Phantasmagoria, photographs, industrial automata, cinema, television and digital technologies look darkly backward and surge restlessly forward in form and effect, new media dressed up in old figures, spectres, fairies, doubles, monsters and vampires. Marshall McLuhan's 'rear-view mirrorism' seems to operate, describing a process whereby 'a new medium explores its potential in terms of the medium it is in the process of supplanting' (Hartley and Fiske 1978: 15). The medium is the machine, anticipatory and terrifying, monstrous and sublime. It'll possess you, disturb you, destroy you ... (*Poltergeist*; *Videodrome*; *The Ring*).

If Shakespeare were alive today he'd be writing *Coronation Street* or *EastEnders* or *Holby City* or *The Bill*.

If Shakespeare were alive today he'd be Stephen Fry ... Melvyn Bragg, Simon Cowell, Russell T. Davies, Germaine Greer or Meera Syal.

If Shakespeare were alive today he'd be Matt Groening, Martin Scorsese, Oprah Winfrey, Will Smith or Morgan Freeman playing God.

If Shakespeare were alive today he'd be the Cookie Monster on *Sesame Street* introducing Masterpiece Theatre.

If Shakespeare were alive today he'd be the Captain of the Starship Enterprise, making it so.

Since absorbing its mass audience, TV has flickered with the spectre of social and cultural decline. The trashing of culture has a longer history, however, and one in which late coming television only has a small and ambivalent part to play. TV does not necessarily destroy cultural values: as a 'social medium' (in McLuhan's terms), it brings groups together, the family, for instance, vocal and positive in their participatory spectatorship just like the audience for traditional Shakespearean theatre (Hawkes 1973: 230). Hawkes takes his bearings from S. L. Bethell's account of the 'multi-consciousness' of Shakespearean drama in which interpretation occurs on various levels as a kind of 'bricolage'. He goes on to suggest that contemporary theatre, in which little interaction occurs, has become bankrupt, while TV's 'new Globe' allows, among the chattering groups watching in various living rooms, a diverse and often complex process of producing social meanings (Hawkes 1973: 234). From Bethell's 'flourishing drama' as 'epiphenomenon of a flourishing and organic national culture' to TV as new Globe and new Bard (Hartley 2003: 49), the cultural studies line culminates in 'bardic television' as the locus for the mediation of cultural codes and conventions and social rituals: it is 'our own culture's bard' (Hartley and Fiske 1978: 85). The position, in which the bardscreen occupies the centre of oral, dynamic and mythical cultural communication, depends on a mass version of the medium, of a communication and reception of televised messages to groups who recognize their unity in the circulation and interpretation of coded messages.

But unity, like a nation, is forged in violence. Historically, bards waged war as well as glorifying martial triumph in song. And TV continues to function as a 'war machine for colonizing the soft mass of electronic mind', its swarmscreens serving a process of 'desensitization' and 'infantilization' and engendering a 're-energization' involving new schemes of sensational violence (Kroker and Kroker 1996: 6). Beyond the reflective frame of the rear-view mirror catching a new medium in the image of the old, swarms replace the shock functions of mechanical cultural reproduction with an anaesthesia of events and an escalation of mediated sensations.

If Shakespeare were alive today he'd be Geraldo Rivera on Fox News (working secretly for Al Jazeera).

11 September 2001

Barely glancing at CNN flickering on wall-mounted screens, B. Murray Bezumi took a sip of strong, black coffee in the Windows of the World restaurant on the 107th floor of the World Trade Center. He was having a breakfast meeting with Mohammed Zibrab, literary scholar from Tunisia. Zibrab was talking about Sheikh Zoubeir's last play, *The Tempest*, and his departure from London shortly after its debut in 1611. 'Most scholars accept that *The Tempest* is Shakespeare's valedictory play, an extended metaphor for his life, art and practice. It is even accepted that here, for the first time, in a play for once without a known literary source, the poet comes somewhere close to the surface, in the form of Prospero, the magician and great playwright, and Zoubeir's shadowy form can at last be discerned. The Americans of course consider the play to be about the colonization of the New World, but it is not so. Prospero, banished by a usurping brother, had set sail from Milan to Tunis, only to be beset by Barbary pirates and a storm. It is the story of Sheikh Zoubeir's trajectory in reverse, presaging his return to North Africa. And while he breaks the staff that conducts the dramatic action of his plays, ending his career in London, this is only to pick up a gun and return to Tunis to foment revolution.'

Bezumi looked incredulous, if not a little bemused.

'Don't take my word for it. Listen to the words of the great Shakespearean scholar Richard Wilson. Zoubeir had been funding insurrectionary pirates in terrorist actions on the Barbary Coast for years. He was in league with the English pirate Jack Ward, who, with Zoubeir's finances, introduced gun powder to the rebels in Tunis. As Wilson says, "Prospero's magic occupies the metaphoric space of gunpowder in the symbolic logic of the play." I quote Wilson:

> Prospero is that 'gentleman of fortune', a king of the pirates: 'The only fear and terror of the cruel pirates of Argier / That damned train the scum of Africa'. … the most obvious discursive context of this brigandage was not American propaganda but the death sentence decreed by James I for 'carrying munition to Algiers and Tunis', and on pirates who 'commit foul outrages, murders, spoils and

depradations within the Mediterranean, to the great offence of our friends and extreme loss to our merchants'.

(Wilson 2004: 208)

Mohammed Zibrab pulled up a briefcase and laid it out before Bezumi on the breakfast table. 'When Zoubeir returned to Tunis, the rebellion did not go well. It failed and he was killed, but certain manuscripts were preserved and kept hidden. Eventually they made it to the Bibliothèque Nationale in Tunis, but have lain neglected for centuries. It is a very ramshackle place. You have to know where to look – and how to steal. I have here the complete works of Sheikh Zoubeir. The complete works of Shakespeare, but in the original Arabic. They are infinitely more beautiful in the original. Those plays the English and the Americans have are barbarous translations, crabbed, crude awkward constructions that – and this is well known and accepted by true scholars – generations of editors have had to labour to clean up, edit and render comprehensible. You will find them quite remarkable.'

Bezumi blinked. 'These are the originals?'

'Yes, they are absolutely incendiary, and they come at a serious price.'

Bezumi leaned forward to take the package just as the first plane hit.

And those cloud-capped towers, like the baseless fabric of his vision, were melted into air, into thin air, leaving not a rack behind.

Cybergothspeare

A ghostly figure haunts the bandwidth of network-centric terror, demanding revenge. What does Shakespeare look like reinvented in the realms of cybergothsphere? Cybergothic seems to look backwards, throwing old dark-dressed figures into the path of barely visible swarms arriving from a machinic future: the necromancy of human histories, fears and horrors becomes a neuromancy of nervous information systems careering beyond cybernetic control circuits. Take the replicants, zombies and terminators of now-passed future dystopias: they look a bit Gothic in their wasted black chic, but apart from their camouflage they have nothing even darkly human about them: they form 'a self organizing insidious traumatism, virtually guiding the entire biological desiring-complex towards post-carbon replicator usurpation' (Land 1993: 479). 'Suddenly it's everywhere: a virtual envelopment by recyclones, voodoo economics, neonightmares, death-trips, skin-swaps, teraflops, Wintermute-wasted Turing cops, sensitive silicon, socket-head subversion, polymorphic hybridizations, descending data-storms, and cyborg catwomen stalking amongst the screens' (Land 1993: 479–82).

Cybergothic returns, not from a past or a comfortably repressed psyche but from a terroristic, terminating and machinic future where an 'affirmative telecommercial dystopianism' holds sway and where 'vampiric transfusional alliance cuts across descensional filiation, spinning lateral webs of haemo-commerce. Reproductive order comes apart into bacterial and intergalactic sex, and libino-economic interchange machinery goes micro-military' (Land 1998: 80; 86–87). More swarms: 'the trauma of exclusions and inclusions was always a spectacular distraction. Only multiplicities, decolonized ants, swarms without strategies, insectoid freeways burrowed through the screens of spectacular time' (Ccru, 'Swarmachines'). Such 'swarms without strategies' burrow, pulse and gather under the screens of gothspeare's cultural war machine where 'the fusion of the military and the entertainments industry consummates a long engagement: convergent TV, telecoms, and computers sliding mass software consumption into neojungle total war' (Land, 'Meltdown'). These swarms, as formless and devastating as the Goths' destruction of empire, cannot be captured as 'multitude', the mirror and other of Empire's global network: they are not recuperable in any, even residually, human form as the basis of a new society. In this respect, Hardt and Negri are far too nostalgic in their vision of 'new vampires' and 'new monsters' being able 'to form new, alternative networks of affection and social organization'. That 'Frankenstein is now a member of the family' is no guarantee of a new monstrous humanity forming itself from the swarms ransacking the networks themselves (Hardt and Negri 2006: 193–95).

Is Cybergothspeare a residual monster bard prattling of lost human heritage? An autopoiOedipal defence against the machinic eclipse of complex human culture (Hamilton Grant)? Or some kind of hamletmachine worn out by its oedipuscidal revenge program? A high cultural alibi, even, for the swarms of sensation-repulsion-horror splattered on the screens of adaptation and revision? Strangely, perhaps, that most complex of cultural creatives becomes, in an age of cybernetics, singularly uninformative: if information is a 'difference that makes a difference' (in Bateson's pithy definition) then the works of the bard are too full of quotations (as Norbert Wiener noted) to send anything like a new message (Bateson 1973: 286). Cybergothspeare – from bardbiz to brandbard and beyond – thus circulates almost homogeneously over unimaginable swarms, absorbing their unbound patterns of bacterial and informational inmixing, without anchor or history, off-message and beyond sense. In the mash-media of cyber-gothspeare, Shakespeare may look the same at the same time as the quotes become de-textualized, rewired and teletargeted to different demographic groups in the manner of an Amazon book recommendation or an online newspaper story selection, sometimes soothing, sometimes the timely topical line and sometimes horror-excitement-thrill.

28 January 2011

Dream team Salahuddin. They attack at dawn with sonic horns, their phonic guns scoring Quranic forms across the Manhattan skyline. Sufis surfing on boards of steel, laser scimitars coded zikr slice through American defences, reformatting all resistance. Takbirs from cyborg mujahids, AI imams electro du'a, robotic maidens of paradise swarm across the Eastern seaboard in mechanoid martyrdom sacrifice. Sunnah troopers from crescent starship shabab clones, ranks of Ibrahim tanks hook up with the Islamic-American insurgency. They activate the Saracens and annihilate the Pharoah's sons, slaying the riba first, the money lenders, the bank elite. The Statue of Liberty falls prostrate.

Now jihadi jetskis patrol the Hudson River on mechanical Moorish tours of duty with Deen machines and replicant Sufis. The Islamic elders consult and direct the citizens, in honour of the martyrs of 9/11, to build a mosque on Ground Zero (Fun'da'mental, 'All is War', 2006).

But there is another suggestion. Opposite the mosque, but within the grounds of the cleared site, plans are made to build a replica of Sheikh Zoubeir's Globe [theatre], the 'Wooden O' inscribing, architecturally, the zero that grounds the new culture of Islamic-America, even as it links it like a ring with the past. Sheikh Zoubir becomes official poet of the Islamic Republic of America. And alongside the sword of Islamic justice, the quality of Sheikh Zoubeirian mercy drops like gentle rain from heaven.

Notes

1 These would become in London the core of the Lord Chamberlain's Men, the company for whom Shakespeare wrote his early plays.
2 It is not certain what happened to the young Shakeshafte, but he did not stay long with the players because by August 1581 he was on his way back to his home town of Stratford. A document in the possession of the Bishop of Worcester's registry dated 28 November 1582, representing a considerable bond enabling the shotgun wedding of young 'William Shagspeare' to 'Anne Hathwey', already three months pregnant, suggests that the libidinal young man quickly lived up to his name only to repent in leisure for the rest of his life in provincial obscurity.
3 What probably appealed to Sheikh Zoubeir about the name was not only its homonymic quality, but the fact that 'Zoubeir' in the Tunisian dialect offers the same bawdy potential as 'spear' or 'shaft' in English.

11 Afterword

The 'grounds' of the Shakespeare–Gothic relationship

Jerrold E. Hogle

Ever since Horace Walpole 'sheltered my own daring under the canon' of the 'genius' Shakespeare in his 1765 Preface to the Second Edition of *The Castle of Otranto* (Walpole 2003: 70), there has been no doubt that the 'Gothic Story', in nearly all the forms it has taken then and since, has been deeply influenced by Shakespeare's plays. Nonetheless, the preceding essays have still revealed many hitherto unnoticed relationships between Shakespeare and the Gothic mode. We shall henceforth have to view both 'the Bard' and 'the Gothic' quite differently than we have – and very much by way of how they illuminate each other. We now see, for example, that the Gothic can help us retroactively define some of Shakespeare's own dramatic and symbolic choices. On the one hand: while we know that many Walpole contemporaries and the eighteenth-century criticism of Shakespeare took ideologically motivated liberties with the already floating term 'Gothic', transposing it from a 'barbarous' negative into an 'authentically old English' positive (see Clery 2002: 25–30), Steven Craig has reminded us that Shakespeare's ideological sense of what 'Gothic' encompasses, as in the Goth characters of *Titus Andronicus* (1593–94), is 'a set of superstitions and enchantments' imposed by 'migrant barbarians who plunged the civilized world into darkness', however complex their actual history, much as Italian Renaissance historiographers had already said in trying to rescue the best of classical Rome from what they thought had decimated and degraded it. The counter-movement that valued *up* a greatly recast 'Gothic' in England after 1740, Craig helps us recall, was part of an anti-Royalist effort of that time to reconstitute the English past and then label its National Poet 'Gothic' so as to re-present both as symbolizing values that some British Whigs, including Walpole among others, were claiming to restore in the face of what they saw as Continental corruptions infecting the English crown.

On the other hand: Elisabeth Bronfen has convinced us here that 'night' is a 'privileged stage for transgressions' of daytime official culture in

Shakespeare and therefore serves as a wide-ranging 'heterotopic counter-site' for him. In his night, there are just as many blurrings of boundaries and beings and just as much drifting of desires across wildly different bodies and images as there are in the most sequestered, unlit, antiquated and dream-like spaces, often the 'subterraneous regions' or primeval woods (Walpole 2003: 82–86 and 127–33), of Gothic fictions from *Otranto* to *Frankenstein* to *Night of the Living Dead*. We do not realize how thoroughly pre-Gothic Shakespeare is, in other words, until we look back through the Gothic to his most similar motifs and tendencies. That is why Robert Miles and Michael Gamer can see the Bard's blatant skewing of historical sources to serve Tudor-era concerns and his own world view appearing behind the same tendencies in W. H. Ireland's *Vortigern* of 1796. After it was presented as one of Shakespeare's recovered plays and once this 'forgery' was discovered, it turns out, *Vortigern* was condemned for being both 'Germanic' and 'Jacobin', as well as too Gothic, in orientation precisely because it really does echo Shakespeare's partial deference and half-resistance to the most settled ideologies of his own day. A similar retrospection also explains why Peter Hutchings can see the generic instability increasingly apparent in post-1930 films that rework Shakespeare and the Gothic, often both of them at once, as reminding us of a near-breakdown of genre-boundaries already there in Shakespeare's own works, the very one about which there were complaints from strict neo-classicists of his time (Greenblatt 2004: 296–98) as well as those of the seventeenth and eighteenth centuries. Retrospective revelations even appear in the daring 'Gothspeare' essay by Fred Botting and Scott Wilson. True, for them the most current, uprooted, commodified and widely circulating fragments from both Shakespeare and the Gothic keep combining and recombining in our cyberspace world, even to the point of blending into 'Gothspeare' at times. By doing so, they show the potentials in these remnants for turning into a cross-cultural mixture of discourses retroactively rewriting the very cultural foundations of the Bard himself. But that is only because Shakespeare, Botting and Wilson admit, crossing between supposedly 'high' and 'low' levels of his culture by slipping between the many different genres of writing and performing he knew, played out to an unusual degree the struggle between the symbolic schemes by which his and any culture always tries to stabilize itself, using both older forms, on the one hand, and the cross-generic re-combination of signs that enables the very reworking of past symbols upon which stability depends, on the other.

At the same time, these and other essays in this collection are equally powerful in redefining what occurs in the Gothic itself when it re-uses Shakespearean ingredients, particularly as they offer the Gothic both the attraction of long-standing traditions and a tradition of transforming older

sources to suit newer systems of belief. Dale Townshend traces the reap-
pearances of the Ghost of Hamlet's Father, a proto-Gothic symbol of the
supposedly quintessential Shakespeare (since the Bard probably played the
part), as it keeps asserting itself amid the many seventeenth- and eighteenth-century attempts to bowdlerize Shakespeare's plays to emerge, particularly in the Gothic, as a figure for the 'culturally patriotic' and 'familiar
and native' even as it is also 'emptied out of spiritual meaning and handed
over to the commercial economies of spectacle and popular entertainment'
in a Europe increasingly controlled by the bourgeois middle-class market.
The nostalgia in this image, heavily used by Walpole in particular, urges
its post-1760 employers to seek a re-grounding of it in verifiable deaths
and bodies that can actually be mourned, rather than in older religious
principles, Townshend shows. Yet this same quest, he goes on to reveal,
turns the neo-Gothic reuuses of such images into marketable 'veilings and
sublimations of death' that never really satisfy the longings underlying
them in the modern subject's movement across symbols so perceptively
analysed in the twentieth century by Sigmund Freud, Jacques Lacan and
Julia Kristeva, among others. Sue Chaplin, in turn, starts with how theatrical performances in Shakespeare are often like juridical trials, whether
or not they are out-and-out courtroom scenes, and how these are refash-
ioned in Walpole's Gothic as 'spectral juridico-literary spaces' pressuring
characters to uncover or reveal long-hidden guilty secrets. For her, the
configurations of these spaces, in part because they refer back to
Shakespeare to authorize them, announce the fictiveness of their construction – and hence the fabricated nature of law and jurisprudence,
despite their claims of a deep-rooted 'authenticity' – even more than
Shakespearean theatricality did. Such Gothic spaces, in fact, need to be
rooted in some prior and invisible crime, retrospectively if not originally,
because that same supposition has proved to be necessary in the 'juridical
discourse' of the eighteenth century (as in Blackstone's 1765 *Commentaries*)
which seeks to 'transform' a supposedly 'authentic national legal romance
tradition' (the mythical 'Gothic constitution' of England) into a seemingly
'enlightened modern rule of law' much as Walpole proposes to 'blend the
two kinds of romance, the ancient and the modern'.

These insights, thankfully, reveal the Gothic, from the eighteenth
through to the twenty-first century, as being far more unsettled, complex,
and in touch with cultural changes (the way we currently see Shakespeare)
than many of its explicators once thought it to be. Angela Wright can now
show us that Ann Radcliffe's frequent uses of Shakespeare during the
tempestuous transition of the 1790s into the 1800s are not as single-
minded and anti-supernatural as some critics have assumed. Wright
recovers evidence that Radcliffe's deployments of Shakespeare changed

204 Jerrold E. Hogle

considerably with her reactions to a Western cultural landscape in constant transformation. What her epigraphs from him suggest in *The Romance of the Forest* (1791) is greatly altered in the more internal echoes of the Bard in her late *Gaston de Blondeville* (ca. 1802–3) published posthumously in 1826 with her important dialogue on the legacy of Shakespeare excerpted in the *New Monthly Magazine* as 'On the Supernatural in Poetry'. In both *Gaston* and the dialogue, Radcliffe embraces, first, even a *Hamlet*-esque ghost as a sign of her sense that the current English government has broken from a more just past that now haunts it and, second, a more deliberate, quasi-Shakespearean staginess in her writing as a hint that a social 'authenticity' has decayed in favour of a sheer 'performativity and artifice' in England as it is coming to be. To be sure, Glennis Byron may seem to be redirecting our attention to a more simplified use of the Gothic and Shakespeare when she turns to the recent and still ongoing 'Twilight' series of teen vampire romances by Stephenie Meyer, which began in 2005. But instead Byron shows that the ideological conflicts embedded into this new cross between *Romeo and Juliet* (1595–96) and an ever-changing Gothic vampire tradition are, however current, just as vexed and unresolved as we find in Radcliffe's self-revisions or in many parts of Shakespeare's own most pre-Gothic dramas.

After all, Byron reminds us, Shakespeare's own Romeo finds his and Juliet's conflicted situation so draining that he laments how much 'Dry sorrow drinks our blood' (3.5.59), and Meyer combines this hint anew with the recent phenomenon of adolescents being rendered as vampires so as to make her young lovers and rivals seem both truly post-Shakespearean and highly marketable as embodiments of present-day cultural quandaries affecting teens especially. Indeed, by linking the Gothicized marketability of a somewhat hollowed-out *Romeo and Juliet* to the very modern belief that teen rebellion and sexuality are just naturally 'in the blood', Meyer can offer us complicated girls and boys caught right now, not just between updated versions of old class or family conflicts, but between 'love as a cultural construction' in popular representations that suck the life out of what they counterfeit and 'love as instinctual, spontaneous, and experi-enced on the body', an agonizing tug-of-war between very different incli-nations. It is no wonder, then, that the essays immediately surrounding Byron's near the close of this collection draw out the 'reversal and dis-solution of' as well as the renewed search for 'cultural values' in Gothic fictions of the last sixty years (to quote Botting and Wilson), particularly as those 'Gothics' simultaneously lose many of their old anchors in Shakespeare and yet play off his works as 'points of demarcation that delegitimize any form of popular cultural expression' (again Botting and Wilson) much as the Bard often did on his own. *That* tug-of-war is what enables Hutchings to celebrate Gothic films since 1930 as both expressing an 'elegy for a lost style' and enacting cross-generic disruptions that address inconsistent 'commercial pressures and audience tastes'. It is also what encourages Botting and Wilson to see the post-modern Gothic as well as revivals of the Bard as 'turning the war machine of modern progress and enlightenment inward', as Shakespeare himself began to in half-affirming and half-questioning the dominant ideologies and class-boundaries of his day, to critique and break down the war-inducing 'borders of all contemporary pseudo-innovations' so as to move them towards the new cultural interrelations that might really change the world for the better.

Even so, I now have to wonder, what are the factors that most fundamentally make these newly revealing arguments about the Shakespeare–Gothic relationship possible from the start? Why, in fact, has this relationship remained so basic both to the genesis of the post-Renaissance 'Gothic' in Walpole and his many successors and to the development of the numerous variations on the Gothic since that never quite silence the echo of Shakespeare in them? I want to bring these discussions to a momentary close by suggesting some of the possible answers to those questions. What I here propose, in fact, may help 'bookend' the pieces between this Afterword and John Drakakis's Introduction by furthering the powerful suggestions that Drakakis makes there as he provides an over-arching history of the different forms taken by the Gothic re-use of Shakespeare. These forms, Drakakis rightly shows, when examined closely, are almost always dialectal and ironic, countering one tendency in them with its opposite or near-opposite, whatever their different emphases. Gothic replays of Shakespeare, to summarize Drakakis's examples, can 'historicize' themselves by alluding to the Bard and yet 'de-historicize' both his work and themselves by presenting their combination as 'universal' in transcending (while invoking) the time-gap between Shakespeare and the Gothic; they can use him to resurrect a past 'ground' that gives the Gothic cultural capital to do what it does, but they can still uproot that source to make it refer to more contemporary concerns, thereby echoing the very Shakespeare the Gothic thus violates; they can invoke a Gothic-ized Bard to call up the ideology of a more 'natural' old England yet also to emphasize the theatrical artificiality of the words and postures being recast; and they can both venerate Shakespeare as a point of departure and proceed to dismantle his assumptions, bringing forward an initially 'canonical' set of quotations to then appropriate them in a way that rejects at least part of the Shakespeare 'canon'. In all these dialectical actions in the Gothic, I find, this literature of terror and horror reveals an interplay of contradictions very much *in* Shakespeare in partly similar and partly different ways. There is a tug-of-war at levels of both ideology and symbology in his plays that the Gothic both repeats and transforms in its own variations on an 'ancient–modern' dialectic. Indeed, we can see self-questioning dialectics always active in both Shakespeare and the Gothic separately and together, at a number of different levels I would now like to specify. These make up the 'common ground' of the Shakespeare–Gothic relationship, I would argue, precisely because each dialectic 'un-grounds' its own 'grounds' internally. Each is driven, after all, by the inconsistent cultural pressures of its time and place and by the creative or re-creative capacities and the conflicted beliefs of the authors involved, be they Shakespeare himself or the most influential figures (including filmmakers) in the long, unstable, and ever-shifting lineage of the 'Gothic Story'.

Walpole's interplays of what he calls 'ancient' and 'modern', we must remember, point in his second Preface and *Otranto* not just to the different styles and assumptions of the once-aristocratic and supernatural romance, such as *The Fairie Queene* of Shakespeare's time, and the middle-class-oriented 'realism' of the eighteenth-century novel from Defoe to Smollett. They also help indicate what *Otranto* is most basically about, as E. J. Clery has shown us: a 'contradiction between the traditional [aristocratic] claims of landed property and the new [increasingly bourgeois] claims of the modern family; a conflict between two versions of economic "personality" that provoke a hesitation over what rightly determines the foundations of the early modern self' (Clery 1995: 77). Within this quandary so key to the genesis of the modern Gothic, which goes on to nearly always combine backward-looking and future-oriented longings all at once, Walpole's enlarged, armoured, fragmented ghost of Alfonso, Otranto's original owner, and the reanimated, silent ghost of the portrait of Prince Manfred's grandfather, ultimately exposed as Alfonso's poisoner, usurper and the counterfeiter of his false will – both of which recall the more fully embodied and speaking Ghost in *Hamlet* – are at best hollowed-out, entirely artificial, and mostly voiceless bearers of the 'true' aristocratic inheritance and descent that are trying to resurface from decades of burial.

As such, Walpole's Gothic ghosts offer, in the words of John Allen Stevenson, 'an image of the immortality of kingship [or at least landed nobility] and of the necessity and justice of removing bad kings' (Stevenson 1990: 107) who may have violated such 'social contracts' as the Magna Carta of 1215, which the Whig Horace Walpole proudly hung near his bed in his quasi-Gothic house at Strawberry Hill (Kallich 1971: 34). Walpole manifestly reworks the 'old but by no means dead idea of a king with two bodies' (Stevenson 1990: 93) that distinguished the natural person of a particular monarch or noble from the ongoing idea or general image of the monarchy itself. This image, as in the encrypted effigy of Alfonso or the portrait of Manfred's grandsire, ensures perpetual social continuity, but with the option for the people to replace any occupant viewed as 'usurping' the role. Walpole in one of his many letters, we find, saw himself as a 'quiet republican' who preferred that the 'shadow of monarchy, like Banquo's ghost [in Shakespeare's *Macbeth*], fill the empty chair of state', and thus maintain a vague grounding in a continuous order of traditions (cit., Clery 1995: 72), instead of its being occupied by a tyrannical denier of legitimate public rights and entrepreneurial initiative. Otherwise, Walpole could hardly say what he does in his second *Otranto* Preface. There he justifies his anachronistic use of 'unnatural … machines' (Walpole 2003: 65), including the medieval Catholic images, such as the effigy, that are declared to be empty 'superstition' in his more guarded (but clearly Anglican) *first* Preface (2003: 59). He declares that he has the entrepreneur's 'liberty to expatiate [with such anachronisms] through the boundless realms of invention' (2003: 65) using a 'fancy' now 'reinstrumentalized by the operations of the [largely middle-class] market' to create a 'new route' in fiction that is 'commercially up-and-coming' (Clery 1995: 65) while not a total rejection of the Shakespearean images that it re-uses in attractive and nostalgic, but also emptied-out, ways.

Shakespeare's Ghost of the Father in the original *Hamlet* (1600–1601), as it happens, is only slightly more substantial than Walpole's hollow and more fragmented recastings of it, primarily because it brings with it its own conflict of sixteenth-century ideologies. Even this recognizable Ghost, as Hamlet says on first seeing him, 'com'st in such a questionable shape' that the Prince hesitates between believing that it bears 'airs from heaven' that offer 'charitable' truth and concluding that it carries 'blasts from hell' that might deceive him because of the 'intents wicked' of a 'goblin damn'd' (*Hamlet* 1.4.40–43).[1] As several scholars have cautioned us (see Curran 2006: 3–14), Shakespeare's Danish Prince and his play were positioned, like most members of their audience in 1600, as caught between a now-unsanctioned, but still popular, Catholic view of ghosts as speakers of truth, especially if they were returnees from Purgatory (as the *Hamlet* Ghost claims to be without using the word) – a concept that the Church of England officially rejected more than many of its members did – and a more Protestant position that sees ghosts as 'demons in disguise who assumed human form in order to achieve a devilish purpose' (Frye 1984: 17; see also Greenblatt 2001). Hamlet later feels he must 'have grounds / More relative than' what the Ghost has told him to prove that his uncle Claudius usurped the throne after poisoning his father (2.2.603–4), because no one on the stage or in the audience ever resolves the irresolution among beliefs through which the Ghost is viewed. Act V of *Hamlet* does invoke a vaguely overarching but hidden 'providence' that may encompass all or only some of these stances (5.2.219–20), but that mystery just momentarily suspends more than it decides the basic contention among beliefs at the end of the sixteenth century, and even this Catholic–Protestant debate is not the only factor in Hamlet's quandaries about the Ghost. Just before he decides his method of establishing 'grounds more relative', Shakespeare's Prince acknowledges that a devilish spirit may have come to him 'Out of my weakness and my melancholy' (2.2.601). He hesitates again, now between Protestant options whereby such a spectre could be the projection of an internal state of mind, like the 'dagger' that Macbeth seems to see before him (2.1.33–35), or could be a way the devil has of externally attaching a 'shape' to 'melancholy' because he may be 'potent with such spirits', as though melancholy were more of a spiritual energy than a personal emotion (2.2.602). To help 'ground' its Janus-faced tug-of-war between conflicting ideologies and the kinds of 'personalities' they envision, Walpole's inaugural 'Gothic Story' alludes to a Ghost in *Hamlet* that was itself a contested symbol into which was projected an earlier but equally unresolved set of contradictory positions.

Indeed, by seeing its primary inspiration as Shakespeare's *Hamlet*, which Alexander Pope had already classified as the Bard's most 'Gothick' work (Pope 1725: xxii–iv), the first Gothic Story takes as a principal reference point a play with a title character who is bedevilled by *many* belief systems pulling in both retrograde and progressive directions. Shortly before he first views the Ghost, Shakespeare's Prince complains about the noisy revels that the new King Claudius has ordered upon his dubious accession to the throne, and he does so by using ideological touchstones of 1600 that could not be more at odds with each other. Hamlet likens this 'heavy-headed' practice in the body politic to a 'vicious mole of nature' in 'particular men' (1.4.17–24). This 'mole' can possibly be a predestined 'stamp of one defect, / Being nature's livery, or fortune's star', the preference of an old aristocratic ideology that saw character as predetermined by the class into which Heaven and Nature placed a person. Concurrently, though, the same 'mole' can be 'some habit, that too much o'er-leavens / The form of plausive manners' and leads to 'general censure' by a person's spectators (1.4.23–36), a more rising bourgeois view in, say, Shakespeare's class that allowed the developing self to become what he or she can persuade an audience he or she was by how personal behaviour (one's chosen 'rhetoric') led to applause or 'censure' for one's 'manners'.

No wonder Walpole's Prince Manfred, like many Gothic heroes and heroines after him, is torn between 'personalities', questioning whether he should be driven more by the 'circumstances of his fortune' or by the 'natural … temper' of what seem his own inclinations (Walpole 2003: 87). His and Walpole's main models are a Prince and a whole setting, vaguely medieval Denmark as reconceived around 1600, that are permeated by ideological contests about the very basis of character as much as the nature of ghosts – and about a great deal more besides. Hamlet's many debates with himself include the pull of family-avenging-attacks-on-family by a waning feudal standard, on the one hand, and the central-monarchy-and-Church-of-England pressure to leave revenge to either heaven or the state, on the other, virtually the same imperatives that tear at each other in *Romeo and Juliet*. Even the idea of the 'king with two bodies', though more fully problematized in *King Lear* (1605), is as contested in *Hamlet* as it is for Walpole. While Hamlet may feel that his father, the figure apparently still visible in the Ghost, embodies a 'combination and a form indeed, / Where every god did seem to set his seal' to establish a standard by which a man may be a monarch, thus making Claudius too like a 'mildewed ear' to embody that divinely-sanctioned idea (3.4.60–64), the same Prince, in endorsing his own royal successor as he dies, finally accepts the process of the 'election' of a King by the same council of representatives that originally put Claudius on the throne, whatever the general standard of the time (5.2.355–56). The main 'Gothick' reference points for Walpole's Gothic, it turns out, are a play, author and cultural milieu that are all as extremely betwixt and between as his new kind of English fiction, its would-be-aristocratic yet also-entrepreneurial author (Clery 1995: 75), and the likely audience for both in 1764–65.

To be sure, being pressured and pulled by conflicting ideologies does not lead Walpole to take exactly the same positions as Shakespeare seems to, even in *Hamlet*; after all, over a century-and-a-half of social changes have intervened between Shakespeare's most pre-'Gothick' writings and *The Castle of Otranto*. While *Hamlet* may defer its ultimate solutions to the workings of a very obscure Providence and at least play with the possibility of some of the Catholic ideas it includes, Walpole in his *Castle* pointedly declares the groundlessness of *all* its Catholic anachronisms, even the quasi-Shakespearean ones, in his first Preface. As a result, the climactic moment in *Otranto* where a kind of providence apparently declares itself – the rising and brief pronouncement of the 'immense', reunified Ghost of Alfonso and its ascent 'towards heaven, where … the form of saint Nicholas was seen … receiving Alfonso's shade' as though that scene were in a fresco on a Catholic dome (Walpole 2003: 162) – is a moment where any metaphysical truth in it is absolutely denied in advance by the author. Even the Ghost's final statement about 'Theodore' as true heir has to be subsequently verified by a supposedly 'authentic writing' (2003: 164), itself as obscure and invisible as *Hamlet*'s 'providence'. The general 'shadow' of sanctioned inheritance, like the vague, ghostly outline of 'monarchy' endorsed in Walpole's letters, retains some validity, however problematic, in *Otranto* while many of this final spectacle's Catholic accoutrements and other links to older institutions are presented and even longed for but are pre-emptively invalidated.

Walpole wrote, not for a Shakespearian audience torn between various Christian interpretations of ghosts and sanctions for kingship, revenge and character, but for an eighteenth-century readership for whom 'mobile property, bound up in the unstable, "imaginary", mechanisms of speculation and credit, was [becoming] a threatening alternative to the [old] system of heritable wealth derived from land … which laid claim to the values of stability … by avoiding the abstraction of capital investment and profit' (Clery 1995: 74). The best ideological solution to *this* tug-of-war, which *Otranto* attempts, since mere deference to a general 'providence' may now mean an endorsement of 'speculation', is an assurance of secure inherited property fictively *analogous* to older aristocratic guarantees. The resulting analogies thus have to employ the figures of receding beliefs, but they do so alongside some more modern independence from strictly kingdom-based and Catholic-church-based controls that were only beginning to loosen in Shakespeare's day. Even so, this way of addressing 'a specific crisis in the experience of [Walpole's] eighteenth-century audience' that was in danger of distancing the aspirations of the 'self' based on older ideologies from the 'social forms' now driven by a pre-industrial market (Clery 1995: 79) locates its starting point in an Elizabethan 'genius' who struggles with an earlier but similar crisis of understanding where retrospective aristocratic and prospective middle-class beliefs were just as much in conflict and just as inclined to divide between them the means by which a viable 'self' could find self-definition and inheritable foundations.

To put all this in a more traditional way: Shakespeare is the premiere dramatist of a major, complex transition between the holdovers of medieval schemes for selfhood and social order and the emergence of early-modern aspirations towards freer-standing and more apparently self-determined modes of self-production and self-marketing. He enunciates the dawn of modernity in the West or what Harold Bloom calls the 'invention of the human' as we know it (see Bloom 1998: 1–17), often through employing older forms of expression, such as Saxo Grammaticus' thirteenth-century history of 'Amleth'. If the Bard does that half-regressively, he also does it at least half-progressively by rejecting some of his sources' founding assumptions, sometimes violating established generic limits in the process, yet always at least minimally within the boundaries usually acceptable to English Renaissance audiences and censors. For the Gothic to be effectively a 'new species of writing' from the 1760s on that can deal imaginatively with what pulls eighteenth-century and subsequent readers towards both 'ancient' and 'modern' beliefs as articulated at *their* time, it can do no better than start at his most 'Gothick' with the best-known and most prestigious articulator of 'clashing realizations' and 'primal ambivalence' (Bloom 1998: 7 and 11). Yes, the Gothic Story must resituate what it echoes for a wider readership of greater literacy across more classes in a more print-based culture driven by less censored and more open-market circulation, all after intervening adaptations and critiques of the Bard have questioned the solidity of Shakespeare's classical and religious groundings and his suitability for emerging middle-class tastes, while also re-establishing him as an English standard both 'Gothick'-ly 'natural' and timelessly enduring. Nevertheless, the Gothic achieves its looking both backwards and forwards by grounding itself in the deracination yet strong recollection of past schemes in Shakespeare when he is at his most inclusive in dramatizing the ideological quandaries of his time.

Even though Walpole was addressing a crisis of cultural and 'economic' self-definition in the England and Europe of the 1760s, it is really no accident that the Gothic mode attains its greatest resonance and popularity in the 1790s, the decade of Ann Radcliffe and Matthew Lewis, surrounded as they were by the stormy political conflicts and changes manifested in revolutions and their aftermaths as well as numerous competitors in 'terror' from blatant imitators of them to Continental rivals and popular Gothic dramatists (see Miles 2002c). The 1790s needed the Gothic as never before to address by symbolic displacement an extremely backward-longing and forward-moving era, and the Gothic was ready to meet the need because it harkened back so thoroughly to the most Janus-faced works of Shakespeare, who rose to his own prominence in the 1590s, another decade full of 'apocalyptic forebodings' as one century was about to give way to another (Bloom 2003: 139). At that turning point too, Anglo-European hopes and fears for the future, given the potent draw of the still-visible and haunting past, were just as contentious and anxious for Western audiences, albeit in somewhat different terms, as they were when Gothic fictions came into their strongest cultural role at another end-of-the-century transition into yet another emergence of a modernity, now a pre-industrial one, though one still nostalgic for some of the grounds of selfhood it feared to lose.

As the foregoing essays have shown, consequently, the centrality of Shakespeare to the Gothic extends far beyond *The Castle of Otranto* – and does so precisely because of what my own accounts of these essays have emphasized in them: the Gothic's drive, basic to its genre-crossing nature, to develop the manifestations in Shakespeare of the most pervasive conflicts between divergent ideological claims. For another example, aside from those offered by my colleagues here, I would suggest Lewis's *The Monk* of 1796, which quotes Shakespeare several times from various plays but also extensively redevelops his proto-Gothic *Tragedy of Macbeth* (1606).

The Monk cites *Macbeth* directly at the start of its Volume II (Lewis 1998: 129) from a point in the play (3.4.92–106) that clearly intrigued Walpole: the appearance of the Ghost of Banquo at now-King Macbeth's banquet where only Macbeth can behold the 'horrible shadow'. While this citation mainly sets the stage for the appearance of the Bleeding Nun ghost in Lewis's subplot, it also points to deeper recollections of *Macbeth* at the heart of *The Monk*'s central story. Just as Macbeth hears a presage of his progress up the noble ranks to the Crown from the seemingly prophetic 'weird sisters' – welcomed by Banquo as either 'fantastical' or 'I' th' name of truth' (1.3.52–53) – so the movement of Lewis's monk, Ambrosio, from apparent sanctity and Catholic obedience to unchecked lust and double murder assisted by Satan himself is apparently prophesied twice in the first chapter: in the early dream of Lorenzo (Lewis 1998: 27–28), where a 'Monster' in priest's habit violates his beloved Antonia on a church altar (as Ambrosio will rape Antonia, not knowing she is his sister, on a tomb in the church's sepulchre), and in the predictions of a weird-sister 'Gypsy' telling fortunes in the streets of Madrid, who warns Antonia that 'Lusty Man and Crafty Devil / Will combine to work your evil' (Lewis 1998: 35–38). Moreover, this last omen appears fulfilled when we discover that Ambrosio's seduction by the succubus Matilda and a 'beautiful' Satan have been entirely pre-planned, even to the point of Ambrosio's incest, by a Satan who had 'watched the movements of [this monk's] heart' and so pre-constructed the means to his venality knowing that he would follow them to his damnation (Lewis 1998: 440).

At the same time, it is left unclear in *The Monk* whether the supernatural is really independent of psychological projection or more the externalized product of it. Lorenzo as he begins to dream is described as entering his own 'delusions' while considering 'the obstacles that might oppose his wishes', which could include Antonia's attraction to the preaching Ambrosio (Lewis 1998: 27); the Gypsy might be referring to a general danger that already exists for Antonia, the severity of which will depend on how any particular suitor of hers chooses to regard her; Satan cannot begin to plot, by his own admission, until Ambrosio has reached a certain state of mind; and all the renderings of Catholic beliefs, with Satan and the supernatural among them, are presented here, as per Walpole's first Preface, as sensuous but false idols, within which a believer, such as Ambrosio, can remain mentally enthralled, especially when he proceeds to resist Catholic authority only within the terms, including Satan, of Catholicism itself. Similarly, Shakespeare in *Macbeth*, though he gestures towards the writings of King James I, as well as Scottish folklore, about witchcraft (see Kinney 2001: 242–58), thereby manages to link the weird sisters to the suspect Catholicism that James has just disavowed, as well as to a quasi-Celtic old cult that supposedly served Satan the Deceiver. The Bard thus raises questions about whether these witches have a totally independent reality or are called up by the same 'imperial' Satanic impulses in his hero (1.3.129) that later project the mental image of an assassin's 'dagger' (see Frank Kermode on *Macbeth* in Shakespeare 1974: 1309). Macbeth has wondered, after first seeing the sisters, after all, if 'My thought, whose murther is yet but fantastical,' leaves him only in a state of 'surmise' where 'nothing is / But what is not' (1.3.140–42).

The Monk, then, continues an irresolution between supernatural and psychological causes quite crucial to Shakespeare originally, with the proviso only that the status of the supernatural has become linked for eighteenth-century Protestants to a Catholic iconography now presented nearly always as discredited and hollow, however attractive. Because of the attachment of the out-and-out supernatural to a Catholic order rejected by authors from Walpole to Lewis and at least implicitly by the great Shakespeare, actual ghostliness in the Gothic Story is more or less inseparable from psychological projection, at least as a possibility, since the very beginning of the Gothic tradition. Oscillations in the Gothic after *Otranto* between the empirically 'explained supernatural' (as in Radcliffe's romances) and the reasserted, often 'Germanic' onslaught of multiple ghosts, but with hints of mental projection (as in Lewis), all across the history of the Gothic – leading at times to completely undecidable hauntings, most famously in Henry James's *The Turn of the Screw* (1898) – thus never really escape from Shakespeare's older hesitations about the supernatural in the face of his and his culture's ideological debates, as much as the Gothic does try more deliberately to evacuate archaic 'certainties' from such preternatural figures without losing their symbolic potentials.

Concurrently, too, the psychological side of this conundrum, as the Gothic develops it, looks back as much to Shakespeare's *un*certainties as the Gothic supernatural does. We have already noted how the many debates with himself in the soliloquies of Hamlet, very much re-enacted in the solitary speeches of Macbeth, are echoed in the internal conflicts of *Otranto's* Manfred and their articulation of competing grounds for self-definition. We now realize, particularly if we recall the thought-patterns at war with each other in Lewis's monk, that these inward dilemmas have become more plentiful and complex in the heroines and heroes (or anti-heroes and heroines) of most Gothic fictions and dramas composed in Walpole's wake. Still, Shakespeare makes these psychological torments possible because of more than just the conflicts among beliefs in his soliloquies. In addition, as Bloom and Greenblatt have both noted in their different ways, he articulates and stages a pre-Enlightenment 'inner structure' by creating a 'strategic opacity' in his later characters (Greenblatt

2004: 324). Right at the point where Macbeth wonders whether the weird sisters have placed 'what [is or] is not' in his mind, he adds that his 'thought', as he projects 'horrible imaginings', 'Shakes so my single state that function / Is smother'd in surmise' (1.3.138–41). He has become divided both within his thinking and from his own understanding of himself, thereby also dividing thought and motive ('surmise') from action ('function'), as though his presumed 'single state' has turned out to be a multiplicity of layers with depths whose bottom he cannot comprehend, as 'Bottom' cannot in *A Midsummer Night's Dream* (1595–96; 4.1.204–16), because some previous level has become obscured (here 'smothered') by another.

This otherness from the self *in* the self, moreover, is intensified by what Joel Fineman has isolated in Shakespeare, especially in the *Sonnets*: how most of his speakers' attempts to turn vision into language run explicitly up against 'the difference between vision and language' (Fineman 1986: 16), not to mention the difference of words from each other, one reason that 'what is' to a speaker suddenly seems 'what it is not' after (s)he has adopted words than can be used by others, as Macbeth and Hamlet have – and Walpole's Manfred and Lewis' Ambrosio must. These multiple differences force every such speaker to place his or her 'ideal of identification … in an imaginary past' held at a distance, so much so that 'a space and a time [must nearly always] open up … for subjective introspection' (Fineman 1986: 25). There is thus a need even in the self to interpret a series of signs sundered from their reference points (and in that sense opaque), signs beset as well by a quandary over whether one's language is attached to or independent of the self. This opacity subjects those signs to possibly contrary interpretations of them, given the range of options available – several, as we have seen, at Shakespeare's time – for explaining the relation of 'thought' to 'function' or would-be 'signified' to any visible 'signifier' (to use the terms of Ferdinand de Saussure 1966: 65–70).

The self-division in haunted Gothic characters beginning with Walpole's is unquestionably founded on this Shakespearean 'rhetoricity that speaks against itself', which Fineman rightly sees (anticipating Bloom 1998 and Greenblatt 2004) as beginning to open up 'the modernist literary self' (Fineman 1986: 29–31) that will come to have the Freudian layers of unconscious, preconscious, consciousness and verbal expression. Further informed by John Locke's late-seventeenth-century empiricism of sense perceptions becoming ideas and remembered ideas becoming associated with other ones to suggest certain foundations for themselves, all subject to re-presentation by the added layer of words, Ann Radcliffe in *The Mysteries of Udolpho* (1794) can therefore quote Shakespeare – 'Unfold the evil which is here wrapped up / In countenance' (*Measure for Measure* 5.1.117–18,

Radcliffe 1998: 331) – to set up her positioning of Emily St. Aubert, whose wholeness of identity with her parents at La Vallée is far in a past now only remembered, between seeming to see 'a malicious triumph in [the villain Montoni's] manner' and 'dismissing the same thought' as different associations cross her mind (Radcliffe 1998: 338). Emily is thus left just as divided about the hidden motives of her chief adversary as Isabella is about the Duke of Vienna in Shakespeare's *Measure* and as Emily herself has long been by now about her deceased father, her family's buried history, and her own obscure motivations and prospects, the most constant situation of conflicted central characters in the suspenseful playing out of most Gothic novels and plays. Indeed, the Gothic's main further development of Shakespearean depth, since at least the novel allows for the verbalization of unspoken thoughts, is to complement the 'strategic opacity' that the Bard has helped begin, not just by uttering inconsistent ideologies about causality or motivation, but by projecting one's own accreting and conflicted associations of ideas, since there is no other 'ground', back into the gaping depth of thought's layers as they face the conscious subject inside itself and in others. Radcliffe's Emily, after all, like Walpole's Manfred and especially Lewis's Ambrosio (despite all of Radcliffe's differences from both these authors), is as likely to be wrong as she is to be right in the end, since she projects her current associations backwards from limited experience, about the final correspondence between one's associations and 'reality', as it later comes to be perceived, just as much as the Macbeth of Shakespeare is as likely to believe 'what is not' as he is to grasp 'what is'.

Gothic fictions and Gothic characterizations, in other words, are enabled in part by an early modernity in Shakespeare that is rooted in the separation of the signifier from the signified, be it object or idea, and hence in the differentiation of 'self' from its signs and the self from all signifiable aspects of itself and others – all of which help make possible and likely the conflicts among systems of belief for interpreting the self, other selves, and their objects as these are all constituted by systems of signs. Here, then, is another common ground based on an un-grounding that links Shakespeare and the Gothic mode irrevocably, and it underlies the previous essays in this book at the level of symbology to the same degree that both the Gothic and Shakespeare are rooted in contradictory schemes at the level of ideology. As I have argued before (starting in Hogle 1994, just as several of these essays note), Walpole's and later Gothic ways of turning Shakespearean ghosts of dead bodies into shades of what is already spectral, such as effigies *or* portraits *or* mental images composed out of multiple perceptions and coloured by associations, are enactments of what I call 'the ghost of the counterfeit' because they are based on and haunted by Shakespeare's earlier uses of what were at his time already 'counterfeit' symbols in which signifiers were no longer viewed as having their previous unalterable connections to people, ideas, or objects.

By employing such terms, I am again accepting the definition of 'counterfeit' offered by Jean Baudrillard in *Symbolic Exchange and Death*, which uses this word to refer to a specific set of assumptions about how signifiers relate to signifieds and thus how signs (including words, images, costumes and other modes of rhetorical self-presentation) relate to people during the early modern era in the sixteenth and seventeenth centuries, the time of Shakespeare. At that time, the sign functioned partly in the way Hamlet sees his father's Ghost: as an 'appearance that is bound to the world' (Baudrillard 1993: 51) – 'I'll call thee Hamlet, / King, father, royal Dane' (*Hamlet* 1.4.44–45) – according the medieval concept of the 'bound sign' in which an image referred to an embodied person, already defined within the Judeo-Christian Chain of Being, who was ensconced in a class and role so predetermined and immutable that there was philosophically no distance between the person's being and the signs of his or her station. Concurrently, however, 'counterfeit' partly refers also, with the connotations of 'fake' now coming forward, to a '*nostalgia* for the natural referent of the sign' without the 'natural referent' being necessarily attached to it (again Baudrillard 1993: 51, emphasis added). During a period when rising bourgeois men, such as Shakespeare himself, could *buy* a Coat of Arms not originally connected to the family, signs for the self, while looking backwards to a 'bound' condition, could be viewed as transferrable across people from different classes so that a person could acquire certain higher-class features ('faking' them) without being pre-entitled to them. Hence the possibility of antiquated images becoming psychological projections of them or sheerly rhetorical self-presentations being regarded (or not) as 'plausive manners'.

Shakespeare plays with both these senses of 'counterfeit' when he has Prince Hamlet confront his mother in her bedroom with 'The counterfeit presentiment of two brothers' (3.4.54). Here the portrait of old King Hamlet, according to his son, shows a match between role and person 'Where every god did seem to set his seal', apparently leaving no distance between sign and person even in the picture (3.4.61), while the portrait of the usurper Claudius presents a gap between the person (or 'mildew'd ear') and the role of monarch to such an extent that he has become 'a Vice of kings' who 'from the shelf the precious diadem stole' (3.4.98–100) without any determined right to it, even though the 'diadem' is clearly transferable from one figure to the other. The mobility of the diadem across reference-points becomes analogous to the distance between self and sign in Claudius's 'counterfeit', and since the portrait of Old Hamlet is a counterfeit as well, the same possibilities are there too, even as they already are in the 'questionable shape' of his Ghost, which may or may not be a 'grounded sign'. This condition explains why the Ghost as signifier refers, like the counterfeit, both back towards a more grounded condition (as an object of desire) and away from such foundations to a conflict among ideologies about ghosts that exacerbates, even as it also stems from, the breach between sign and substance in the counterfeit that also longs for no breach at all (now in the past). When the Walpolean Gothic centres itself on the *ghosts* of such counterfeits, we thus have to say, it is referring back to a early-modern division in the sign that is already in force, an un-founded foundation of the wider cultural condition in which Shakespeare's characters *as* counterfeits oscillate between regressive and progressive schemes for defining selfhood and its many relationships.

The appearance of the many ghosts of such counterfeits, starting with the shades of statues or portraits, in the Gothic of Walpole and his successors, then, links this 'new species' since 1764 to signs *of* signifiers (what symbols of legality in the Gothic turn out to be in the essay here by Chaplin). The earlier signifiers, too, as in the Ghosts of Old Hamlet and Banquo, are already Janus-faced hesitations between the 'ancient' and the 'modern' and thus between belief-systems that tend in both directions. Like an oft-recovered and often bowdlerized, and so ever-receding, Shakespeare, such counterfeits, now re-ghosted, haunt the eighteenth century and subsequent Gothic with an un-grounded play across different belief systems and a longing for foundations prior to those, as in the de-Catholicized bric-a-brac of Walpole's Strawberry Hill, in which original underpinnings are irrecoverably distanced into an inaccessible, albeit beckoning, past. Consequently, Gothic characters have to be confronted by apparitions that are possibly but not clearly mental projections filled with conflicting associations, as indeed they already are. Behind these, the definition of the self and its grounds pursued through those 'others' is almost infinitely withdrawn and yet is always sought through layers of backward-looking signification (such as 'authentic writings') that can only be interpreted via later signifiers that may project more origins 'back there' that can actually be reached, all as parts of a much later stage of the 'early modern' human condition rendered in Shakespeare. For these reasons, the Theodore who is restored to his birthright as Alfonso's descendent at the end of *Otranto* must seek his now-dead true love (Matilda) through the more present signifier of such a being (the still-living Isabella), so much so that he is left, not so much in possession of his long-sought selfhood, 'but in the society of one with whom he could forever indulge the melancholy that had taken possession of his soul' (Walpole 2003: 165), the eerily revealing way that the first Gothic Story ends without the 'rest' that Hamlet is granted as his 'story' goes on to at least be re-told (*Hamlet* 5.2.349–60).

This concatenation of paradoxes, on the one hand, leaves the post-Renaissance self as depicted in the Gothic dependent for self-fulfilment on substitute-signifiers for the most desired Other in a potentially endless drift from one to another (the Lacanian condition that Townshend here sees in the *Hamlet*-esque Gothic in and after Walpole). On the other hand, it also permits Walpole's and others' uses of now hollowed-out shapes to be signs of very generalized continuities, 'like Banquo's ghost' in separating the form of kingship from the body of a king, from which old tyrannies can seem to be evacuated and to which can now be attached transformative 'expatiations' of it by way of both older and newer signs (as in Walpole 2003:65). These will allow for the entrepreneurial replacement of older significations by newer associations of thoughts and signifers now given the status and pedigree, if not the meanings, of the old ones – which therefore still haunt their users with their ghosted-counterfeit forms, as Walpole's Theodore finds, much as a reinterpreted Shakespeare and his spectral figures continue to haunt the Gothic. In addition, the fact that ghosted counterfeits are really cut mostly adrift from their former foundations, while also holding out vaguely foundational spaces calling their viewers back to them, means that authors, characters and readers of a Gothic thus focused on multi-directional and self-obscuring symbols can use these figures or spaces as half-concealing and half-revealing repositories, the way Radcliffe's Emily does in projecting her associations into the sixteenth-century Europe that she observes, both to deal with and to hide the conflicted foundations (such as the ongoing captivity of women, in Radcliffe's case) of the authors' and readers' more modern existence. This Gothic sublimation is what allows David Punter to see a 'middle-class' readership making use of the Gothic for over two centuries now because it 'displaces the hidden violence of present social structures, conjures them up again as past, and promptly falls under their spell' (Punter 1980: 418) in part because that Gothic recalls the Shakespeare who used 'counterfeits' of medieval figures to incarnate the ideological conflicts of his time.

All of this is why Gothic spectres and monsters, from Walpole's ghosts of counterfeits and Lewis's Bleeding Nun or Satan to Frankenstein's creature, Dr. Jekyll's Mr. Hyde, Stoker's Count Dracula, and beyond, have been sites, as critics have seen since 1988 (beginning with Gordon that year), for what Kristeva has called 'abjection' (see Kristeva 1982: esp. 3–10): the 'throwing off' into a symbolic 'otherness' and the 'throwing under' the gaze of social authority the most fundamental multiplicities and inconsistencies connected with the self-in-formation (starting with its being half-inside and half-outside the mother and being half-dead and half-alive at the moment of birth), including the cultural multiplicities and conflicting ideologies crossing boundaries between gender, race, class, and more out of which a 'self' attempts to emerge with a supposedly coherent identity by projecting that amalgam of inconsistencies somewhere else, leaving it all 'unconscious' and apparently outside the self deeply rooted in it. Just as Bronfen has shown us in this collection, Shakespeare 'set the stage' for even this 'heterotopic' re-location of interpenetrating and blurred differences, at least in his uses of 'night', but the full potential in such symbolic sites of mixed conditions (partly artificial/partly real, partly dead/partly alive, partly internal/partly external, etc.) to become locations for abjected multiplicities does not come about until the Shakespearean 'counterfeit', itself drawn in multiple directions as a nodal point for conflicts of belief, becomes the ghost of the counterfeit in the Gothic in and after Walpole. Only by that time has the 'counterfeit' symbol become so removed from its earliest reference points and so widely circulated as a hollow figure waiting to be filled up by its re-users, even as it keeps calling us back to lost origins, that it can serve perfectly as a useful, but also self-obscuring, locus for what is terrifyingly or even horrifically non-identical in the West and for the Western sense of 'identity' at the time a particular 'Gothic' work is produced. This combination of symbolic turns is what allows Walpole's ghosts, as examples, to be antiquated-yet-open figures for focusing the conflict he faced between different 'economic personalities'. His spectres do combine regressive calls towards inheritance and continuity with an emptied-out artificiality that can be circulated and transfigured in a newer kind of market. Abjection as a process needs especially this drawing backwards to what can never be fully reached *and* this pulling away from that draw towards a newer movement into the modern interplay of more mobile signifiers so that this latter drive can then 'throw' its inconsistencies back into the regressive side of this multiple process in order to seem consistent. In other words, abjection at its fullest needs the 'double bind' that the ghost of the counterfeit alone can perform in being even more Janus-faced than the counterfeit at Shakespeare's time.

The symbolic mode (really an interplay of conflicting genres) that most allows this degree of abjection to be frequently enacted, then, is quite aptly called 'Gothic', even though that term has not always been used for this sort of fiction-making. 'Gothic' always looks back to an old cultural moment, as it does to Shakespeare and the Crusades in *Otranto*, but the term is also mobile enough to join that nostalgia to many newer contradictions in human experience, given that it too is the ghost of a counterfeit, a re-symbolizing of the already merely symbolic, from a very early point. Even in Shakespeare, as Craig has shown, and certainly in the Renaissance historians who used 'Gothic' to refer pejoratively to a non-classical medieval architecture that had nothing to do with Goths, 'Gothic' has been a term that loads a quite vague past-ness with later ideological and political content (unquestionably in *Titus Andronicus*), and that past-ness has become even more remote and empty by the time the 'Gothic Story' starts abjecting into that multi-directional depth the multi-directional conflicts and most fearsome psychological quandaries of its own times. Realizing that none of this, ideologically or symbolically, would have come about in literature, drama, or film if Shakespeare had not helped to coalesce what the 'Gothic Story' then modified is therefore essential to seeing how 'the Gothic' performs its 'cultural work' for us all in the Western world and how it reflects back, in so many of its variants, on the cross-currents in Shakespeare that made the Gothic's symbolizing of its own cross-currents possible. The foregoing essays can all say what they do and this collection can have its considerable cultural value, we must therefore conclude, because of a retrospective *and* prospective complexity in the Gothic at its best that stems from a quite similar complexity in Shakespeare that has vividly brought us into our modernity with all its contradictions on symbolic display, both in successive reproductions of his work and in the ongoing production of Gothic fictions.

Notes

1 All further references to Shakespeare's plays in this essay will be taken from *The Riverside Shakespeare* (Shakespeare 1974).

References

Abraham, Nicolas and Torok, Maria (1994) *The Shell and the Kernel: Renewals of Psychoanalysis Vol. I*, ed. and trans. Nicholas T. Rand, Chicago and London: Chicago University Press.

Addison, Joseph (1965) *The Spectator*, ed. Donald F. Bond, 5 vols, Oxford: Clarendon.

——(1980) *The Freeholder*, ed. James Lehany, Oxford: Clarendon.

Aikin, Arthur (1797) Review of *The Italian*, *Monthly Review* March, 22.

Altman, Rick (1999) *Film/Genre*, London: British Film Institute.

Anon. (1797) Review of *The Italian*, *Analytical Review* May, 25: 516–20.

Ascham, Roger (1967) *The Scholemaster*, Menston: The Scolar Press Ltd.

Auerbach, N. (1995) *Our Vampires, Ourselves*, Chicago: University of Chicago Press.

Austen, Jane (2003) *Northanger Abbey, Lady Susan, The Watsons, Sanditon*, ed. James Kinsley and John Davie, Oxford: Oxford University Press.

Bailey, Helen Phelps (1964) *Hamlet in France: From Voltaire to Laforgue*, Geneva: Libraire Droz.

Baillie, Joanna (1804) *Miscellaneous Plays*, London: Longman, Hurst Rees & Orme.

Baines, Paul (1999) *The House of Forgery in Eighteenth-Century Britain*, Brookefield, Singapore and Sydney: Ashgate.

Bakhtin, Mikhail (1981) *The Dialogic Imagination*, trans. Caryls Emerson and Michael Holquist, Austin: Texas University Press.

—— (1984) *Rabelais and His World*, Bloomington: University of Indiana Press.

Baldick, Chris (1993) 'Introduction', in *The Oxford Book of Gothic Tales*, ed. Chris Baldick, Oxford: Oxford University Press, xi–xxiii.

Barrell, John (2000) *Imagining the King's Death: Figurative Treason, Fantasies of Regicide 1793–1796*, Oxford and New York, Oxford University Press.

——(2006) *The Spirit of Despotism: Invasions of Privacy in the 1790s*, New York and Oxford: Oxford University Press.

Barthes, Roland (1977) 'The Death of the Author', in his *Image Music Text*, ed. Stephen Heath, London: Fontana Press, 142–48.

Bartholomeusz, Dennis (1969) *Macbeth and the Players*, Cambridge: Cambridge University Press.

Bassingthwaite, D. and Kilpatrick, N. (1995) *As One Dead*, Clarkston, GA.: White Wolf.

Bataille, Georges (1988) *The Accursed Share I: Consumption*, trans. Robert Hurley, New York: Zone Books.

Bate, Jonathan (1989a) *Shakespeare and the English Romantic Imagination*, Oxford: Clarendon Press.

——(1989b) 'Shakespeare and Original Genius', in Penelope Murray (ed.) *Genius: The History of an Idea*, Oxford and New York: Basil Blackwell, 76–98.

——(1995) 'Introduction to *Titus Andronicus*', in William Shakespeare, *Titus Andronicus*, ed. Jonathan Bate, The Arden Shakespeare, 3rd series, London and New York, Routledge, 1–123.

Bateson, Gregory (1973) *Steps to an Ecology of Mind*, London: Paladin.

Baudrillard, Jean (1993) *Symbolic Exchange and Death*, trans. Iain Hamilton Grant, London: Sage.

Blackstone, William [1765] (1966) *Commentaries on the Laws of England*, London: Dawsons.

Blagdon, Francis William (1805) Review of *Gondez the Monk*, *The Fowers of Literature for 1805*, 423.

Blanchot, Maurice (1981) *The Gaze of Orpheus and Other Literary Essays*, trans. Lydia Davis, New York: Station Hill.

Bloom, Harold (1998) *Shakespeare: The Invention of the Human*, New York: Riverhead Books.

——(2003) Hamlet: *Poem Unlimited*, New York: Riverhead Books.

Boaden, James (1794) *Fontainville Forest, A Play in Five Acts*, London: Hookham and Carpenter.

Boswell, James (1924) *Letters of James Boswell*, vol. 2, ed. Chauncy Brewster Rinkers, Oxford: Clarendon Press.

Botting, Fred (2002) 'Aftergothic: consumption, machines, and black holes', in J. Hogle (ed.) *The Cambridge Companion to Gothic Fiction*, Cambridge: Cambridge University Press, 277–300.

Boydell, John (1789, 1790, 1791) *A catalogue of the pictures in the Shakspeare Gallery, Pall-Mall*, London.

Braudel, Fernand (1972) *The Mediterranean and the Mediterranean World in the Age of Philip II*, trans. Sian Reynolds, 2 vols, London: Collins.

Brontë, Charlotte [1847] (1985) *Jane Eyre*, ed. Q. D. Leavis, Harmondsworth: Penguin.

Burke, Edmund (1790) *Reflections on the Revolution in France, and on the proceedings in certain societies relative to that event*, London: J. Dodsley.

——[1790] (1969) *Reflections on the Revolution in France*, ed. Conor Cruise O'Brien, Harmondsworth: Penguin.

Castle, Terry (1987) 'The Spectralization of the Other in *The Mysteries of Udolpho*', in Laura Brown and Felicity Nussbaum (eds) *The New Eighteenth Century*, London: Methuen, 231–53.

Cavell, Stanley (1969) 'The Avoidance of Love: A Reading of *King Lear*', in his *Must We Mean What We Say?*, Cambridge: Cambridge University Press, 267–353.

Chaplin, Sue (2007) *Gothic and the Rule of Law, 1764–1820*, Basingstoke: Palgrave Macmillan.

Chibnall, Steve (1998) *Making Mischief: The Cult Films of Pete Walker*, Guildford: FAB Press.

Chiu, Frances (ed.) (2006) Ann Radcliffe, *Gaston de Blondeville*, Chicago: Valancourt Books.

Clark, Alice (2005) 'Voltaire', in Michael Dobson and Stanley Wells (eds) *The Oxford Companion to Shakespeare*, Oxford: Oxford University Press, 513–14.

Clery, E. J. (1995) *The Rise of Supernatural Fiction*, Cambridge: Cambridge University Press.

——(2000) *Women's Gothic: From Clara Reeve to Mary Shelley*, London: Tavistock.

——(2002) 'The Genesis of "Gothic" Fiction', in Jerrold E. Hogle (ed.) *The Cambridge Companion to Gothic Fiction*, Cambridge: Cambridge University Press, 21–39.

Clery, E. J and Miles, Robert (eds) (2000) *Gothic Documents: A Sourcebook, 1700–1820*, Manchester, Manchester University Press.

Coleridge, Samuel Taylor (1951) *Selected Poetry and Prose of Coleridge*, ed. Donald A. Stauffer, Princeton: Princeton University Press.

——(1962) *Shakespearean Criticism*, ed. T. M. Raysor, 2 vols, London: J. M. Dent.

——(1975) *Biographia Literaria*, ed. George Watson, London: Dent.

——(1983) *Biographia Literaria, or Biographical Sketches of My Literary Life and Opinions*, vol. II, ed. James Engell and W. Jackson Bate, London and New Jersey: Routledge and Kegan Paul.

——(1987) *Lectures, 1808–1819*, vol. II, ed. R. A. Foakes, Princeton: Princeton University Press.

Connolly, L. W. (1971–72) 'The Censor's Wife at the Theatre: The Diary of Anna Margaretta Larpent, 1790–1800', *Huntington Library Quarterly* 35: 49–64.

——(1976) *The Censorship of English Drama, 1737–1824*, San Marino: Huntington Library.

Cox, Jeffrey N. and Gamer, Michael (2003) 'Introduction', in their edition *The Broadview Anthology of Romantic Drama*, Peterborough, Ont.: Broadview Press, 2003, xviii–xxii.

Crowl, Samuel (2000) 'Flamboyant realist: Kenneth Branagh', in Russell Jackson (ed.) *The Cambridge Companion to Shakespeare on Film*, Cambridge: Cambridge University Press, 222–38.

Curran, John E., Jr. (2006) Hamlet, *Protestantism, and the Mourning of Contingency: Not to Be*, Burlington, Vermont: Ashgate.

Cybernetic culture research unit, 'Swarmachines', *Abstract Culture: Swarm 1*. Online. Available at http://ccru.net/swarm1/1_swarm.htm (accessed 4 May 2007).

Davis, L. (2001) '"Death-marked love": Desire and Presence in *Romeo and Juliet*', in R. White (ed.) *Romeo and Juliet: New Casebooks*, Basingstoke: Palgrave, 28–46.

Dean, Jodi (2004) 'Žižek on Law', *Law and Critique* 15: 1–24.

Deleuze, Gilles (1986) *Cinema 1*, trans. Hugh Tomlinson and Barbara Habberjam, London: Athlone Press.

Deleuze, Gilles and Guattari, Felix (1986) *Kafka: Towards a Minor Literature*, trans. Dana Polan, Minneapolis: University of Minnesota Press.

de Man, Paul (1984) 'Autobiography as De-Facement', in his *The Rhetoric of Romanticism*, New York: Columbia University Press, 67–81.

Derrida, Jacques (1986) 'Mnemosyne', in his *Memoires for Paul de Man*, trans. Cecile Lindsay, New York: Columbia University Press, 3–43.

——(1992) 'Before the Law', in Derek Attridge (ed.) *Acts of Literature*, London: Routledge, 181–220.

——(1994) *Specters of Marx: The State of Debt, the Work of Mourning, and the New International*, trans. Peggy Kamuf, New York and London: Routledge.

——(1995) 'Passions', in *On the Name*, ed. Thomas Dutoit, trans. David Wood et al., Stanford: Stanford University Press.

——(2000a) 'The Double Session', in *Dissemination*, trans. Barbara Johnson, London: Athlone Press, 173–226.

——(2000b) 'Plato's Pharmacy', in *Dissemination*, trans. Barbara Johnson, London: Athlone Press, 63–171.

Dobson, Michael (1994) *The Making of the National Poet: Shakespeare, Adaptation and Authorship, 1660–1769*, Oxford: Clarendon.

Dolar, Mladen (1996) 'At First Sight', in Renata Salecl and Slavoj Žižek (eds) *Gaze and Voice as Love Objects*, Durham, NC: Duke University Press, 129–53.

Döring, Tobias (2006) *Performances of Mourning in Shakespearean Theatre and Early Modern Culture*, London and New York: Palgrave.

Douzinas, Costas and Greary, Adam (eds) (2005) *Critical Jurisprudence: The Political Philosophy of Justice*, Oxford: Hart Publishing.

Drakakis, John (2007) 'Present Text: Editing *The Merchant of Venice*', in Hugh Grady and Terence Hawkes (eds) *Presentist Shakespeare*, Accents on Shakespeare, Abingdon and New York, Routledge, 79–95.

Drake, Nathan (1798) *Literary Hours, or Sketches Critical and Narrative*, London: T. Cadell and W. Davies.

Dutton, Thomas (1800) *The Dramatic Censor* 2.xvii: 98.

Feibel, Juliet (2000) 'Vortigern, Rowena, and the Ancient Britons: Historical Art and the Anglicization of National Origin', *Eighteenth-Century Life* 24: 1–21.

Fenton, Harvey and Flint, David (eds) (2001) *Ten Years of Terror: British Horror Films of the 1970s*, Guildford, Surrey: FAB Press.

Finch, M. B. and Allison Peers, E. (1920) 'Walpole's Relations with Voltaire', *Modern Philology* 18.3: 189–200.

Findlater, Richard (1967) *Banned! A Review of Theatrical Censorship in Britain*, London: MacGibbon and Kee.

Fineman, Joel (1986) *Shakespeare's Perjured Eye: The Invention of Poetic Subjectivity in the Sonnets*, Berkeley: University of California Press.

Foakes, R. A (1993) *Hamlet Versus Lear: Cultural Politics and Shakespeare's Art*, Cambridge: Cambridge University Press.

Forsyth, Neil (2000) 'Shakespeare the Illusionist: Filming the Supernatural', in Russell Jackson (ed.) *The Cambridge Companion to Shakespeare on Film*, Cambridge: Cambridge University Press, 274–94.

Foucault, Michel (1977) 'Language to Infinity', in *Michel Foucault: Language, Counter-Memory, Practice*, trans. Donald F. Bouchard and Sherry Simon, Oxford: Blackwell, 53–67.

——(1998) 'Different Spaces', reprinted in James Faubion (ed.) *Aesthetics, Method, and Epistemology: Essential Works of Foucault, 1954–1984*, London: Penguin Books, 175–85.

Freedman, Barbara (1991) *Staging the Gaze: Postmodernism, Psychoanalysis, and Shakespearean Comedy*, Ithaca: Cornell University Press.

Freud, Sigmund (1900) *The Interpretation of Dreams*; reprinted in James Strachey (ed.) *Standard Edition of the Complete Psychological Works*, vols 4–5, London: Hogarth Press, 1953.

——(1919) 'The Uncanny'; reprinted in James Strachey (ed.) *Standard Edition of the Complete Psychological Works*, vol. 17, London: Hogarth Press, 1955, 217–56.

Frye, Northrop (1957) *Anatomy of Criticism*, Princeton: Princeton University Press.

Frye, Roland Mushat (1984) *The Renaissance Hamlet: Issues and Responses in 1600*, Princeton: Princeton University Press.

Gamer, Michael (1997) 'National Supernaturalism: Joanna Baillie, Germany, and the Legitimation of Gothic Drama', *Theatre Survey* 38.2: 49–88.

Garber, Marjorie (1990) 'Shakespeare as Fetish', *Shakespeare Quarterly* 41.3: 242–50.

——(2004) *Shakespeare After All*, New York: Pantheon Books.

Gelder, Ken (1994) *Reading the Vampire*, London: Routledge.

Genette, Gérard (1982) 'Proust Palimpsest', in *Figures of Literary Discourse*, trans. Alan Sheridan, Oxford: Basil Blackwell, 203–28.

Golder, J. D. (1971) '"Hamlet" in France 200 Years Ago', *Shakespeare Survey* 24: 79–86.

Goodrich, Peter (1990) *Languages of Law: From Logics of Memory to Nomadic Masks*, London: Weidenfeld and Nicolson.

Gordon, Marci M. (1988) 'Kristeva's abject and sublime in Brontë's *Wuthering Heights*', *Literature and Psychology* 34: 44–58.

Goux, Jean-Joseph (1998) 'Subversion and Consensus: Proletarians, Women, Artists' in Jean-Joseph Goux and Philip R. Wood (eds), *Terror and Consensus: Vicissitudes of French Thought*. Stanford: Stanford University Press, 135–44.

Grazia, Margreta de (1991) *Shakespeare Verbatim: The Reproduction of Authenticity and the 1790s Apparatus*, Oxford: Oxford University Press.

Grebanier, Bernard (1966) *The Great Shakespeare Forgery: A New Look at the Career of William Henry Ireland*, London: Heinemann.

Greenblatt, Stephen (1997) 'Introduction to *A Midsummer Night's Dream*', in Stephen Greenblatt (ed.) *The Norton Shakespeare*, New York and London: Norton & Company, 805–11.

——(2001) *Hamlet in Purgatory*, Princeton, NJ: Princeton University Press.

——(2004) *Will in the World: How Shakespeare Became Shakespeare*, London: Jonathan Cape.

Greene, Donald (ed.) (1984) *Samuel Johnson: The Major Works*, Oxford: Oxford University Press.

Griffith, Elizabeth (1971) *The Morality of Shakespeare's Drama Illustrated*. London: Frank Cass.

Groom, Nick (2002) *The Forger's Shadow: How Forgery Changed the Course of Literature*, London: Picador.

Hall, Stuart (1992) 'Notes on Deconstructing the Popular', in *People's History and Socialist Theory*, ed. Raphael Samuel, London: Routledge, 277–94.

Hamilton-Grant, Iain, 'Burning AutoPoiOedipus', *Abstract Culture: Swarm 2*. Online. Available at http://www.ccru.net/swarm2/2_auto.htm (accessed 9 May 2007).

Hardt, Michael and Negri, Antonio (2006) *Multitude*, London: Penguin.

Hartley, John (2003) *A Short History of Cultural Studies*, London: Sage.

Hartley, John and Fiske, John (1978) *Reading Television*, London: Methuen.

Hawkes, Terence (1973) *Shakespeare's Talking Animals*, London: Edward Arnold.

Haywood, Ian (1986) *The Making of History: A Study of the Literary Forgeries of James Macpherson and Thomas Chatterton in Relation to Eighteenth-Century Ideas of History and Fiction*, London and Tornonto: Associated University Press.

Hazlitt, William (1818) *Characters of Shakespeare's Plays*, 2nd edn, London: Taylor and Hessey.

Hobsbawm, E. J. (1990) *Nations and Nationalism Since 1780: Programme, Myth and Reality*, Cambridge: Cambridge University Press.

Hogan, Charles Beecher (1968) *The London Stage 1600–1800; Part V: 1776–1800*, Carbondale, Southern Illinois University Press.

Hoggart, Richard (1958) *The Uses of Literacy*, Harmondsworth: Penguin.

Hogle, Jerrold E. (1994) 'The Ghost of the Counterfeit and the Genesis of the Gothic', in Allan Lloyd Smith and Victor Sage (eds) *Gothic Origins and Innovations*, Amsterdam and Atlanta: Rodopi, 23–33.

——(1998) '*Frankenstein* as Neo-Gothic: From the Ghost of the Counterfeit to the Monster of Abjection', in Tilottama Rajan and Julia Wright (eds) *Romanticism, History, and the Possibility of Genre*. Cambridge: Cambridge University Press, 176–210.

——(2001). 'The Gothic Ghost of the Counterfeit and the Progress of Abjection', in David Punter (ed.) *A Companion to the Gothic*, Oxford: Blackwell, 293–304.

——(ed.) (2002) *The Cambridge Companion to Gothic Fiction*, Cambridge: Cambridge University Press.

Howard, Tony (2000) 'Shakespeare's Cinematic Offshoots', in Russell Jackson (ed.) *The Cambridge Companion to Shakespeare on Film*, Cambridge: Cambridge University Press, 295–313.

Howard, Tony (2007) *Women as Hamlet: Performance and Interpretation in Theatre, Film and Fiction*, Cambridge: Cambridge University Press.

Howells, Coral Ann (1982) 'The Gothic Way of Death in English Fiction, 1790–1820', *British Journal for Eighteenth-Century Studies* 5: 207–15.

Hume, Robert D (1997) 'Before the Bard: "Shakespeare" in Early Eighteenth-Century London', *English Literary History* 64.1: 41–75.

Hurd, Richard [1762] (1963) *Letters on Chivalry and Romance* (1762), Augustan Reprint Society no. 101–2, University of California.

——[1765] (1972), *Moral and Political Dialogues; with Letters on Chivalry and Romance*, Westmead: Gregg International Publishers.

Hutcheon, Linda (2000) 'Irony, Nostalgia and the Postmodern', *Studies in Comparative Literature* 30: 189–207.

Hutchings, Peter (2004) *The Horror Film*, London: Pearson.

Ireland, William Henry (1796) *Vortigern. A Tragedy in Five Acts*. Larpent MS1110, Huntington Library.

——(1799) *Vortigern, An Historical Tragedy, in Five Acts, Represented at the Theatre-Royal, Drury Lane. And Henry the Second, an Historical Drama*, London: J. Barker, B. White, T. Egerton, R. Faulder.

——[1805] (1969) *Confessions of William–Henry Ireland Containing the Particulars of His fabrication of the Shakespeare Manuscripts*, ed. Richard Grant White, New York: Burt Franklin.

——(1832) *Vortigern; An Historical Play; With an Original Preface*, London: Joseph Thomas.

Irwin, Megan. (2007) 'Charmed', *Phoenix New Times News*, 12 July. Online. Available at http://www.phoenixnewtimes.com/2007-07-12/news/charmed/ (accessed 20 July 2007).

Jacobs, Edward H. (2000) *Accidental Migrations: An Archaeology of Gothic Discourse*. London: Associated University Presses.

Johnson, Claudia L. (2003) 'Introduction to *Northanger Abbey*', in Jane Austen *Northanger Abbey, Lady Susan, The Watsons, Sanditon*, ed. James Kinsley and John Davie, Oxford: Oxford University Press, vii–xxxv.

Johnson, Samuel (1765) 'Preface', in his edition of *The Plays of William Shakespeare*, vol. 1, London: Tonson, Woodfall et al., v–lxxii.

Kahan, Jeffrey (1998) *Reforging Shakespeare: The Story of a Theatrical Scandal*, Cranbury, NJ Lehigh University Press, 1998.

Kallich, Martin (1971) *Horace Walpole*, Boston: Twayne.

Kalman, Matthew (2005) 'Bethlehem's star-crossed lovers', *San Francisco Chronicle*, May 15. Online. Available at http://sfgate.com/cgi-bin/article.cgi?file = /c/a/2005/05/15/MNGAICPIMS1.DTL (accessed 20 July 2007).

Keane, Angela (1995) 'Resisting Arrest: The National Constitution of the Picturesque and Gothic in Ann Radcliffe's Romances', in Tony Pinkney et al. (eds) *News from Nowhere: Theory and Politics of Romanticism*, Keele: Keele University Press, I: 96–119.

Keen, Paul (1999) *The Crisis of Literature in the 1790s*, Cambridge: Cambridge University Press.

Kinney, Arthur F. (2001) *Lies Like Truth: Shakespeare, Macbeth, and the CulturalMoment*, Detroit: Wayne State University Press.

Kirschling, Gregory (2007) 'Stephenie Meyer's "Twilight Zone"', *Entertainment Weekly*, August. Online. Available at http://www.ew.com/ew/article/0,20049578,00.html (accessed 4 August 2007)

Kliger, Samuel (1952) *The Goths in England: A Study in Seventeenth- and Eighteenth-Century Thought*, Cambridge, MA: Harvard University Press.

Kristeva, Julia (1982) *Powers of Horror: An Essay on Abjection*, trans. Leon S..Roudiez, New York: Columbia University Press.

——(1989) *Black Sun: Depression and Melancholia*, trans. Leon S. Roudiez, New York: Columbia University Press.

Kroker, Arthur and Kroker, Marilouise (1996) 'Code Warriors', *CTheory*. Online. Available at www.ctheory.net/articels.aspx?id=78 (accessed 27 November 2006).

Lacan, Jacques (1977) 'Desire and the Interpretation of Desire in *Hamlet*', *Yale French Studies* 55.56: 11–52.

——(1981) *The Four Fundamental Concepts of Psycho-Analysis*, ed. Jacques-Alain Miller, trans. Alan Sheridan, New York: W. W. Norton.

Lambarde, William (1970) *A Perambulation of Kent*, Trowbridge: Redwood Press.

Land, Nick (1993) 'Machinic Desire', *Textual Practice* 7.3: 471–82.

——(1998) 'Cybergothic', in Joan Broadhurst et al. (eds), *Virtual Futures*, New York and London: Routledge, 79–87.

——'Meltdown', *Abstract Culture: Swarm 1*. Online. Available at http://www.ccru.net/swarm1/1_melt.htm (accessed 16 April 2007).

Legendre, Pierre (1985) *Leçons IV: L'inestimable object de la transmission: Étude sur le principe généalogique en Occident*, Paris: Fayard.

Lewis, Matthew Gregory [1796] (1973) *The Monk: A Romance*, ed. Howard Anderson, The World's Classics, Oxford: Oxford University Press.

——[1796] (1998) *The Monk*, ed. Howard Anderson and Emma McEvoy, Oxford: Oxford University Press.

——[1797] (1992) *The Castle Spectre: A Drama in Five Acts*, in Jeffrey N. Cox (ed.) *Seven Gothic Dramas, 1789–1825*, Athens, Ohio: Ohio University Press, 149–224.

Lewis, W.S. (ed.) (1944) *The Yale Edition of Horace Walpole's Correspondence*, vol. 24, New Haven: Yale University Press.

Litten, Julian (2002) *The English Way of Death: The Common Funeral Since 1450*, London: Robert Hale.

Liu, Marjorie M. (2005) *A Taste of Crimson*, New York: Dorchester.

Longueil, Alfred E. (1923) 'The Word "Gothic" in Eighteenth-Century Criticisn', *Modern Language Notes* 38: 453–56.

Lounsbury, Thomas R. (1902) *Shakespeare and Voltaire*, London: David Nutt.

Lynch, Jack (2004) 'William Henry Ireland's Authentic Forgeries', *Princeton University Library Chronical* 66: 79–96.

——(2005) 'The Truth, the Whole Truth, and Anything but the Truth: What Can You Say about William Henry Ireland?', First Annual David Hosford Lecture, Rutgers University, Newark, 11 April.

——(2007a) *Inventing Shakespeare: The Unlikely Afterlife that Turned a Provincial Playwright into the Bard*, New York: Wallace.

——(2007b) 'The Picaresque Biography: William Henry Ireland', in Christoph Ehland and Robert Fajen (eds) *Das Paradigma des Pikaresken: The Paradigm of the Picaresque*, Heidelberg: University of Heidelberg Press, 147–57.

Mackenzie, Henry (1790) 'Account of the German Theatre', in *Transactions of the Royal Society of Edinburgh*, vol. II, London: T. Cadell; Edinburgh: J. Dickson, 154–92.

Madoff, Mark (2004) 'The Useful Myth of Gothic Ancestry', in Fred Botting and Dale Townshend (eds) *Gothic: Critical Concepts in Literary and Cultural Studies*, vol. 1, London: Routledge, 27–37.

Maguire, Nancy Klein (1991) 'Nahum Tate's *King Lear*: "the king's blest restoration"', in Jean I. Marsden (ed.) *The Appropriation of Shakespeare: Post-Renaissance Reconstructions of the Works and the Myth*, Hemel Hempstead: Harvester Wheatsheaf, 29–42.

Mair, John (1938) *The Fourth Forger: William Ireland and the Shakespeare Papers*, London: Cobden-Sanderson.

Mallett, P.-H. [1770] (1847) *Northern Antiquities*, trans. Thomas Percy, ed. I. A. Blackwell, London: Bohn's Library.

Malone, Edmond (ed.) (1790) *The Plays and Poems of William Shakspeare […]*, 10 vols., London, J. Rivington et al.

——(1796) *An Inquiry into the Authenticity of Certain Miscellaneous Papers and Legal Instruments, published Dec. 24, MDCCXCV and Attributed to Shakespeare, Queen Elizabeth, and Henry, Earl of Southampton […]*, London: Bladwin, Cadell and Davies.

Marks, Richard and Paul Williamson (eds) (2003) *Gothic: Art for England 1400–1547*, London: V&A Publications.

Martin, Peter (1995) *Edmond Malone, Shakespeare Scholar: A Literary Biography*, Cambridge: Cambridge University Press.

Mathias, Thomas James (1798) *The Pursuits of Literature, A satirical poem in four dialogues with notes*, 7th edn, London: T. Becket.

——(1805) *The Pursuits of Literature*, 13th edn, London: T. Becket.

Maturin, Charles Robert. [1820] (2000) *Melmoth the Wanderer*, ed. Victor Sage, Harmondsworth: Penguin.

Meyer, Stephenie (2005) *Twilight*, London: Times Warner.

——(2006) *New Moon*, New York: Little, Brown.

Mighall, Robert (1998) 'Sex, history and the vampire', in William Hughes and Andrew Smith (eds) *Bram Stoker: History, Psychoanalysis and the Gothic*, London: Macmillan, 62–77.

Milbank, Alison (1995) 'Introduction', in Ann Radcliffe *The Castles of Athlin and Dunbayne*, ed. Alison Milbank, Oxford: Oxford University Press, ix–xxix.

Miles, Robert (1995) *Ann Radcliffe: The Great Enchantress*. Manchester: Manchester University Press.

——(2001) 'Abjection, Nationalism and the Gothic', in Fred Botting (ed.) *The Gothic: Essays and Studies*, Cambridge: D. S. Brewer, 47–70.

——(2002a) 'Europhobia: the Catholic Other in Horace Walpole and Charles Maturin', in Avril Horner (ed.) *European Gothic: A Spirited Exchange*, Manchester: Manchester University Press, 84–103.

——(2002b) *Gothic Writing, 1750–1820: A Genealogy*, 2nd edn, Manchester: Manchester University Press.

——(2002c) 'The 1790s: the effulgence of Gothic', in Jerrold E. Hogel (ed.) *The Cambridge Companion to Gothic Fiction*, Cambridge: Cambridge University Press, 41–62.

——(2005) 'Trouble in the Republic of Letters: The Reception of the Shakespeare Forgeries', *Studies in Romanticism* 44: 317–40.

Montagu, Elizabeth (1769) *An Essay on the Writings and Genius of Shakespear [sic], Compared with the Greek and French Dramatic Poets. With Some Remarks Upon the Misrepresentations of Mons. De Voltaire*, London: J. Dodsley.

Montrose, Louis Adrian (1998) '"Shaping Fantasies": Figurations of Gender and Power in Elizabethan Culture', in Stephen Greenblatt (ed.) *Representing the English Renaissance*, Berkeley and Los Angeles: University of California Press, 31–57.

Nochinson, M. (2001) 'Titus', *Cineaste* 26.2: 48–50.

Norton, Rictor (1999) *The Mistress of Udolpho: The Life of Ann Radcliffe*, London and New York: Leicester University Press

Novy, Marianne L. (1998) *Engaging with Shakespeare: Responses of George Eliot and Other Women Novelists*, Iowa: University of Iowa Press.

Nuttall, A. D. (2007) *Shakespeare the Thinker*, New Haven and London: Yale University Press.

Ovid (1988) *Tristia ex Ponto*, 2nd edn, trans. Arthur Leslie Wheeler, London: Heinemann.

Pearlman, E. (1987) '*Macbeth* on Film: Politics', in Stanley Wells (ed.) *Shakespeare Survey* 39, Cambridge: Cambridge University Press, 67–74.

Percy, Thomas [1765] (1966) *Reliques of Ancient English Poetry*, 3 vols, ed. Henry B. Wheatley, New York: Dover Publications.

Poole-Carter, Rosemary (2007) *Juliette Ascending*, Dallas: Top Publications.

Poovey, Mary (1979) 'Ideology in *The Mysteries of Udolpho*', *Criticism* 21: 307–30.

Pope, Alexander (ed.) (1725) *The Works of Mr. William Shakespear*, Vol. 1, London: Tonson.

Price, Matthew (2007) 'Star-crossed Lovers Quit West Bank', *BBC News*, 28 February. Online. Available at http://news.bbc.co.uk/2/hi/middle_east/6405799.stm (accessed 20 July 2007).

Punter, David (1980) *The Literature of Terror: A History of Gothic Fiction from 1765 to the Present Day*, London: Longman.

Radcliffe, Ann (1790) *A Sicilian Romance*, 2 vols, London: T. Hookham.

——(1795) *A Journey Made in the Summer of 1794 through Holland and the western frontier of Germany with a return down the rhine: to which are added observations during a tour to the lakes of Lancashire, Westmoreland and Cumberland*. London: G. G. and J. Robinson.

——(1826a) *Gaston de Blondeville, or the Court of Henry III keeping festival in Ardenne, A Romance, to which is prefixed a memoir of the author, with extracts from her journals*, London: Henry Colburn.

——(1826b) 'On the Supernatural in Poetry', *New Monthly Magazine*, 16.1, 145–52.

——[1794] (1966) *The Mysteries of Udolpho*, ed. Bonay Dobrée, Oxford World's Classics, Oxford: Oxford University Press.

——[1794] (1980) *The Mysteries of Udolpho*, ed. Bonamy Dobrée, Oxford World's Classics, Oxford: Oxford University Press.

——[1791] (1986) *The Romance of the Forest*, ed. Chloe Chard, Oxford's World's Classics, Oxford: Oxford University Press.

——[1789] (1995) *The Castles of Athlin and Dunbayne*, ed. Alison Milbank, Oxford World's Classics, Oxford: Oxford University Press.

——[1794] (1998) *The Mysteries of Udolpho*, ed. Bonamy Dobrée and Terry Castle, Oxford World's Classics, Oxford: Oxford University Press.

——[1797] (2000) *The Italian, or the confessional of the black penitents*, ed. Robert Miles, Harmondsworth: Penguin.

Ravenscroft, Edward (1969) *Titus Andronicus, or the Rape of Lavinia*, London: Cornmarket Press.

Ray, Jeanne (2000) *Julie and Romeo*, New York: Harmony Books.

Reeve, Clara [1778] (1977) *The Old English Baron: A Gothic Story*, ed. James Trainer, Oxford: Oxford University Press.

Regis, Pamela (2003) *A Natural History of the Romance Novel*, Philadelphia: University of Pennsylvania Press.

Reno, Robert P. (1984) 'James Boaden's *Fontainville Forest* and Matthew G. Lewis' *The Castle Spectre*: Challenges of the Supernatural Ghost on the Late Eighteenth-Century Stage', *Eighteenth-Century Life* 9.1: 95–106.

Romance by You (2007) 'Vampire Kisses'. Online. Available at http://www.bookbyyou.com/vampire/default.asp (accessed 2 July 2007).

Romance Writers of America (2007) 'About the Romance Genre'. Online. Available at http://www.rwanational.org/cs/the_romance_genre (accessed 2 July 2007).

Royster, Francesca T. (2000) 'White-Limed Walls: Whiteness and Gothic Extremism in Shakespeare's *Titus Andronicus*', *Shakespeare Quarterly* 51.4: 432–55.

Sanders, Julie (2006) *Adaptation and Appropriation*, London: Routledge.

Saussure, Ferdinand de (1966) *Course in General Linguistics*, ed. Charles Bally and Albert Sechehaye, trans. Wade Baskin, New York: McGraw-Hill.

Schimel, Lawrence (1994) 'Swear Not By the Moon', in K. Kerr and M. Greenberg (eds) *Weird Tales from Shakespeare*, New York: Daw, 192–94.

Schlegel, Augustus William (1815) *A Course of Lectures on Dramatic Art and Literature*, vol. I, trans. John Black, London: William Blackwood; Dublin: John Cumming.

Schoenbaum, S. (1991) *Shakespeare's Lives: New Edition*, Oxford and New York: Oxford University Press.

Scott, Walter Sir (1932) *The Letters of Sir Walter Scott*, ed. H. J. C. Grierson, 12 vols, London: Constable.

Scouten, Arthur H. (1945) 'Shakespeare's Plays in the Theatrical Repertory when Garrick Came to London', *University of Texts Studies in English*: 257–68.

Sedgwick, Eve Kosofsky (1986) *The Coherence of Gothic Conventions*, New York: Methuen.

Shakespeare, William (1967) *A Midsummer Night's Dream*, ed. Stanley Wells, New Penguin Shakespeare, London: Penguin Books.

—— (1974) *The Riverside Shakespeare*, ed. G. Blakemore Evans et al., Boston: Houghton Mifflin.

——(1986a) *The Complete Works*, ed. Stanley Wells *et al*, Oxford: Clarendon Press.

——(1986b) *The Complete Works: Original Spelling Edition*, ed. Stanley Wells, Oxford: Clarendon Press.

——(1989) *Hamlet*, ed. Harold Jenkins, The Arden Shakespeare, London and New York: Routledge.

——(1995) *Titus Andronicus*, ed. Jonathan Bate, The Arden Shakespeare, 3rd Series, London: Thomson.

——(1997) *The Norton Shakespeare*, ed. Stephen Greenblatt, New York and London: Norton & Company.

——(1998) *The Arden Shakespeare Complete Works*, ed. Richard Proudfoot, Ann Thompson and David Scott Kastan, Walton-on-Thames: Thomas Nelson and Sons Ltd.

Shelley, Mary [1831] (1994) *Frankenstein: Or, The Modern Prometheus*, Harmondsworth: Penguin.

Sickelmore, Richard [1798] (2005) *Edgar; Or, The Phantom of the Castle*, ed. James D. Jenkins, Chicago: Valancourt Books.

Sinyard, Neil (2000) 'Shakespeare Meets *The Godfather*: The Postmodern Populism of Al Pacino's *Looking for Richard*', in Mark Thompson Burnett and Ramona Wray (eds) *Shakespeare, Film, Fin de Siècle*, London: Macmillan, 58–72.

Skal, David J. (1990) *Hollywood Gothic: The Tangled Web of Dracula from Novel to Stage to Screen*, London: André Deutsch.

Smith, D. Nichol (ed) (1963) *Eighteenth-Century Essays on Shakespeare*, Oxford: Clarendon.

'Stephenie Meyer talks about *Eclipse*', Amazon.com. Online. Available at http://www.amazon.com/o/ASIN/0316160202/104-5937882-2074343? SubscriptionId = 0F3WXJ7VXVY8YP775TG2 (accessed 3 August 2007).

Stephens, John Richard (ed.) (1997) *Vampires, Wine and Roses*, New York: Berkeley Books.

Stevenson, John Allen (1990) *The British Novel, Defoe to Austen: A Critical History*, Boston: Twayne.

Stewart, Susan (1984) *On Longing: Narrative of the Miniature, the Gigantic, the Souvenir, the Collection*, Baltimore: The Johns Hopkins University Press.

Sutherland, John (1995) *The Life of Sir Walter Scott*, Oxford: Blackwell.

Taylor, Anthony Brian (1996) '"The Goths Protect the Andronici, Who go Aloft:" The Implications of a Stage Direction', *Notes and Queries* 241.2: 152–55.

Taylor, Neil (1994) 'The Films of *Hamlet*', in Anthony Davies and Stanley Wells (eds) *Shakespeare and the Moving Image: the plays on film and television*, Cambridge: Cambridge University Press, 180–95.

Thomson, James [1730] (1981) *The Seasons*, ed. James Sambrook, Oxford: Clarendon Press.

Vasari, Giorgio (1978) *The Lives of the Artists*, trans. George Bull, Harmondsworth: Penguin.

Vickers, Brian (ed.) (1975) *Shakespeare: The Critical Heritage Vol. 3, 1733–1752*, London and Boston: Routledge & Kegan Paul.

——(ed.) (1976) *Shakespeare: The Critical Heritage Vol. 4, 1753–1765*, London and Boston: Routledge & Kegal Paul.

——(ed.) (1979) *William Shakespeare: The Critical Heritage Vol. 5, 1765–1774*, London and New York: Routledge.

——(ed.) (1981) *William Shakespeare: The Critical Heritage Vol. 6, 1774–1801*, London and New York: Routledge.

Vineyard, Jennifer (2007) 'Re-Buffed: New Comic Book Series Resurrects Vampire Slayer'. Online. Available at http://www.mtv.com/news/articles/1551286/20070131/index.jhtml (accessed 5 July 2007).

Walker, Shiloh. (2005) 'The Blood Kiss', in Emma Holly et al. *Hot Spell*, New York: Penguin, 303–98.

Walpole, Horace [1764] (1968) *The Castle of Otranto*, in Peter Fairclough (ed.) *Three Gothic Novels*, Harmondsworth: Penguin, 37–148.

——[1764] (1982) *The Castle of Otranto: A Gothic Story*, ed. W. S. Lewis, Oxford, Oxford University Press.

——[1764] (1996a) *The Castle of Otranto*, ed. E. J. Clery, Oxford World's Classics, Oxford: Oxford University Press.

——[1764] (1996b) *The Castle of Otranto*, ed. W. S. Lewis, Oxford World's Classics, Oxford: Oxford University Press.

——(2003) *The Castle of Otranto and The Mysterious Mother*, ed. Frederick S. Frank, Peterborough, Ontario: Broadview Press.

Warwick, Alexandra (2007) 'Feeling Gothicky?' *Gothic Studies* 9.1: 5–15.

Watt, James (1999) *Contesting the Gothic: fiction, genre and cultural conflict, 1764–1832*, Cambridge: Cambridge University Press.

White, R. S. (2001) 'Introduction: What is this thing called love?' in R. H. White (ed.) *Romeo and Juliet: New Casebooks*, Basingstoke: Palgrave, 1–27.

Williams, Anne (1995) *Art of Darkness: A Poetics of Gothic*, Chicago: Chicago University Press.

Williams, Deanne (2004) 'Mick Jagger Macbeth', in Peter Holland (ed.) *Shakespeare Survey* 57, Cambridge: Cambridge University Press, 145–58.

Williams, Ioan (ed.) (1970) *Novel and Romance: A Documentary Record, 1700–1800*, London: Routledge and Kegan Paul.

Williams, Raymond (1961) *Culture and Society, 1780–1950*, Harmondsworth: Penguin, 1961.

Wilson, Richard (2004) *Secret Shakespeare*. Manchester: Manchester University Press.

Wollstoncraft, Mary [1790] (1989) *A Vindication of the Rights of Man*, in Janet Todd and Marilyn Butler (eds) *The Works of Mary Wollstonecraft*, vol. 5, London: William Pickering, 1–77.

Wordsworth, William (1920) 'Preface to *Lyrical Ballads*', in Thomas Hutchinson (ed.) *The Poetical Works of Wordsworth*, London: Oxford University Press.

——(1974) *The Prose Works of William Wordsworth*, vol. I, ed. W. J. B. Owen and Jane Worthington Smyser, Oxford: Clarendon Press.

Wright, Angela (2004) '"To live the life of hopeless recollection:" Mourning and Melancholia in Female Gothic, 1780–1800', *Gothic Studies* 6.1: 19–29.

——(2007) *Gothic Fiction: A reader's guide to essential criticism*, Basingstoke: Palgrave.

——(2008) '"How do we ape thee, France!" The cult of Rousseau in women's Gothic writing of the 1790s', in Avril Horner and Sue Zlosnik (eds) *Le Gothic*, Basingstoke: Palgrave, 67–83.

Wright, J. (ed.) (1815) *The Speeches of the Rt. Hon. C. J. Fox in the House of Commons*, vol. II, London: Longman, Hurst, Rees, Orme and Brown.

Young, Edward [1759] (1966) *Conjectures on Chivalry and Romance*, Leeds: Scholar Press.

Zimmerman, Susan (2005) *The Early Modern Corpse and Shakespeare's Theatre*, Edinburgh: Edinburgh University Press.

Žižek, Slavoj (2001) *Enjoy Your Symptom!*, London: Verso.

Index

240   *Index*

Milton, J. 5, 7–9, 13, 67, 72–3, 76,
    111
mimesis 98–9, 104–10
Mimique 99, 106–7, 110
minor literature 10–12, 18
minstrels 126
*Miscellaneous Observations on the Tragedy of
    Hamlet* 66, 71
Miscellaneous Plays 134
mise-en-scène 154, 161
The Mistress of Udolpho 119
money lenders 200
The Monk 8, 10–12, 77, 84, 136–7,
    145, 211–13
Montagu, E. 43–4, 65, 67–8, 71, 102
More, T. 76
Morland, C. 1–3
Morley, R. 163
Mormons 181
La Mort de César 63
MTV 159
Much Ado About Nothing 18
multi-consciousness 196
multinational corporations 171
Murphy, A. 62–3
The Mysteries of Udolpho 6, 46, 56–8,
    88–91, 93, 116–17, 184, 214

Nachträglichkeit 73
Nashe, T. 6
nationalism 4, 6, 113–14, 122, 142
Nature 124, 188
Nazis 160
necromancy 198
Negri, A. 199
neo-classicism 4, 63, 70, 72, 89, 188,
    190–2, 202
neo-Gothicism 203
New Monthly Magazine 121–2, 204
New Moon 167–8, 177–9, 185
New World 197
new world order 189
New York Times 167
Night of the Living Dead 161, 202
nihilism 160
The Ninth Gate 156
Nochinson, M. 157–8
nocturnal world 21–41
nomads 186, 188–90
Normans 150

The North Briton 146
Northanger Abbey 1–2, 12, 14
Northern Antiquities 190
Northern Hive 189
Norton, R. 116, 119, 121, 125
nostalgia 109–10, 142, 199, 203, 207,
    216, 219
Novy, M. 16
Nuttall, A.D. 8

Oedipus complex 72, 199
The Old English Baron 79–81
Olivier, L. 4, 157
'On the Supernatural in Poetry' 116–
    18, 121, 124, 204
opium 6
origins 100–4, 110, 139, 162, 189
Orphelin de la chine 64
Osorio 133
Othello 2, 8, 15–16, 63, 138, 164–5
Ottomans 186
Ovid 48, 186
Oxford edition 52

pageantry 126
Paine, T. 193
paranormal 172–3
parliaments 190
Perambulation of Kent 50
Percy, T. 190–1
performance 61, 72, 124, 126, 142,
    188
Petrarch 176–7, 179
phantasmagoria 195
The Phantom of the Castle 86–7
Philips, A. 187
Picts 146
pirates 186, 197
Pit and the Pendulum 157
Pitt, B. 172–3
Pizarro 133
plagiarism 8, 61, 103, 143
Plato 106, 110
Playboy Productions 160
*The Plays and Poems of William
    Shakespeare* 113
Plutarch 49, 186
Poe, E.A. 157–8
Poets Laureate 61, 83, 132
Poland 160